T0272391

ADDITIONAL PRAISE FOR *THE ITALIAN SQUAD*

"As the grandson of Black Hand victims, I thank Paul Moses for vividly telling the story of those courageous Italian American policemen, and others, who despite resistance, valiantly strove to protect them."
—**JEROME KRASE**, former president of the American Italian Historical Association

"Moses shows how a group of early twentieth-century pioneers in the New York City Police Department—Italian immigrant detectives—worked to earn the trust of their own community while solving crimes, a daunting challenge heightened by interference from Tammany Hall and a growing marketplace for lurid crime reporting, supplied by the city's multitude of daily newspapers. Paul Moses does his own brilliant detective work in *The Italian Squad*, reconstructing long-forgotten criminal cases that highlight changing relationships of politics, law enforcement, and ethnicity in the nation's largest city."
—**JAMES FISHER**, author of *On the Irish Waterfront: The Crusader, the Movie, and the Soul of the Port of New York*

"*The Italian Squad* reads like a great mystery thriller with the sweep of important history. Paul Moses uses his masterful skills as a storyteller to cast new light on this extraordinary time in New York City and in the lives of Italian Americans fighting for clean and honest government everywhere. Readers will be fascinated by the inspiring heroic cops who battled the evilness of the 'Black Hand' mobsters terrorizing innocent newcomers in America. As a great lesson for today, *The Italian Squad* reminds us of how virtue can triumph over vice but at a deadly cost. As a Pulitzer Prize-winning writer, Paul Moses brings his deep understanding of the Italian American experience in New York to reveal one of the most compelling stories from our past."
—**THOMAS MAIER**, author of *Mafia Spies: The Inside Story of the CIA, Gangsters, JFK, and Castro*

THE ITALIAN SQUAD

THE ITALIAN SQUAD

THE TRUE STORY OF THE IMMIGRANT COPS WHO FOUGHT THE RISE OF THE MAFIA

PAUL MOSES

WASHINGTON MEWS BOOKS

An Imprint of

NEW YORK UNIVERSITY PRESS

New York

WASHINGTON MEWS BOOKS

An Imprint of

NEW YORK UNIVERSITY PRESS

New York

www.nyupress.org

Please contact the Library of Congress for Cataloging-in-Publication data.

ISBN: 9781479814190 (hardback)

ISBN: 9781479814213 (consumer ebook)

ISBN: 9781479814244 (library ebook)

New York University Press books are printed on acid-free paper, and their binding materials are chosen for strength and durability. We strive to use environmentally responsible suppliers and materials to the greatest extent possible in publishing our books.

Manufactured in the United States of America

10 9 8 7 6 5 4 3 2 1

Also available as an ebook

To Pete, Charlie, Minna, and Owen

and in memory of

Leonard T. Muscato

CONTENTS

CHARACTERS

The Italian Immigrant Detective Commanders

JOSEPH PETROSINO—Named first commander of the Italian Squad when it was founded in 1904. Murdered in Palermo, Sicily, on March 12, 1909. Born in Padula, Campania.

ANTHONY VACHRIS—Lieutenant named commander of the Italian Squad's Brooklyn branch in 1907. Traveled to Italy to complete Petrosino's mission in 1909. Headed headquarters-based Italian Squad, 1910 to 1911. Born in Paris to parents from Liguria.

CHARLES CORRAO—Led the Brooklyn Italian Squad, 1910 to 1911. After the Italian Squad was officially abolished, he played a key role in the Detective Bureau in coordinating investigations of "Black Hand" crimes. In 1912, he became the first recipient of the NYPD's Medal of Honor. Born in Palermo.

MICHAEL FIASCHETTI—Family friend of Petrosino, led the Italian Squad from when it was reinstated in 1919 until its merger with the Bomb Squad in 1922. Born in Morolo outside Rome.

Under Petrosino's command on the original Italian Squad in 1904

JOHN ARCHIOPOLI, MAURICE BONNOIL, ROCCO CAVONE, PETER DONDERO, JOSEPH DIGILIO, MICHAEL MEALLI, RALPH MICELLI, PAUL SIMONETTI.

Also on the Italian Squad

EDWARD CASTANO, JOHN CROWLEY, LOUIS DARDIS, LIBORIO GAMBARDELLA, LT. ARTHUR GLOSTER, BERNARDINO GROTTANO, FRANK MUNDO, JAMES PELLEGRINO, JOSEPH PUCCIANO, SILVIO REPETTO, EUGENE SCRIVANI, ANGELO TREZZA, FRANCIS UPTON.

Other notable sleuths

RAE NICOLETTI of the Women's Precinct. AMEDEO POLIGNANI of the
Bomb Squad.

JAMES MCCAFFERTY—Chief of detectives from 1907 to 1910.

WILLIAM J. FLYNN—Agent in charge of Secret Service in New York, then
second deputy police commissioner in charge of Detective Bureau, 1910–
1911. Later served as director of the Secret Service and director of the
federal Bureau of Investigation.

GEORGE S. DOUGHERTY—Second deputy commissioner in charge of
Detective Bureau, 1911 to 1914.

EDWARD HUGHES—Inspector and chief of detectives, 1911–1912.

JOHN COUGHLIN—Brooklyn-Queens detective commander, served as chief
of detectives, 1920–1928.

THOMAS J. TUNNEY—First commanding officer of the Bomb Squad.

JAMES J. GEGAN—Bomb Squad commander.

BALDASSARE CEOLA—Police chief in Palermo who led Italian investigation
of Joseph Petrosino's assassination; removed after making arrests.

Mayors and their police commissioners

GEORGE B. MCCLELLAN, JR.—Democrat; mayor, 1904–1909. Appointed
former New Jersey Congressman WILLIAM MCADOO as police
commissioner from 1904 to 1905, then retired brigadier general
THEODORE BINGHAM, 1906 to 1909. Fired Bingham, replacing him
with WILLIAM F. BAKER.

WILLIAM J. GAYNOR—Former judge who pledged to end policing abuses
and maverick Democrat mayor from 1910 to 1913. Appointed Brooklyn
attorney JAMES C. CROPSEY as police commissioner in October 1910.
Socialite and Fire Commissioner RHINELANDER WALDO became
police commissioner in May 1911. He shut down the Italian Squad and
demoted Vachris for testifying in opposition.

ARDOLPH KLINE served as interim mayor after Gaynor died in September
1913. He fired Waldo on the last day of his term.

JOHN PURROY MITCHEL, Republican-Fusion mayor from 1914 to 1917, appointed Progressive reformer ARTHUR H. WOODS as police commissioner.

JOHN F. HYLAN—Mayor from 1918 to 1925, he was elected with support from unlikely allies William Randolph Hearst and Tammany Hall. His initial commissioner, FREDERICK BUGHER, resigned during his first month in office. RICHARD ENRIGHT, promoted from police lieutenant to commissioner, led the department from 1918 to 1925. He reinstated the Italian Squad, then later merged it into the Bomb Squad. Demoted Fiaschetti to patrolman.

Notable crimes, criminals, and their victims

Suspects in the 1903 "Barrel Murder" of BENEDETTO MADONIA were later believed responsible for the unsolved murder of Joseph Petrosino. The gang was led by brothers-in-law IGNAZIO LUPO and GIUSEPPE MORELLO, who were convicted of counterfeiting in 1910, along with ANTONIO CECALA and GIUSEPPE CALICCHIO. Printer ANTONIO COMITO testified against them. Gang members CARLO COSTANTINO and ANTONINO PASSANANTI were suspects in the Petrosino murder. VITO CASCIO FERRO, a Sicilian Mafia don, had connections to the Lupo-Morello gang and late in his life claimed to have been the one who shot Petrosino.

ANTONIO CINCOTTA and ANTONIO MISIANI—Convicted in attempt to extort $15,000 from opera star ENRICO CARUSO in 1910. CINCOTTA'S conviction was overturned on appeal; MISIANI jumped bail.

MICHAEL SCIMECA, three-year-old son of MARIANO and LEONILDA SCIMECA, was kidnapped in 1910. VITO MICELLI was later convicted.

JOSEPH LONGO, age eight, and MICHAEL RIZZO, age six—kidnapped on the same night in 1910. Convictions of STANISLAO PETTANZA and MARIA RAPPA were overturned.

GIUSEPPE COSTABILE—Considered an important figure behind "Black Hand" bombings, he was convicted in 1911. Was suspected of 1908 bombing of FRANCESCO SPINELLA's home.

Giovanni Rizzo—Milk delivery man caught in the act of bombing a tenement in 1911.

Frank Cirofici—One of the four gunmen arrested and executed in the 1912 slaying of gambler Herman Rosenthal, who was prepared to inform on Lieutenant Charles Becker, also executed.

Angelo Settimana—Also known as Angelino Sylvestro, was convicted in 1913 for his role in a gang that carried out dozens of bombings on a contract basis; he attempted to bomb the apartment of Ciro Pecoraro for refusing to let his daughter marry hoodlum Joe Fay. Associates "Zump," Rocco Puccielli; "Burke," Anthony Sadaitys; and "Schmitty," Alfred Lehman, testified against him.

Oresto Shilitano—Fatally shot Patrolmen William Heaney and Charles J. Teare on Mulberry Street in 1913. Convicted, based on testimony of eyewitness neighbor Nellie De Carlo, and executed in 1916.

Frank Abarno and Carmine Carbone—Anarchists convicted of conspiring to bomb St. Patrick's Cathedral in 1915.

Giosue Gallucci—East Harlem–based "King of Little Italy," he was murdered in 1915.

Leopoldo Lauritano, Alessandro Vollero—Leaders of Navy Street gang. Allied with Coney Island gang leader Pellegrino Morano in a murderous mob war in 1916 with the Morello gang, all three were convicted on homicide charges. Informant Ralph Daniello testified against them, and gave police details of twenty-three murders.

Rosario Borgia and underlings Pasquale Biondo, Paul Chiavaro, and Frank Mazzano—Executed in connection with the murders of four Akron, Ohio, police officers in 1917 and 1918. Lorenzo Biondo and Anthony Manfriedo were sentenced to prison.

Michael Casalino and Joe Zambelli—Executed in connection with the 1919 murder of Joseph and Helen Holbach, owners of a Queens nightspot. Paul Ricci was sentenced to prison.

VINCENZO PAPACCIO, a.k.a. James Papaccio, was tracked to Italy and tried and convicted there in connection with the 1919 slaying of teenagers LENA SPINELLI and JOSEPHINE GENTILE, bystanders to a Little Italy gun battle.

SANTO CUSAMANO, ANTHONY MARINO, and ROBERTO RAFFAELE were convicted in the 1921 kidnapping and death of five-year-old JOSEPH VAROTTA, son of SALVATORE and ANTOINETTE VAROTTA.

BARTOLO FONTANA admitted to the 1921 murder of CAMILLO CAIOZZO and turned informant, telling authorities of at least sixteen slayings linked to a Sicilian Mafia dispute. Charges were dropped against his alleged co-conspirators, including future Buffalo crime boss STEFANO MAGADDINO and VITO BONVENTRE. Newspapers claimed the "Good Killers" gang was responsible for scores of murders.

JOE MASSERIA, early mob boss who won 1922 war with slain bootleg rival UMBERTO VALENTI. Murdered in 1930, on losing end of the Castellammarese War.

Other notables

LORENZO C. CARLINO, lawyer whom Fiaschetti roughed up. He was representing MARIA IAVARONE.

CARLO BARSOTTI, influential newspaper publisher who opposed existence of an Italian Squad with attorney FRANCIS L. CORRAO, brother of Charles Corrao, and JUDGE JOHN J. FRESCHI. Journalist and professor ALBERTO PECORINI spoke out in favor of keeping the squad.

JUDGE CHARLES C. NOTT, JR.—Judge in the Abarno-Carbone bomb conspiracy trial, his home was later bombed.

WILLIAM HENRY BISHOP—US consul in Palermo who assisted the NYPD in 1909, with help from LLOYD C. GRISCOM, ambassador to Italy.

HOMER M. BYINGTON—US consul in Naples during Fiaschetti visit there.

"BIG TIM" SULLIVAN—Powerful Tammany figure and state legislator who won passage of a pioneering gun-control law in 1911; known to have ties to illegal gambling.

"LITTLE TIM" SULLIVAN—Cousin and political ally of "Big Tim," blocked funding of a "secret service" while serving on Board of Aldermen.

HENRY CURRAN—Republican-Fusion alderman who led 1913 investigation into police corruption.

PROSPER BURANELLI—Writer who published exaggerated accounts of Fiaschetti's exploits.

PART ONE

1904 to 1909

1

"Dies Martyr"

THE skies had darkened even before sunset as a driving rain shot through Palermo's waterfront district. But after a two-hour pour, the pounding paused at 7:30 p.m. and he saw a chance to leave his hotel room and get dinner again at the trattoria on the other side of the Piazza Marina. He left his rusty, unloaded .38-caliber Smith & Wesson revolver in a yellow leather valise in his room, number 16, at the Hôtel de France. And he left a letter to his wife on the table: "Dearest wife, I arrived in Palermo, I find everything confused . . . I do not like all of Italy at all . . . I'll explain to you when I come. God, God, what a misery!"

Before long, he was taking the edge off a tense day with a half liter of wine and *piatti* of pasta and tomato sauce, grilled fish, and cheese. He sat with his back to the wall, by now a familiar stranger in busy Caffè Oreto after dining there throughout his thirteen days in Sicily. People thought he was a tourist or perhaps a relatively prosperous businessman, dressed as he was in a black jacket and matching vest, with a gold chain linking the second buttonhole of the vest to a gold watch nestled in the pocket, and an elegant brown silk tie around his neck. He had the newspapers, *Giornale di Sicilia* and *La Tribuna*, which carried early results of the national elections, and then there was a visit from two men who stood by his table and spoke to him respectfully.

It was past 8:30, and he'd had a long day, having caught the 6:30 a.m. train to Caltanissetta, a city in the interior where he'd spent several hours combing through paperwork in the local courthouse before returning to Palermo in the afternoon. During the day, he made his customary notes in the notebook he carried, including an entry that referred to a Vito Cascio Ferro, "dreaded criminal." It had already been a busy day, but these two men were supposed to help, so he indicated he would see them outside. After finishing his repast, he paid the bill, picked up his umbrella, and stepped into the night in his long, dark gray coat and black derby. The wind was still blowing strong, rustling the trees in the Garibaldi Garden at the heart of the piazza, and he walked in the shadowy gaslight alongside an iron fence that enclosed the park.

8:45 p.m. on Friday, March 12, 1909: As he reached the southwest corner of the garden, three gunshots thundered in the night, and then a fourth. One bullet sliced into his back just below his right shoulder blade and ripped both of his lungs. Another, again from behind, caught him in the neck. A third bullet exploded into his left temple as he turned his head toward the two assailants who'd ambushed him. He held up a hand as if to shield his face, reached for the iron railing to his left, took several steps, stumbled and fell forward into the street, gashing the right side of his forehead. Two men fled; one of them threw his handgun beside their victim. It was a .38-caliber revolver made in Liege, Belgium; only one of its six chambers was discharged.

Alberto Cardella, a sailor from the warship *Calabria*, which was in port, heard the shots and was the first who dared to be at his side. By then the two men had fled toward Palermo's alleys, and the sailor observed their bloody victim, who lay chest down. The gaslights on the piazza flickered and died, and the victim was cast in darkness until someone in the crowd that now gathered went for candles. Then a medical officer from the ship stepped through the knot of people and confirmed that the man was dead. No one knew who he was; everyone knew he was not from Palermo. An investigator arrived and, with the help of some guards, cordoned off the crowd to a respectful distance. In the candlelight, he searched the man's pockets: he still had cash, including a fifty-lire note and four five-lire bills, plus a booklet of blank checks. He still had the gold watch. Then there was the gold New York City detective shield, No. 285. There were thirty business cards. And a postcard to New York with the message, "A kiss for you and my little girl."

His identity was now obvious: this was none other than Giuseppe Petrosino, the American detective whose exploits in New York were so celebrated that, even in Italy, the government had granted him honors five months earlier in appreciation for his arrests of fugitives from Italian justice. This man was a legend for his clever disguises, his dogged determination to thwart the menace of the "Black Hand," and the brilliant arrests that had made him a hero in the melodramatic mass media of the day—the sensationalist newspapers, widely read muckraking magazines, a series of novels written in Italian, and even moving pictures, with a leading American studio's release one month before of *The Detectives of the Italian Bureau*. And there was the derby he so often wore in newspaper photos and illustrations, on the ground next to his body.

At 11 p.m., three Italian police officials visited the home of William Henry Bishop, the sixty-two-year-old American consul in Palermo. They didn't need to say a word: "Their gloomy faces announced to me that poor Petrosino was slain," Bishop later wrote to his superiors at the State Department. Bishop, a former Yale professor and a popular novelist, had feared for the detective's safety, especially since he refused backup from local police. They'd spoken daily for the past week, with Bishop helping Petrosino navigate the Sicilian bureaucracy to secure official criminal records that could be used to deport dangerous criminals from the United States. He came to realize that Petrosino's secret mission was no secret in Palermo. Now, the writer-turned-diplomat had walked into a story much bigger than any of those that ever passed through his typewriter.

After midnight, the shaken consul went to Palermo's main telegraph office to cable New York City's police commissioner, General Theodore Bingham, and the US ambassador in Rome, Lloyd Griscom. Then he sent a telegram to the *New York Herald* office in Paris, "the latter as the best means of bringing this deplorable murder quickly before the civilized world."[1]

Six time zones and an ocean away, the *Herald* city desk reacted to that middle-of-the-night news via Paris and Palermo. Shortly before 1 a.m. New York time, the newspaper had a reporter knocking on the Petrosino family's door at 233 Lafayette Street, a five-story brick building on the western edge of Little Italy in lower Manhattan. The reporter asked Petrosino's wife, Adelina, if she'd received any news from her husband. In that awkward moment, it became clear that Mrs. Petrosino had no idea of her husband's fate. "I am sure that my husband is all right," she told the reporter, standing in her doorway and holding her infant daughter in her arms. "Or I should know."

Whether from panic or misinformation, the reporter stopped short of the awful truth. He blurted out that Lieutenant Petrosino had been seriously injured in Palermo. Adelina, a widow when she married Joe fourteen months earlier, quickly alerted her brother Louis, who lived upstairs with his wife, Angelena, and their two sons, aged four and five. Louis Saulino, a thirty-four-year-old postal clerk, rushed over to police headquarters at 300 Mulberry Street, a five-minute walk, to see if he could find out more. But the police on duty didn't know anything about it, and suggested the newspaper was wrong.

At dawn, the *Herald* hit the streets with a devastating article reporting that Petrosino had been slain in Palermo, a morning paper exclusive. Still, Adelina hoped that it was all a mistake. A reporter from the Italian-language *L'Araldo Italiano* found the grieving widow seated at the foot of the couple's bed later in the morning in her third-floor apartment, circled by friends. "Tell me, for pity, that it's not true," Adelina beseeched. The reporter had no good news for her. "Is it not true, signore, that he will come back?" she asked, adding that her husband would never leave this "little creature"—*creaturina*—their fourteen-week-old daughter, also named Adelina.

For much of the day on Saturday, March 13, the Palermo-datelined *Herald* article was the only evidence anyone in New York had that the star detective had been slain. When detectives lined up at police headquarters that morning, Inspector James McCafferty read the newspaper's account of the death of this "fine, conscientious, honest and efficient member of the force," his voice cracking. The Central Office detectives already had read all about it, of course.

McCafferty, who had gumshoed with Petrosino in the celebrated "Barrel Murder" case of 1903, then got to work contacting other police departments in cities with Black Hand violence—Pittsburgh, Detroit, Chicago, Baltimore, Boston, New Orleans, and San Francisco, among others—asking for leads. Petrosino had helped the chiefs in many other cities.[2]

Police Commissioner Theodore Bingham was visiting friends in Washington. He telegrammed Secretary of State Elihu Root, a fellow New Yorker, at 9:41 a.m. on March 13—nearly nineteen hours after the slaying: "Can you get confirmation and particulars of reported murder of Lt. Petrosino of Police Department in Palermo, Sicily." It's not clear why there was such a delay in delivering the original telegram from Bishop, but a new version came from the US ambassador in Rome, received at the State Department in Washington. With the garble included, it read:

> *Consul Palermo requests me to inform you as follows:*
> *Quote Petrosino shot, instantly killed, near his hotel early this evening. Assassins unknown. Dies martyr to of protecting peaceful Italian in America. End quote.*
> *G R I S C O M*

That message was in turn cabled to New York, where the first deputy police commissioner acknowledged it in a telegram received at 12:26 p.m.:

> *Despatch received Consul Palermo confirming murder Lieutenant Petrosini.*
> *Request good offices State Department to ask Italian Government to notify us promptly and fully if indications are discovered that plot was made in New York. Use vigorous action.*[3]

Bingham returned on the 11 a.m. train. Communicating with his deputy commissioners via long-distance telephone, he went straight to his apartment at the Iroquois Hotel on West Forty-Fourth Street after his arrival in New York. He had nothing to say.

A Martyr To His Duty

Lieut. Joseph Petrosino, New York.
New York Police Department,
1869-1909
Assassinated in discharge of his duty,
At Palermo, Italy, March 12, 1909.

FIGURE 1.1. Postcard in memory of Lieutenant Joseph Petrosino following his murder in Palermo on March 12, 1909. Photo credit: Petrosino family archive.

As Saturday morning dawned in New York, Lieutenant Anthony Vachris was the man of the hour. With his close friend Joe Petrosino dead, Tony Vachris was "now regarded as the leading police authority on Italian criminals in the city" and his "probable successor," as the *Tribune* would put it.[4]

The two men, both in their forties, had much in common. Both were immigrants who had come to New York as children—Giuseppe arriving at Castle Garden with his father, Prospero, in 1872 at the age of twelve, and Vachris, born Antonio Vaccarezza, with his parents in 1870 at age four.[5] They were stocky, tough-minded men. Both balded early. Both loved opera. Both excelled as cops, but had to struggle against anti-Italian bias to win promotions. Petrosino's breakthrough had come in 1895 when Theodore Roosevelt, head of the Police Board of Commissioners, promoted him to detective as part of an anti-corruption shakeup in the Detective Bureau. Vachris had to win a court order in 1902 to gain a promotion to detective sergeant that he'd already been found qualified for. By 1909, both men had become household names because of their crime-fighting exploits against the dreaded Black Hand—which was imagined in the newspapers to be a massive criminal conspiracy rooted in the Old World, but which was actually more of a brand name adopted by disconnected bands of thugs who blackmailed Italian immigrant merchants with the threat of bombings and kidnappings. Petrosino was chief of the Italian Squad of the Detective Bureau, a unit created in 1904 when it became painfully obvious that the NYPD had failed to police the city's rapidly expanding Italian population. Vachris led the Brooklyn branch of the Italian Squad.

Now, Vachris was thinking about their last conversation. He had accompanied a moody Petrosino to the dock on February 9; they spoke before he boarded the *Duca di Genova*, a big, two-funneled, double-masted vessel. Petrosino, posing as Jewish businessman Simone Velletri, was heading for Genoa and then to Rome to start his journey. Vachris knew Petrosino's penchant for going it alone when he pursued dangerous investigations—he'd achieved so much that way—and urged him to consult with the local officials everywhere he went in Italy, especially in the south.

"Joe, you may be safe and all right up in the North, but look out for yourself as you never did before in the South," Vachris later recalled telling him. Petrosino, who was born in Padula in the southern Italian region of Campania, brushed off the concerns from his brother officer, whose parents were from Genoa, further north. Vachris himself was born in Paris, where his family stayed before migrating to New York, but, as the *Brooklyn Daily Eagle* put it in one of the hundreds of stories it carried about him, "he is Ligurian from the crown of his picturesque bald head to the soles of his brogans."

"I'm no fool, Tony, and I'll be ready for anything that happens down there," Petrosino responded. Vachris reminded Petrosino that it had been nearly four decades since he was last in Italy. "I begged him to remember that he did not have as many friends where he was going as he had here," he told reporters hours after learning of his friend's death. "But he shrugged his shoulders and gave that queer little laugh of his. So what could I do? Besides he felt it was his duty, and knowing that he believed so, I said nothing more."

Vachris was convinced that the culprits in Petrosino's assassination were criminals he had chased back to Italy, whether through the legal mechanism of deportation or simply by letting them know, in very blunt terms, that he was on to them. "Palermo is the worst hole in Southern Italy for the Mafia," he told reporters who came to see him at Brooklyn's police headquarters. "There are at least a hundred criminals of the most desperate type there who knew Petrosino, many of them having been deported from this country because of his work." Vachris suspected that someone in the local police force in Palermo had tipped off Petrosino's enemies.[6]

Charles S. Corrao—Charlie to the other men on the Italian Squad—thought so, too. A well-built thirty-six-year-old man with fine dark hair and a handsome, clean-shaven face, he was the only Sicilian member of the Italian Squad. Corrao and his family had migrated from Palermo; his father, Luigi, worked on the Brooklyn docks as a ship caulker. Charlie worked the same job until he was able to join the police force in Brooklyn in 1896. After seven years on patrol duty—during which the City of Brooklyn became part of New York City—he caught the attention of a fellow immigrant who served as the highest-ranking Italian in the Police Department, Captain Charles A. Formosa, the detective commander in Brooklyn. Needing sleuths who could speak Italian, Formosa arranged Corrao's transfer to the Detective Bureau.

Corrao tended to go at his job quietly, leaving the histrionics to his older brother Francis L. Corrao, who made headlines as the first Italian assistant district attorney in Brooklyn and as the leading political organizer of the borough's growing Italian community. Charles Corrao spoke through his actions, and the public took note. "Corrao's wide acquaintance among the Italians of Brooklyn and his long experience as a detective there make him a formidable man for criminals of the Italian districts of the borough," the *Herald* said in a front page article about his 1904 arrest of a kidnapping suspect, Vito LaDuca.[7]

When Frank Corrao had an opinion, you read it in the newspaper. He certainly had one on Petrosino's death: "Corrao Holds Italian Government Largely Responsible for Murder," the *Brooklyn Standard Union* headlined the following day. He had traveled to Italy the previous summer with Brooklyn district attorney John F. Clarke. Corrao's aim was to research loopholes that criminals exploited in the generally harsh Italian legal system; Clarke was more interested in a three-month Italian vacation. Recalling his trip, Corrao raised the possibility that cozy ties between the Mafia and Italian officialdom played a role in Petrosino's slaying. "It seemed to me when I was over there last summer that the Government assists in maintaining the spirit of the Mafia."[8]

Petrosino's slaying hit one of the younger investigators on the Italian Squad hardest that morning. Michael Fiaschetti had found a mentor in Petrosino, and was awestruck by him. "Walking in on him was like taking a bow before a king," he later wrote, describing his first visit to the detective's office. Petrosino was a family friend who fascinated him with his stories about detective work. At six feet tall, the brash, dark-haired, blue-eyed twenty-eight-year-old Fiaschetti was a sort of apprentice to the stout, five-foot, three-inch Petrosino. Fiaschetti called himself a Roman—he seemed like a gladiator—although he was born not in the Eternal City but in Morolo in the Lazio region of Italy, forty-three miles southeast of Rome. He came to America with his father, Domenico, an accomplished musician and band leader, when he was eleven years old, settling first near North Adams in western Massachusetts, then moving to New York when he was sixteen. Petrosino, who loved to play the violin, was friendly with Fiaschetti's father, who sat at the piano on Sunday afternoons and performed piano scores for the operas he loved. So Petrosino was there to aid his friend's son when the young man's life fell apart.

Michael Fiaschetti had married the love of his life, slender, dark-eyed Jennie Cavagnara, in 1905; Jennie gave birth to their daughter Anna the following year. But in 1907, Jennie died suddenly of an infection from a needle prick, and Fiaschetti took to drinking. Petrosino straightened him out, telling him he needed discipline, and urging him to join the NYPD. Within six weeks after he was hired as a patrolman in Brooklyn in September 1908, Fiaschetti was transferred to the Italian Squad in Manhattan; he was still officially a patrolman, but he was to learn detective work from the master. "We who had served under Petrosino swore we would get his murderers," he later wrote. "I, in particular, whom he had befriended so much, made my vow."[9]

Vachris shared that sentiment. He didn't say so, but despite the obvious danger, the wheels were already turning in the NYPD to send him. On the afternoon of March 13, 1909, Commissioner Bingham wrote to the the secretary of state: "We have heard this morning that Lieut. Petrosino was murdered in Palermo. It is the intention of the Department now to send another officer to Italy to make the same sort of investigation that Lieut. Petrosino was sent to carry on."[10]

2

"On the Dead Quiet"

JOSEPH PETROSINO and the Italian Squad were the Police Department's answer to a summer of humiliating news coverage. In the sweltering heat of July and August 1904, Newspaper Row fixated on the "Society of the Black Hand." There was plenty to write about as one "Black Hand" crime after another exploded: a grocery at 252 Elizabeth Street was demolished in a bombing; a beer party at 456 151st Street ended with an explosion that injured twenty people; Joseph Stravalli's barber shop at 417 Third Avenue was bombed to bits; eight-year-old Tony Mannino's kidnapping in Brooklyn was national news. In the face of this "epidemic of crime," as the *World* put it, the NYPD was accused repeatedly of incompetence. Italian merchants held big public meetings to plead for more help from police, for more Italian cops, and for their fellow Italians to step forward to tell detectives what they knew about Black Hand threats. And yet the blackmail letters continued: telling the public that police were helpless emboldened the extortionists.

The crimes of a few Black Handers cast suspicion on all of the close to two million Italians who disembarked in the Port of New York in the first decade of the twentieth century. "We have too many bad Italians already, and since the good Italians so generally refuse to give any information to the police which might assist them in their efforts to run down criminals of their race, we may be unable in any protective measures we adopt to distinguish in every case the good Italian immigrant from the bad Italian immigrant," the *Times* threatened. "That will make no difference—protect ourselves we must."[1]

Press-savvy Petrosino tried to change this mindset, a mission his Italian Squad detectives inherited. He complained to a writer from the Italian-language newspaper *Il Progresso Italo-Americano* of being "besieged as usual these days by so-called 'reporters' from American newspapers who insist that every stupid scam or criminal act committed by an Italian must be attributed to the now-famous 'Black Hand.'" He recounted a conversation with a *Harper's* editor: "I wanted to give it to them straight, the facts, but they wouldn't even notice, interested only in enormously exaggerating the facts of the story which, if related honestly would not at all put our compatriot immigrants in anything but a benevolent light."

To Petrosino, "the facts" meant that 97 percent of Italian immigrants were law-abiding and hardworking, a number he arrived at by scrutinizing data for arrests and the prison population. Contrary to the typecasting in the newspapers, Italians were not overrepresented on the criminal dockets. Where there was crime, Petrosino said many of the offenses grew from "passion, impulsiveness, the defense of trampled honor: premeditated crimes are very rare among Italians." He acknowledged that immigrants from southern Italy arrived with the "painful inheritances" of poor education and deep poverty, but said that with improved education, literacy would increase and crime decrease.[2]

Italian-born police officers tried to make this case before Petrosino, and his successors would take up the task. "When an Italian does anything, it is printed in big type," Augustus Sbarbaro, perhaps the NYPD's first Italian-born officer when he was hired in 1873, told the *Sun*.[3]

Southern Italian immigrants were viewed as a "problem," lawyer and journalist Gino C. Speranza wrote in his 1904 article "How It Feels to Be a Problem," a title that echoes a question W. E. B. Du Bois raised in an 1897 essay on "The Strivings of the Negro People."

Considering how many foreign-born residents the United States had, Speranza wrote, "it is a strange fact how few Americans ever consider how very unpleasant, to say the least, it must be to the foreigners living in their midst to be constantly looked upon either as a national problem or a national peril." That hostility, he added, led Italian immigrants to insulate themselves. "It is with this in mind that I say that if my countrymen here keep apart, if they herd in great and menacing city colonies, if they do not learn your language, if they know little about your country, the fault is as much yours as theirs. And if you wish to reach us you will have to batter down some of the walls you have yourselves built up to keep us from you."[4]

The immigrant detectives who would lead the Italian Squad during its on-and-off existence from 1904 to 1922—Petrosino, followed by Anthony Vachris, Charles Corrao, and Michael Fiaschetti—faced a daunting task. A handful of cops on a force of ten thousand needed to persuade a community numbering in the hundreds of thousands that an obviously biased criminal justice system could treat Italian immigrants fairly. When they caught those who blackmailed, kidnapped, and bombed their fellow Italians, the cases were sensationalized in the press—which strengthened the idea that Italians were dangerous and unfit to be American citizens.

The growing political movement to pass laws aimed at halting Italian and Jewish immigration—ultimately successful in the 1924 immigration act—made full use of Black Hand fears, and that influenced lawmakers. A 1907 US Department of Commerce and Labor report that called for new restrictions on immigration stated: "The current history of the perpetration of heinous crimes throughout the United States by foreigners domiciled therein, especially by members of the 'Black Hand' and other like societies, is evidence that needs no special comment." Petrosino's assassination served to underscore the peril: if criminals could do in the famously tough detective from New York, they seemingly had the power to reach anyone.[5]

"Among the Italians, the event strikes like a moral disaster," a New York correspondent for the Milan-based newspaper *Corriere della Sera* observed. "Americans had finally learned to recognize the many peaceful Italians who want only to earn their bread honestly and perhaps save a little. But the periodic crimes of a few desperate people, emboldened by the freedom they abuse, severely embarrasses the attempt to resurrect the Italian name."[6]

Already internationally famous before his death, Petrosino was sainted after it—"dies martyr," as the US consul in Palermo put it in his

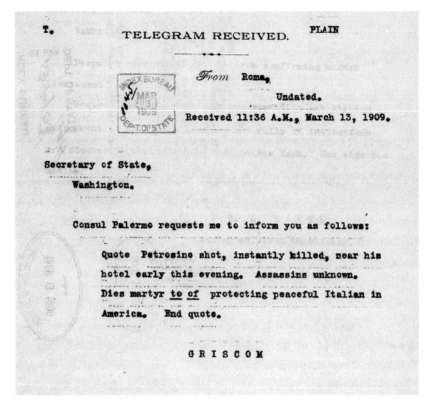

FIGURE 2.1. The US ambassador to Italy, Lloyd Griscom, relayed word of Joseph Petrosino's assassination from the consul in Palermo, William Henry Bishop, to the State Department. From there, it went to the New York Police Department. Photo credit: National Archives and Records Administration.

telegram that night. It's interesting to see that a small and somewhat disjointed portion of Bishop's cable did not appear in news accounts; the newspapers' quote ends at "dies martyr." The version in State Department files continues, identifying for whom the martyr died: "protecting peaceful Italian in America. End quote."[7]

This book will tell the story of how Petrosino's successors continued that mission. His death is often treated as the end of a story, but here, it is the beginning. For the Italian Squad detectives who worked with him, his memory was always there: his example shaped their tactics; his murder confronted them with a mystery they yearned to solve; his death reminded them of the danger they faced.

The squad was created to serve as a bridge between a Police Department that failed to protect the Italian immigrant community and an Italian community that distrusted police and the court system. The celebrity status of Petrosino, Vachris, Corrao, and Fiaschetti showed how Italian immigrants were already making great contributions to American society. The irony was that their successes against "Black Hand" criminals were reconfigured in the New York newspapers—a key player in this story—as evidence that southern Italians were especially prone to violent crime and therefore unfit to be American citizens. The alarming depiction of a sinister, foreign-controlled Black Hand "society" boosted the nativist movement. A century later, the storm over crime and immigration—"crimmigration"—has blown into national politics once more.

* * *

The first *Mano Nera*—Black Hand—case in New York dates to August 3, 1903, an attempt to blackmail fifty-year-old Brooklyn contractor Nicola Cappiello. Shakedowns had occurred before then, of course, but in this case the extortionists decided to send the victim a letter signed *Mano Nera*. It demanded that Cappiello hand over $10,000—the original meeting place was to be Thirteenth Avenue and Seventy-Second Street in Brooklyn—or else his home at 107 Second Place in Brooklyn would be dynamited. Vachris made arrests, and two men were quickly sent up the river to Sing Sing prison. But the newspapers, especially the *World*, played up the Black Hand angle. Suddenly, there was a mysteriously powerful "Society of the Black Hand." In a splashy spread, the broadsheet sketched out a black-gloved fist thrusting a dagger toward the heart of a sad-eyed Cappiello. It was an early chapter in the years of sensationalized and often inaccurate coverage of the so-called Black Hand, which the papers thoroughly confused with the Sicilian Mafia and Neapolitan Camorra—all leading to the notion that Italians were inherently criminal and thus unfit to be American citizens. Petrosino tried to set the story straight: the Black Hand was not some centralized organization but small, unconnected bands of small-time criminals. "The idea that there is a big criminal club in this city called the 'Black Hand' is all a myth," he told the *Times* in 1908. "It has grown out of the custom of the newspapers of calling every crime committed by an Italian a 'Black Hand' outrage."[8]

With one of American journalism's great newspaper wars under way in New York at the time, there was money to be made by cashing in on the public's fear of the enormous surge of immigrants into the nation's largest city. The hype was free advertising for blackmailers: "Black Hand" became a powerful brand name that allowed small-time thugs to appear invincible. It was as if a few local blacksmiths were able to pass themselves off as U.S. Steel. Soon enough, criminals in every city with a concentration of Italian immigrants used the Black Hand logo.[9]

It became obvious that the Police Department, which had a handful of Italian-speaking cops, wasn't up to the task of ending the violence. "The average policeman of Irish or German descent is as helpless to deal with conditions as an American traveler set down for the first time in Naples or Milan," a *Survey* magazine writer asserted. "A Black Hand plot may be hatched out under his very face and he be none the wiser." Joseph Pulitzer's *World* upbraided the Detective Bureau, accusing it of "grave neglect of duty." The Brooklyn magistrate who presided over arrests in the Tony Mannino kidnapping case advocated creating a "secret service" of Italian undercover sleuths. "No English-speaking policeman can get any information from an Italian, and the few Italian policemen we have in the department are so well known that they have come to be spotted by their countrymen," James Tighe said. And Joseph Petrosino kept pushing for a squad of Italian detectives; he couldn't do it alone.[10]

Police Commissioner William McAdoo, a Democrat and former New Jersey congressman, knew that the Tammany-controlled Board of Aldermen had powerful members who were allied with criminal gangs, including Italian ones. They were certainly opposed to creating a "secret service" that would report to the commissioner outside the chain of command in the Detective Bureau, which Tammany (the Manhattan Democratic organization) manipulated.

Petrosino warned the commissioner that if the freelance extortionists weren't stopped, professional criminals from Italy—the Sicilian Mafia or Neapolitan Camorra—would come to town to organize and control the lucrative racket. He had already seen the Mafia insinuate itself into counterfeiting rings; Vito Cascio Ferro, perhaps the most powerful leader of a Sicilian mob *cosca*, or clan, was arrested in Manhattan in 1902 in connection with a thriving operation in Hackensack, New Jersey. He beat the federal case, which originated from a tip Petrosino received. The following year, he fled the city to elude arrest in connection with a murder investigation.[11]

When McAdoo gave in and established an Italian Squad, Petrosino told him it was not enough; the commissioner insisted it was the best he could do. City records show that, in mid-September 1904, the officers who formed the core of the squad were transferred in from other assignments: Ralph Micelli, Paul Simonetti, Peter Dondero, Michael Mealli, John Archiopoli, and Joseph DiGilio. One was new: Rocco Cavone, a twenty-seven-year-old family friend Petrosino had persuaded to leave a job as a production manager in a factory. Detective Sergeant Maurice Bonnoil, French-born and able to speak Italian, was already working in the headquarters Detective Bureau when he became part of the squad.[12]

In addition, McAdoo transferred fourteen other patrolmen to plainclothes duty at precincts in the Italian neighborhoods of lower Manhattan and Harlem. The plan was that Petrosino would be able to call on these officers, who included Charles Corrao, James DiGilio, and Hugh Cassidy (who'd Hibernized his name from Ugo Cassini).

In announcing his Italian Squad on September 13, 1904, McAdoo criticized the Italian community for not cooperating with police. "The trouble now is that an Italian criminal at once seeks refuge behind racial and national sympathy, and many of his countrymen, otherwise honest, believe it a sort of patriotic duty to shield him from officers of the

Det. Rocco Cavone

Det. Ralph Micelli

Det. Joseph D...

Lieut. Joseph Petrosino

Office of Italian Squad
316 Lafayette St.

Lieut. Maurice ...

Det. Peter Dondero.

Det. Michael Meali.

Det. Paul Simonelli.

Det. John T. Archiopoli.

Original Italian Squad
· 1904 ·

FIGURE 2.2. The original Italian Squad as established in 1904, shown in a photo collage that was among Joseph Petrosino's possessions. The photo at the center depicts the Italian Squad's office at 316 Lafayette Street. Photo credit: Petrosino family archive.

law," he said. McAdoo created the Italian Squad in response to a political need—he had to do something about the public's alarm from newspaper coverage of the "Black Hand." But, he argued, the problem was with the Italian community, and not incompetent or indifferent policing.

In a letter to the *Times*, Gino C. Speranza explained that southern Italians were reluctant to cooperate with police because law enforcement had been used for centuries in their homeland to oppress, not protect:

"Witnesses become spies and informers and are universally despised." (The Donegal-born McAdoo had elsewhere used a similar explanation for why New York cops of Irish origin wouldn't inform on each other.) But beyond that, Speranza charged, immigrants were reacting to bias. "I have heard a Judge charge a jury that there was a presumption that an Italian went always armed," he wrote. ". . . When a murder cannot be unraveled the police always find that 'an Italian-looking tramp' was

FIGURE 2.3. Police Commissioner William McAdoo initiated the Italian Squad in 1904. The mayor who appointed him commissioner considered McAdoo to be a failure at the job; he later became the city's chief magistrate, shown here in 1910. Photo credit: Library of Congress.

seen in the neighborhood, or, 'a knife was found resembling an Italian stiletto.'" Such grievances would be echoed in the complaints of future minority groups.[13]

Petrosino tried time and again to show that the crime problem did not stem from some kind of inherent flaw among Italians, but from immigration laws that allowed criminals wanted in Italy to escape their homeland's harsh justice by finding safe harbor in New York. He found a willing ear in the commissioner Mayor McClellan installed after dumping McAdoo in December 1905. McClellan, whose father was a lackluster Civil War general and 1864 Democratic candidate for president, had just won his second term by edging out newspaper publisher William Randolph Hearst's anti-corruption mayoral campaign. McClellan, who won with under 40 percent of the vote in a three-way race, ran with Tammany support, as he had in his first term. He realized that reform was in the air and backed away from the Tiger, the symbol political cartoonists used to satirize Tammany's Boss Tweed and his successors as voracious beasts. "McAdoo, as a police commissioner, was a failure," McClellan later wrote. "He had no control over the force, which was really run by the inspectors." McClellan found his man in General Bingham, as people usually referred to him.[14]

When Bingham took office in January 1906, the forty-seven-year-old West Point–trained military engineer promised to "raise hell." He wasn't a man Tammany could buy or intimidate; he still stood ramrod-like despite the artificial limb he wore after the loss of his left leg in a construction accident in 1904. A tall gentleman with disappearing, sandy gray hair and a handlebar mustache, Bingham was a man of action with a genteel background as a Yale-educated New England blue blood whose ancestors served in the Revolutionary War. The commissionership marked his return to public life after a nearly fatal accident; a derrick crushed his knee, causing a perilous infection. McClellan, who was serving in Congress when he met Bingham, had made a surprise choice. Bingham was not a cop but a brigadier general—his friend Teddy Roosevelt promoted him to a general's rank on the next-to-last day before his disability required him to retire from the Army.

There was much angst within the Police Department about Bingham's appointment, but the Italian Squad detectives had found someone they could work with; Bingham had big plans for their unit. After he took office on January 1, 1906, he listened closely to Petrosino and invited him to submit a plan for squelching crime in the Italian community.

Bingham quickly expanded the Italian Squad. But he wanted something more: a "secret service" that would infiltrate the Italian community and report back to him on it. The *New York Times* had suggested this in an editorial. "Such a body is utterly distasteful to American ideas, and its existence would almost certainly lead to evils and abuses nearly as bad as those it would cure, but the alternative is hard to find," the paper acknowledged. However, it warned, "Sooner or later the immigrant bandits will attempt to extend their operations beyond the circle of their own countrymen, and then the measure of equanimity with which we now regard their killings of men more or less like themselves will suddenly disappear, as it did in similar circumstances in New Orleans." The *Times* was alluding to lynch law, which it endorsed after residents of New Orleans murdered eleven Italians in 1891 when a jury issued an acquittal in the slaying of the city's police chief, David Hennessy.[15]

The precedent for a "secret service" came from a private investigation that destroyed the "Molly Maguires," Irish immigrants who were suspected of violence against coal mining companies in northeast Pennsylvania in the 1870s. In December 1906, the *Times* reported that Bingham had ordered the creation of a "secret service" under Petrosino's direction. But Bingham still needed money to fund it. On January 5, 1907, he wrote to McClellan to propose hiring civilians to snoop on the "Italian Black Hand" and anarchists. These employees could be "engaged and discharged at will by the Police Commissioner, to be composed of the best men who can be found anywhere in the world, regardless of any conditions but efficiency." It was necessary, Bingham maintained, because Petrosino and his detectives were easily recognized in the Italian community.[16]

When the Tammany-led Board of Aldermen opposed him, Bingham fought back. "It would be utterly impossible to obtain results when the members of the force are known to 'professional' crooks, or even to 'crooked' politicians," he wrote in the NYPD's 1907 annual report. "The men of the force to-day are not yet quite sure as to who is their real 'boss'—whether it is the 'machine' or the Commissioner."

Even without a "secret service," Bingham expanded the Italian Squad to twenty-three detectives in Manhattan and ten in a Brooklyn unit formed under Vachris in 1907. In that year alone, the squad would work on 424 "Black Hand" cases, including forty-four bombings. The aldermen were not about to be impressed with anything Bingham did, however.

If McClellan had set out to design a police commissioner who would repel Tammany, he could not have done better than Bingham. With his engineer's precision, his Anglo-Irish Yankee Protestant, upper-class, Ivy League–educated ways, and his admissions that he'd never lived in New York before and that he voted Republican for president: everything about him raised the hackles of Tammany's Irish Catholic, up-from-the-streets, deal-making, graft-chasing political brawlers. Routine city budget requests to fund new police station houses turned into a cat-and-mouse game—and Bingham was not used to playing the mouse. He struck back in a threatening newspaper interview:

> I'd hold a mass meeting in some big hall and I'd pick fifty or sixty of the biggest and huskiest men at the meeting. I would select men from each of the districts of the city, and with these men I'd storm the City Hall, take out the aldermen and stick them up against a wall, and I'd say to them: "What are you going to do for me? Are you going to play politics or are you going to give us what we want?" It seems to me that this is the only solution of the problem. The people don't run the city anymore. It's run by the Board of Aldermen and a pack of fools.

FIGURE 2.4. Police Commissioner Theodore Bingham (left) and Mayor George B. McClellan, Jr., distribute awards at New York's annual police parade in 1908. McClellan fired Bingham the following year. Photo credit: Library of Congress, George Grantham Bain Collection.

When a reporter suggested that Bingham was calling for a riot his officers would have to police, he continued, "Well, let's have a riot call. We could cope with it."[17]

McClellan would later write of Bingham: "He had the press with him in the beginning, for he was 'good copy,' as is always any official who bangs his desk and swears a great deal, until the public tires of him." Alderman Timothy P. "Little Tim" Sullivan, cousin of the powerful State Senator "Big Tim" Sullivan, Tammany boss on the Lower East Side, rose from his seat and accused Bingham of lying. "I place him in the same category as Tom Pepper and Mr. Ananias," he said, showing his erudition. (Ananias was an early Christian who dropped dead after lying to St. Peter, according to the Acts of the Apostles. Tom Pepper was a Mark Twain character who was a "preposterous liar.")

"Little Tim," a pale, clean-shaven, dark-haired thirty-six-year-old whose height was actually average and whose political clout was heavyweight, moved to discard Bingham's letter in the trash. The aldermen deemed that inappropriate. Instead, "the letter was received and ordered not placed on file."[18]

No one was surprised to see Sullivan mock Bingham; the newspapers said quite openly that the Sullivans opposed Bingham because he threatened their illegal gambling interests. Although he had on-and-off alliances with the Sullivan clan, McClellan knew it too. "He was part-owner of a very successful vaudeville circuit, the head of a syndicate that controlled and exacted tribute from every prize fight in the city, and the head of another syndicate that received regular payments from the city's gambling establishments," he wrote of "Big Tim" Sullivan. According to McClellan, the Sullivan cousins were corrupt, "frankly and unashamedly." "Big Tim" once told him: "I don't hold for any man taking the stuff from them poor women, but the liquor dealers and the gamblers ought to pay and they do."[19]

The *Brooklyn Eagle* explained why the commissioner's requests for a secret service were rejected: "The motive for the move was hostility to General Bingham combined with an instinct for petty politics. General Bingham has been harassing the gamblers and he re-established the two-platoon system. The policemen do not like this latter move, while friends of the Sullivans were supposed to be hurt by activity against gambling houses."[20]

One might think that creating a "secret service" composed of anonymous civilian investigators known only to two or three top police officials—as Bingham desired—would alarm progressives as well because of the civil liberties implications. That was not the case, however. The reform movement was anti-Tammany and to an extent anti-immigrant.

Bingham displayed his own bias against immigrants. It came through most clearly when he published a 1908 article article claiming, falsely, that Jewish immigrants committed 50 percent of the crimes in New York (and Italians 20 percent, albeit more violent offenses). It was an obvious exaggeration, as anyone familiar with the criminal dockets should have known. It was also a gift for the growing anti-immigration movement.

Bingham set out to raise private money, using the specter of Black Hand violence to attract donors. Actually, though, his plan went well beyond policing crimes among Italians. He spoke of employing secret agents to spy on anarchists and socialists, and even politicians who stood in his way. "Give me the money and I would put certain men behind the bars," he warned.[21]

The Italian Squad detectives at least appreciated the commissioner's willingness to stand up to politicians. "Since he has been in office, I have had a much easier time of it than I had before," Petrosino said. "Now I do not have politicians bothering me. It would surprise the public if it knew the names of some of the men in both parties who have come to me to intercede for some Italian criminals."[22]

It was easy for the aldermen to take the high road in rejecting Bingham's plan for civil liberties reasons: the idea of a secret squad, targeted at one ethnicity, raised obvious concerns. They've been echoed in present-day controversies over the NYPD's surveillance of the city's Muslim community. The private funding troubled even the supportive *Times* editorial board; it mumbled that "the procedure is irregular."[23] Meanwhile, he got into another scrap with the aldermen on February 19, 1909, this time over personnel moves that offended politicians from Brooklyn (a separate city until 1898); they contended he had favored Manhattan. "Several Aldermen wanted to tackle Gen. Bingham at once," the *Sun* observed.

Bingham let a routine City Hall complaint provoke him. "I am the boss. I have complete and entire supervision over my department," he told a committee. "As long as I am police commissioner, I will be commissioner. I hold my men in the hollow of my hand, and I will be absolute."

Having gotten that off his chest, Bingham gleefully announced to reporters later that morning that he'd succeeded in raising enough private money to start a fifteen-person "secret service." The donors' names were not disclosed, but news accounts said they were a mix of wealthy Italian immigrant businessmen and a leading industrialist who'd been plagued with Black Hand extortion threats, most likely John D. Rockefeller, Sr. Petrosino would be the commanding officer, and another lieutenant, Arthur Gloster (and not Vachris, it was quickly noticed), would replace him as commander of the Italian Squad. The commissioner told reporters that he faced no restrictions on how the money could be used, implying that his political opponents could find themselves under investigation.

And then Bingham let slip what ought to have been a closely guarded secret: that Petrosino was at that moment on a secret mission to Italy. Papers, including the Italian-language *Il Progresso*, noted it in various ways; the *Herald* was the most specific. "As a first step in the undertaking Lieutenant Petrosino has gone to Italy and Sicily, where he will procure important information about Italian criminals who have come to this country," it reported. "At present the New York police know of many criminals in the city whom they would like to deport, but they lack definite information about their records in Europe necessary to prove their case." The *Herald* was the American newspaper most followed in Europe; the story was picked up in the Italian press.[24]

Petrosino's journey was supposed to be kept quiet—that was how the plan's architect, Fourth Deputy Commissioner Arthur H. Woods, conceived it. As secretary of the Citizens Union, Woods had played an important role in the high-minded if elitist good-government movement, specializing in police reform. Bingham hired him in 1907, putting him in charge of reshaping the problematic Detective Bureau.

In the same year, Congress passed a law allowing authorities to deport immigrants who had a criminal record in their homelands, provided that they had been in the United States less than three years. Petrosino targeted those he suspected of continuing to commit serious crimes after migrating, and his squad was able to deport twenty-seven in 1908. New York's chief federal immigration officer, Robert Watchorn, said Ellis Island officials got to know Petrosino well and respected him for being "very methodical and matter of fact in his methods of procedure." Petrosino was convinced that if the worst Black Hand criminals could be deported, he could deal with the rest of the problem, according to Watchorn.[25]

Bingham sent periodic letters to the State Department requesting that it ask Italian authorities for the criminal records of dozens of Italians charged in New York with serious crimes—felony assault was the most common offense. But it was an agonizingly slow process. So Petrosino was sent to do his own research in Italian criminal records, to coordinate better with Italian police, and to recruit operatives for the "secret service."

Woods's intent is seen in a back-channel letter he wrote in January 1909 to his friend Robert Bacon, number two official in the State Department. "I am writing this unofficially to ask you unofficially just what we ought to do about this thing," he wrote, asking Bacon's help. "We do not want to make this a formal visit. We want to send Lt. Petrosino over rather on the quiet in order to get information which takes forever if we ask for it officially." Woods took responsibility for an earlier letter Bingham sent to the State Department asking for the "cop" to be introduced to Italy's minister of foreign affairs. "The Commissioner's previous letter to the State Department put the thing on entirely too high a plane," Woods wrote. "It is not our intention at all to have any sort of official visit; in fact we want to keep it on the dead quiet." Woods closed his letter with chummy chatter—"Hammy Hadden was telling me the other day that he had had a good letter from Gaspar"—and a bit of politics: "I had you slated for the Postmaster Generalship, myself." (Bacon became secretary of state later in 1909.)[26]

Woods was cleaning up for Bingham—but there was nothing he could do about the commissioner's impulsive remarks to the press a month later: the first mission of Bingham's "secret service" was no secret.

"The Same Fate as Petrosino"

I‌T was a huge risk to rush another star detective to Italy—but there was a lot of pressure on Bingham to act, for he carried a heavy responsibility for Petrosino's disastrous mission. "At police headquarters, 'I told you so' was on everyone's lips, and, while the assassination caused much sorrow, it was not entirely unexpected," the *Tribune* said. Everyone knew that Bingham had blundered by telling reporters about Petrosino's mission. (It was overlooked that *L'Araldo Italiano* ran an advance story on Petrosino's trip two weeks before the commissioner blabbed to reporters.)

Furthermore, the Police Department had failed to provide a promised second detective to help Petrosino. Correspondence shows that Petrosino continued to believe the department would keep its pledge but that, in fact, the police brass had not yet applied for diplomatic approval for a second investigator. The original plan for the mission had been that Michael J. Galvin, a decorated detective captain at the Elizabeth Street station house, would also go, according to the *Herald*. But there wasn't enough money to send him.

One day after Petrosino's murder, the Police Department declared that all ten thousand of its officers were empowered to act as detectives on the case. But for practical purposes, it fell to the Italian Squad to give the probe direction. "There was no concealment of the fact that the police were resentful and revengeful in the arrests, for the murder of Joe Petrosino in Sicily has stirred up the members of the force as no other case has stirred them up in years," the *Eagle* said. "The police, and particularly the members of the Italian squads, will now keep up a continual warfare."[1]

Vachris and other Italian Squad detectives believed that Petrosino's enemies in New York had initiated the scheme. There were many possible candidates, but the suspects who beat charges in the 1903 Barrel Murder case topped the list; Petrosino had continued to hassle them. The eleven defendants arrested in that case were part of a counterfeiting ring; at the time, they were believed to have murdered Benedetto Madonia after he tried to drop out of the enterprise, then stuffed his corpse in a barrel found on the Lower East Side. The leaders of the gang were two of New York's most notorious criminals, brothers-in-law Giuseppe Morello and Ignazio Lupo, who both had checkered pasts in Sicily before migrating to New York. Petrosino worked closely on the case with the chief of the US Secret Service office in New York, William J. Flynn, who already had the gang under surveillance as he tried to break its counterfeiting operation. The case fell apart despite that, in part because Petrosino's police superiors ordered arrests too soon.

Six years later, Vachris tried to shake information loose from either members of the Barrel Murder gang itself or from people who knew their whereabouts. But the Barrel Murder suspects had mostly vanished. Some had gone underground in the face of the Italian Squad's harassment, US Secret Service surveillance, and—probably most important—a string of apparent revenge slayings picking off the Barrel Murder suspects one by one. Petrosino had been piecing together these slayings, which began in 1905, two weeks after the Barrel Murder victim Madonia's brother-in-law, Giuseppe De Priemo, was released from Sing Sing. He'd begun his sentence on a counterfeiting conviction a month before Madonia's murder; it may well have been the case that the gang had murdered Madonia because it couldn't get at De Priemo while he was in prison. Flynn would later write that the lawman staged a scene in front of a co-conspirator that made it look as if he had struck a deal with De Priemo. (Flynn didn't express any regrets.)

The first to die was the suspected assassin, Tomasso Petto, called *il bove*, "the ox," because of his brute strength. Petrosino picked up on street talk that De Priemo had been seen hunting for Petto, and then learned that Petto was ambushed and shot five times outside his hideaway home in Brownston, Pennsylvania. Newspapers dubbed it the

"Benedetto vendetta." Another Barrel Murder suspect, butcher Vito La-
Duca, fled to Palermo and was murdered there, as Vachris learned early
in 1908.[2]

A key figure, grocery and wine importer Ignazio Lupo, had recently
skipped town; he carted away nearly all the goods from his warehouse
at 210–214 Mott Street one night, leaving creditors to fight for the remaining scraps in bankruptcy court. While Bingham pursued diplomatic channels to get rid of immigrant criminals, Petrosino employed
extra-judicial methods against Lupo, who was Morello's brother-in-law.
"Lupo's alleged connection with the Mafia here was uncovered by Petrosino, and it was during the later stages of the detective's investigations
that he incurred the bitter hatred of Lupo," the *Times* said. "According
to the story told by several men who knew both Lupo and Petrosino
well, the latter heard that Lupo had made threats against him." Petrosino
paid a visit to Lupo, who was described by one investigator as a "well-
dressed, soft-spoken, slick-looking 'gent' of pretended refinement." After
speaking quietly to Lupo outside his business, Petrosino drew close and
punched the stocky, jowly, black-haired hoodlum—a bigger man at five
feet, six inches, 182 pounds—to the ground and pummeled him. "He
did not see Lupo again, and after a few weeks, Lupo disappeared" in
November 1908.[3]

Another suspect arrested in the Barrel Murder, forty-nine-year-old
Pietro Inzerillo, was shot in the face in New York on December 27, 1908.
Petrosino had rushed to St. Vincent Hospital to interview him and, not
surprisingly, Inzerillo concocted a dubious story. The Italian Squad detectives knew that unlike the typical Black Handers they dealt with, the
Morello gangsters had not only the motive but the means, including
connections with Sicilian mafiosi, to assassinate Petrosino during his
travels. Detective Ralph Micelli, Petrosino's closest friend in the Police
Department—he was the one assigned to give Adelina Petrosino the official word that her husband had been slain—also thought it possible
that De Priemo was tied in with the slaying because Petrosino had been
trying to get him deported following his release from prison.

Inzerillo, who owned a pastry shop on Elizabeth Street, had the misfortune to be one of the few members of the Barrel Murder gang in plain sight. He was easily recognizable by his long, dour face, and detectives quickly arrested him down the block from his business on the suspicion that he could provide evidence, if not about Petrosino's death, then about a December 20 bombing at 20 Prince Street, around the corner from his cafe. He was released on bail.[4]

On the other side of the East River, Vachris, Michael Fiaschetti, and two other detectives were making arrests at Sicilian mob hangouts in the Williamsburg and Bushwick sections of Brooklyn. Vachris had become familiar with the Morello gang in the summer of 1904 when investigating the kidnapping of young Tony Mannino; Barrel Murder suspect Vito LaDuca was again under suspicion. The eight-year-old boy was freed, but police never found the evidence to arrest anyone in the Morello gang.

Vachris stayed out all night, eyeing a crowded Sicilian social club at 195 Johnson Avenue in the Williamsburg section. As detectives raided, the twenty to thirty men inside scrambled; one was hauled in as he scaled a fence. The raid led to three arrests and the seizure of three revolvers, a sawed-off shotgun, and a knife. Elsewhere, a man arrested on a vagrancy charge, Antonio La Rosa of East New York, Brooklyn, had been overheard applauding Petrosino's death and boasting of what he himself would like to do to the Brooklyn Italian Squad detectives. "This morning Vachris paid his respects to La Rosa in a strenuous interview held in the lieutenant's office," the *Eagle* said.[5]

This case was small-time in comparison to what awaited Vachris. Bingham planned to send him to complete Petrosino's work in Italy. A second Italian Squad detective, John R. Crowley, a son of Irish immigrants, was to accompany him. Crowley had learned to speak Italian on the job in Brooklyn's waterfront neighborhoods. Bingham faced up to the risk he was asking his detectives to take, asking the State Department to alert the Italian government "and to ask for them the fullest measure of personal protection that can be afforded."

It would be needed: the plan was so widely known that, on March 18, *Il Progresso* published a front-page item from Palermo that warned, "The news that other American detectives are on their way to Sicily, in order to fulfill Petrosino's plans, has created the most lively excitement in this city. The Mafia openly threatens that the new detectives will meet the same fate as Petrosino."[6]

"We Are on the Ground and He Is Not"

THREE days after learning that Joseph Petrosino had been assassinated in Palermo, Anthony Vachris set out for Italy. His path began in unaccustomed finery, at an elegant, brownstone-front townhouse at 224 Madison Avenue where he met Deputy Commissioner Woods at 9:30 p.m. It was an unlikely meeting place: the home of Charles A. Peabody, wealthy president of the Mutual Life Insurance Company; his wife, Charlotte, a prominent socialite; their three children and six servants. Woods was from the upper crust: in 1916, he would marry Helen Morgan Hamilton, J. P. Morgan's granddaughter and a great-great granddaughter of Alexander Hamilton.

Crowley was also there to receive instructions. Vachris had some reservations about Woods, who had no policing experience before becoming a deputy commissioner in 1907. He was, however, on the way to a reputation as one of the leading police reformers of the Progressive Era, and brimmed with ideas. After graduating from Harvard in 1892, the young Bostonian studied sociology at the University of Berlin, researching the police detective bureaus of London, Paris, and Berlin. Afterward, he became a schoolmaster at the Groton School for a decade; his students included Franklin Delano Roosevelt. Meanwhile, he continued studying and writing on police reform, and then in 1905 took a fifteen-dollar-a-week job as a reporter for the *New York Evening Sun*. He also became active on a police reform committee at the Citizens Union, hub of the anti-Tammany good-government movement. Bingham, who moved in these same circles, liked Woods's ideas and hired him as deputy commissioner.

Woods wrapped his arms around this opportunity to bring modern policing to the nation's largest city, starting the department's first homicide squad, the canine corps (four Ghent puppies and one English Airedale, rather than the bloodhounds Bingham preferred), and a card system that allowed him to keep track of each detective's work daily.[1]

Arthur Carey, a star detective who was the first commander of the homicide squad, opined favorably on Woods. "The idea of a Harvard graduate and former English instructor in a fashionable private school coming in from the outside to run the Detective Bureau was received with various reactions by members of the force," he wrote in his memoir. "Woods soon convinced the men by his democratic manner and his practical knowledge of police methods that he was fitted for the job. He put on a workingman's shirt and went out on jobs; lay all night on important plants with the men."[2]

After meeting with Woods, Vachris and Crowley headed straight for the Cunard line's *Mauretania*, which was docked on the Hudson River at Fourteenth Street. The story of their journey has been known only through sketchy, and often wrong, newspaper reports. But thanks to a twenty-six-page handwritten journal that Vachris kept for his trip, and which his descendants preserved, much more of it can be told.

At the gangplank, Vachris was startled to spot Brooklyn police captain William Knipe in uniform, a sight that worried him since his journey was supposed to be kept secret even from police superiors. Knipe tried to speak to Vachris, but the detective cut him off with a quick motion. In his clear cursive script, Vachris wrote in his journal: "he seemed to understand. I hope he had brains enough to keep his mouth shut."

The two detectives shared room 25 on one of the fastest steamships on the ocean, and went to sleep immediately. In the morning, coffee and rolls were brought to their room, and once the vessel departed the harbor, they took a brisk walk on the deck, with mild weather bringing many passengers out. Vachris was on the watch, since police believed that Petrosino's assailants had likely followed him from New York. "I look them over very closely and fail to see anyone I know," he wrote. ". . . At lunch time the passenger list is on the table, even our assumed names are not on it which shows me that the arrangements have been

FIGURE 4.1. Lieutenant Anthony Vachris (right) was sent to Italy to complete Joseph Petrosino's mission. He is shown here between 1910 and 1915. Photo credit: Library of Congress, George Grantham Bain Collection.

well managed." But Vachris was apprehensive; news on "Marconi's wireless" told him that the life of consul William Henry Bishop had been threatened: "this is not very encouraging news. but it has no effect on our determination to carry out our orders given us by our Police Commissioner."

After a record crossing—four days, eighteen hours, and thirty-five minutes—Vachris and Crowley arranged transport to London, where Vachris once again feared his secret had been revealed.[3] A former *New York Evening World* reporter, Charles Murray, "recognized me and began to ply me with questions," Vachris wrote. "I begged of him to keep mum." There was time to see Buckingham Palace before taking a small ship across the English Channel, and then catching a train to Paris, where the detectives transferred for Milan, enjoying Alpine vistas on the way. Then through to Genoa, pausing overnight in Chiavari in the Ligurian countryside.

Rising at 7 a.m. on March 26, Vachris caught a carriage to Carasco, filled with nostalgia—"O how my heart trills"—as he climbed a winding mountain road to his family's ancestral village, which he cherished as the place where he met his wife, Rafaella Scholastica Clesta. Since he'd been born in Paris and migrated to the United States at the age of four, it's not clear when Vachris had been to Carasco before. But, ready to start his dangerous mission, he warmed himself with memories of family. Petrosino had done likewise; on the way to Sicily, he visited Padula, the village of his childhood, and saw his brother for the first time since he'd left as a boy.

"The scenery is just as beautiful as ever," Vachris wrote, adding that he stopped at "the old homestead" where his grandparents had lived, pausing for a glass of wine with the current residents. Then "I request to be taken out to the wood, and I recognize the first place where I met my little Raf. and I pick up a few flowers. oh what a grand smell of country through that wood." He followed a path through the woods to the Church of Santa Maria in Sturla, "the same old little church, the same benches, and oh, how it makes me think of Raf. I really wish she was here to see it." Then he made his way back by carriage, down the slope to Chiavari. Late in the evening, he and Crowley caught the train for Rome, arriving at 8:30 a.m. on March 27.[4]

* * *

Vachris and Crowley took to the youthful US ambassador in Rome right away. Lloyd C. Griscom, the sandy-haired thirty-six-year-old son of a shipping magnate from a prominent Quaker family in Philadelphia, was an up-and-coming lawyer with strong Republican connections. The ambassador, class of 1891 at the University of Pennsylvania, which he entered at the age of fourteen, was very much at home in the gilded social world found in the novels of Edith Wharton, one of his wife Elsa's best friends. He was acclaimed in Italy for his response to the December

FIGURE 4.2. Lloyd C. Griscom, US ambassador to Italy, smoothed the way for Lieutenant Anthony Vachris to obtain important criminal histories from Italian authorities. "Fine man and I consider him very clever," Vachris observed. Photo credit: Library of Congress, George Grantham Bain Collection.

28, 1908, earthquake in Messina and subsequent tsunami; he'd headed straight to Sicily and Calabria to see the result of the cataclysm himself, and was the pivot of a strong American relief effort. "No disaster in recorded history matched this one—a hundred and fifty thousand dead, a half-million homeless, unknown thousands wounded and in need of help," he wrote in his memoir. "Who was to help them?" The earth's upheaval further fractured the fragile life of southern Italy, creating even more incentive for desperately poor residents of Sicily and Calabria to migrate to America.

By the time the two detectives met Griscom, he already knew that newly elected president William Howard Taft had chosen his successor as ambassador, and he looked forward to returning home to get involved in New York Republican politics (after a summer spent at J. P. Morgan's invitation in the Adirondacks). Although occupied with the earthquake and an upcoming visit to Italy from his friend Theodore Roosevelt en route to his African safari, he gave close attention to the detectives' mission in Rome. Having once worked at drafting indictments for the Manhattan district attorney, Griscom had a good sense for the Police Department's needs. "Fine man and I consider him very clever," Vachris wrote.[5]

Griscom had been working with the Italian government to find a way for the New Yorkers to accomplish their mission without getting killed. Vachris approved. John W. Garrett, first secretary at the embassy and another up-and-coming young diplomat of independent means (Princeton graduate, 1895, grandson of a former president of the Baltimore & Ohio Railroad, future ambassador to Italy), brought them to meet Italy's director of public security.[6]

His office was in Rome's Palazzo Braschi, grand home of the Italian Ministry of the Interior, located just south of the Piazza Navona. The monumental two-story staircase near the entrance, lined with eighteen red granite pillars that had originated in a portico Emperor Caligula built in the first century, set a certain tone, and the chief of police was at home there.

Francesco Leonardi, a forty-year veteran of the Interior Ministry, had met Petrosino there on February 20 and later professed to be unimpressed. He had given Petrosino a letter asking regional police prefects to assist him in "investigations and research necessary for the study of the various manifestations of crime in international relations." That hardly described the mission Petrosino intended; he wanted to target big-time criminals and build a network of spies who would report back to him in New York.[7]

Leonardi was not about to help any more American police officers wander around areas of Italy that he himself disdained as overrun with crime. Vachris was inclined to agree, but he was under pressure from

Bingham and Woods to complete Petrosino's mission as planned—and that meant going to Sicily. The only difference was that, this time, the commissioner decided that his detectives would accept protection from the Italian national police, the carabinieri. Secretary of State Philander Knox personally endorsed Bingham's plan. Vachris "is expected to work mainly in Sicily and the Southern part of Italy, and desires to obtain his information quietly from the chiefs of police of the various towns and cities," he wrote to Griscom.[8]

Diplomats from the two governments exchanged polite notes, but the detectives quickly discovered what the Italians actually meant: no police protection if they went anywhere south of Rome. On the other hand, Leonardi pledged that if they stayed in Rome, he would make sure that the records they wanted were brought to them.

Vachris and Leonardi had a long talk, finding some common ground in their antipathy for Sicily. This northern Italian bias against the south of Italy, and especially Sicily, was baked into Italian politics, both in Italy and in the immigrant communities in the United States. Vachris, with his Ligurian roots and his constant exposure to the foulest crimes of Sicilian migrants to New York, shared it. The same applied to Leonardi, who was from a village near Trent. Leonardi insisted that Vachris and Crowley avoid Sicily. "He is evidently not in love with the place himself," Vachris noted. "Finally, a plan is mapped out between us, and of course I must try."

Back in New York, Bingham and Woods followed developments closely, if at a safe distance. Huntington Wilson, an assistant secretary of state, contacted Bingham on April 2 to break the news that his detectives would not be going to Sicily, as he'd planned.[9]

Shortly before Easter on April 11, Vachris received two letters on the same day from Woods complaining that the Italian authorities had yet to turn over sensitive information that Petrosino was carrying: the names of the men he targeted for record requests. That confirmed Vachris's suspicions of police in Palermo: "am surprised, no, not surprised, but now convinced that the P [Palermo] . . . officials are not on the level because

Pet. list [the list of those whose records Petrosino sought] was never spoken of, either to Leonardi, or anyone else and will dwell on this in my weekly report to Commissioner." But overall, Vachris was upbeat: "our working is commencing to turn out pretty good. certificates are coming in."[10]

Bingham made the opposite claim to Secretary of State Knox in a May 1 letter: "It now seems that we are brought to a standstill by this unwillingness or inability of the Italian Government to afford protection to our agents. . . . Furthermore, the Director General has stated that he cannot get the information for us." His men could retrieve the necessary records from police in Sicily if they went in person, he contended, but would need protection from Italian police. It was left unstated, but there was reason to wonder if the government of Prime Minister Giovanni Giolitti would help if it meant disturbing political allies in Sicily. Giolitti also held the position of interior minister, making him Leonardi's direct superior.

Bingham reminded the secretary that the records he wanted would also help police in other cities "to get rid of a large number of Italian criminal aliens who are here in violation of our laws." He added: "It is rather a work which should be taken up by the national government than by a municipal police force." Bingham closed on a scathing note:

> If this is officially refused we shall know where we stand . . . this Government may have to consider the question as to whether Sicilians are proper persons to admit into this country, since their own Government takes the position that they are of such a lawless nature and have so little respect for the law in their own country that it is not safe to entrust them among police officers from a foreign country on official business.[11]

Meanwhile, Vachris's biggest concern seemed to be what Bingham and Woods might do if he failed to get to Sicily. He thought it would be "foolhardiness" to disregard Leonardi's warnings, writing in his jounal:

I hope the P. [Police] Commissioner will not misunderstand our reasons for remaining here [in Rome]. We are simply trying to use good judgement in obeying both the American ambassador, and the General Director of Public safety although we feel a little hurt at the tones of the 4th Deputy Commissioner's letter. still we are on the ground and he is not. if he was here, and had seen and heard the tone of this grand old man Mr. De Leonardi the General Director he would have done just as we have done . . . it doesn't look as if we have a fighting chance, if we go down there, and to ask anything beyond that is unreasonable, however we are awaiting further developments and shall be guided by them.[12]

Back in New York, Bingham and Woods were frustrated with their two detectives' work. William Henry Bishop discovered that upon returning to the US for a much-needed leave of absence.

The sixty-two-year-old novelist-diplomat was having a difficult year. As 1909 dawned, he and his wife, Sheba, were missing and presumed dead after the Messina earthquake: "Little Hope Left," a *Boston Globe* headline declared. Then came Joseph Petrosino's assassination, and several written death threats that followed. Italian police guarded the Bishops constantly. During the final week of his life, Petrosino had been to his office nearly every day, seen by the visitors who waited on line for paperwork. Of particular concern to Bishop was that he had signed the letters Petrosino sent to police chiefs around Sicily, asking for detailed information about local criminals. Men like Petrosino and Vachris were hardened to the threats they received. But Bishop, who was living the literary life as a professor of romance languages at Yale before his consular appointment, was not. The *Boston Globe* noted that Bishop, author of close to twenty novels often drawn on his travels in Europe, "is having a good chance now to gather material for a Mafia novel."

For Bishop, it was no joke. On March 18, two days before the *Globe* item appeared, he sent a telegram to Griscom in Rome: "Warned that am threatened from dangerous source with same fate—to be sent back dead to America. . . . I cannot, single-handed, combat a mysterious state of things too difficult even for the authorities." Griscom asked what he could to to help, and then took the matter straight to the Italian foreign minister, who promised to brief Prime Minister Giolitti on the threat. On March 21, the panicked consul cabled Griscom: "I don't see how you can help me, unless you could send someone . . . to manage part of the outside work. Shall keep going, but was not well even before earthquake, and may breakdown."[13]

Meanwhile, Bishop immersed himself in the details of Petrosino's murder, reporting them in his diary. He was struck that a letter Petrosino had drafted to Bingham said "am on dangerous ground" and that "I have already met criminals who know me from N.Y." He especially wanted to secure the cipher, or code—he used the Italian word, *cifrario*, in his notes—that Petrosino had used to communicate with the Police Department. He pressed to get Petrosino's effects from the Italian authorities, especially the cipher, "which I much needed to communicate early with the Police Commissioner of N.Y. but all this time has been used by the Court," he wrote in his diary on March 26, two weeks after the murder. He adapted to having bodyguards—two Italian policemen, who, he noted, took an hour off for breakfast at 10 a.m. and another hour for dinner at 3 p.m., and who were well recognized on the streets "though in civilian costume." Meanwhile, he became so frustrated by the Italian authorities' delay in handing over Petrosino's belongings that he went to court on April 1. The petition was rejected eleven days later on grounds that it was written in English rather than Italian. Bishop responded immediately in a testy letter to Cavalier Luigi Orestano, president of the Corte d'Appello of Palermo, suggesting repercussions if he couldn't get records crucial to the police investigation in New York.

Bishop was granted a leave of absence. He and his wife departed from Palermo on April 27 on board the Cunard liner *Carpathia*, bodyguards accompanying them on board until the vessel left the harbor. (The Italian officers left on a smaller craft.)

Arriving in New York on May 12, the Bishops went uptown to stay with Sheba's mother in the Bronx. Immediately, Woods arranged to meet. The next day, in the midst of some "very sultry heat," Bishop sat down with Woods, Bingham, and the commissioner's secretary, Daniel Slattery, for luncheon at 1 p.m. in the Manhattan Hotel at Madison Avenue and Forty-Second Street. It was, he wrote, "a very pleasant and interesting interview."

Bingham, he wrote, was knowledgeable about Italians because he'd served as a military attaché in Rome. Bishop also took note of how Bingham dismissed the Manhattan Democratic political machine: "The Commissioner thinks Tammany as bad and murderous as the Mafia." Woods impressed the diplomat: "a gentlemanly fellow, most intelligent and energetic." He praised an article Woods had just published in *Mc-Clure's*, "The Problem of the Black Hand," which called once again for a "secret service" for investigating Black Hand crimes.

Bishop was struck at how dissatisfied Bingham and Woods were with the Vachris mission to Rome. "The two detectives, Vachris, Ital, and Crowley, Irish, are in Rome on this case but are getting nothing," Bishop wrote. "The Ambassador consulted the Minister of Foreign Affairs, and he the Questore at Palermo, and was informed by latter that he could not guarantee the safety of the American detectives if they went to Palermo. They were therefore ruled out from attempting to trace the assassins."[14]

* * *

Nonetheless, Vachris and Crowley were accumulating hundreds of penal certificates for convicted Italian criminals who had entered the United States illegally. In a May 22 letter, Leonardi tried to assure American diplomats that the process was on track. He said Italian authorities had "acquiesced willingly" to the American request for records, which he had passed on to his police chiefs in Sicily. He'd sped the process by telling the prefects of seven provinces in Sicily to send the records to Rome as they were gathered, rather than wait to submit the entire batch, and also asked for photographs and descriptions where available. Vachris informed Bingham of that, and the commissioner warily accepted the latest assurance.[15]

Settling into a routine, the New York detectives found time to explore the Eternal City. Here, Vachris's journal veers from cop talk to what sounds like the diary of any American tourist. "Crowley and I can now walk to any point" of interest, Vachris wrote. They went to the "superb" St. Peter's Basilica several times and observed that "the more it is visited the more it is interesting." The grandest occasion was the beatification of Joan of Arc on April 18, attended by some thirty thousand people. "Also, we had a good look at the Pope, looks like a very amiable man." Vachris was close enough to note the large emerald ring on the middle finger of Pius X's right hand as he was carried aloft in his chair.

On the other hand, Vachris lamented lacking the comforts of home and hearth, and in particular the company of his wife, Rafaella. They lived in a two-story, one-family semi-attached brick home at 636 Thirty-Ninth Street in the Sunset Park section of Brooklyn, with a driveway, picket fences, and a detailed cornice. Vachris's seventy-four-year-old father, Domenico Vaccarezza, had died there recently, on February 20. He was, the *Eagle* said, "a leading and respected merchant of the Italian colony." Vachris's mother, Maria, continued to live there, as did his son Charles, twenty-three, a contractor on his way to establishing a major construction company, and daughter Lena, nineteen, a stenographer. While her husband was trying to maintain a low profile in Rome, Rafaella made the news through her community activism. With two of her neighbors, she blocked workers from installing telephone poles, jumping into the four-foot-deep holes they'd dug before work could be completed. A crowd gathered, police officers arrived, court papers were filed in the women's behalf, and friends brought out lunch and umbrellas to shade them from the afternoon sun. The three women—including Julia Simonetti, wife of Detective Paul Simonetti—held their ground until the bemused workers quit for the day.

In Rome, Vachris grumbled. "These marble floors & stone walls may look all right but if we escape without getting Pneumonia we will call ourselves lucky," he wrote during the damp days of early April, also complaining that he hadn't yet received mail from home: "more blues for me." He'd switched hotels to stay in a cheaper place, and found it "cold and clammy."

Traffic was poorly managed, he found, and even the Roman food and drink failed to meet his standard. "Both Crowly [sic] and I miss the good american coffee and tea"; the espresso served in Rome was "thick and undrinkable," and "sugar is a luxury and is always very measured." Plus, "everything here is macaroni with a big M. Every time you ask for soup you get macaroni water."[16]

Given such complaints, it's evident the immigrant detective was a fully assimilated American visiting Rome.

* * *

Griscom wanted to make sure Bingham appreciated the progress Vachris and Crowley were making. "Their efforts have been largely responsible for bringing about the new order and a great improvement in the manner in which the Italian authorities treat our requests for criminal records," he wrote to Secretary of State Knox.[17]

For the detectives, the big question was whether they would go to Sicily—if not to seek out records or look for Petrosino's killers, then to please their bosses. But suddenly, their bosses were no longer on the city payroll: Mayor McClellan fired Bingham on July 1, 1909, and Woods then resigned. On the same day, Vachris and Crowley received a cable from the new commissioner, William F. Baker, to return to New York.

What happened next has been the subject of confusion ever since, misrepresented in the newspapers and then in historical accounts. It need not be, since Vachris testified about this publicly before an aldermanic committee investigation on February 21, 1913:

Q: Did you come back immediately?
A: I was about to get out some records at that time and I telegraphed back for them to give me twenty days. There were some important records I

wanted to get out. Well, they extended to me that time, and instead of going back about on the 6th or 7th of July, I think it was, we came back—we
started on the 5th or 6th of August and came back 30 days afterward.

That is, he continued his fruitful work in Rome rather than try to ven-
ture into Sicily for an undercover mission aimed at nabbing Petrosino's
killers, as news accounts suggested.[18]

The two detectives sailed from Naples on August 4, arriving in Jersey
City on the 19th. After their return, many New York newspapers said
they had ventured into Palermo. Vachris "went freely about Palermo
and into the haunts of the very men who would have been only too
pleased to run a knife into him had they realized his identity," the *Times*
said, adding that it was believed the mission would result in the cap-
ture of Petrosino's assassins. The *Telegram* called the trip "probably the
most hazardous of any undertaken by members of the Police Department since its inception. . . . They stayed in Palermo for several weeks,
visiting the rendezvous of many secret bands." The *Tribune* said that the
detectives "slipped quietly out of Rome and into Sicily with the help of
W.H. Bishop, the American Consul." On the other hand, the *Sun*, under
the headline "Vachris Gets Back Alive," said Bingham ordered that the
detectives not go to Sicily.[19]

Commissioner Baker put the lid on, putting out a short official statement and at the same time ordering Vachris and Crowley not to discuss
their work with anyone. Newspaper reporters relied on headquarters
gossip, resulting in many erroneous stories. The sworn testimony Vachris gave to an investigative committee of the Board of Aldermen in
1913 made clear that he thought the Italian government was cooperative.
Since this differed from what appeared in many newspapers, the committee counsel asked a second time:

Q: They were really willing?
A: They were really willing all the way through, yes, sir.
Q: Did you meet with any obstructions?

A: Not at all.

Q: And how widely did you travel about Italy on this matter?

A: Well, when we went from here, we were down in Rome for quite some time. The Italian Government was not willing to risk that we should go to Sicily and told us that any record we wanted they would supply; so they did. They told us that any record that we wanted throughout Sicily, or through any other part of Italy they could get it quicker for us than if we went there to look for it ourselves, and they did not care to assume the risk of having us killed, or something to that effect.[20]

Nor does Vachris's journal include observations from any visit to Sicily. There is one line in his final entry, dated July 29, that could be taken as a hint he did go there, briefly at the very end of his trip. It comes as he makes the impassioned argument that Sicilians should be barred from entering the United States until they can show "that the only way to enjoy real liberty is to assist in maintaining law and order." If the reader has any doubt, he continues, "then he should send for some of the court records here in Sicily, daily assassinations plunder and Robbery cases go by default because the prosecuting officials cannot get the necessary evidence and these bloodthirsty people knowing that no one will talk continue to commit these crimes." Did "here in Sicily" mean he was in Sicily when writing the passage? The "here" could also refer to records from Sicily that he reviewed in Rome—the process he later affirmed under oath.

The bulk of the evidence says that there was no side trip to Sicily. While news accounts said consul Bishop helped sneak the detectives into Palermo, his private diary says nothing of meeting the two men. Instead, it describes how he was spending a restful summer in rural Connecticut as he unwound during his leave from late April to November. Nor is there any reference in State Department correspondence for what would have been a sensitive diplomatic matter; instead it concerned efforts to build on the connections Vachris had made with Italian police. As a practical matter, it is hard to imagine the strapping Irish American

Crowley and Vachris, a Genoese who disdained Sicily, passing as Sicilians, whose "dialect" is really a language of its own.

Had Vachris and Crowley sneaked off to Sicily, the State Department's top diplomat in Italy at the time, chargé d'affaires John W. Garrett, would never have written this glowing letter to Knox:

> I have the honor to call your attention to the efficiency and usefulness of the work done by these men. They got into close touch with the local police officials; arranged a cipher for use between the police of New York and Rome and were able greatly to expedite the securing of Italian criminal records desired by the police not only in New York but in other cities in America. . . . I respectfully suggest the advisability of having either a man from the [US] Secret Service or someone designated by the New York Police Department stationed in Rome so long as the great necessity continues for securing these criminal records speedily.[21]

* * *

The hyped news coverage helped to create a mythology about the trip: that Vachris and Crowley thirsted to travel to Palermo to avenge their colleague's murder, while Bingham tried to hold them back. Likewise, the Italian government was portrayed as an obstacle to their mission. The opposite was so in both cases. The sensationalized depiction of the detectives' journey furthered the false narrative that the "Society" of the Black Hand was a single enormous conspiracy, masterminded by the Sicilian Mafia and Neapolitan Camorra. The braver the Italian Squad detectives could be made to appear in their journey to the belly of the beast, the more it expanded the aura of menace from that mysterious alien monster called the Black Hand—fuel for the growing political movement to stop Italian immigration. Vachris and Crowley were certainly brave when they needed to be, and also prudent—more so than their bosses.

Vachris's accomplishment in retrieving records that Petrosino died for—he came back with penal certificates that documented the Italian convictions of about four hundred suspects, and arranged for three hundred more—demonstrated, or should have, that the "Black Hand" could be beaten by targeting individual criminals rather than through wholesale rejection of a people.

Although Vachris was barred from giving interviews after he arrived back in New York, his hometown newspaper, the *Brooklyn Eagle*, carried what amounted to one, without direct quotes. As head of the Brooklyn branch of the Italian Squad, Vachris enjoyed a special relationship with Brooklyn's major newspaper, which cherished any institution based in the borough. The paper's account squares, better than any other, with the information recorded in State Department documents and the private diaries of Vachris and Bishop. "Vachris declares that he has succeeded beyond his most sanguine expectations in getting what he was sent after, and in finishing up the work that Joseph Petrosino had undertaken," the paper reported. "He has made more headway with the Italian police authorities than any other American agency, and he was congratulated on his success by the American ambassador in Rome." The *Eagle* added, accurately, "Concerning the murder of Petrosino the mission of Vachris and Crowley, it is believed, has been without fruit. In a letter, which Vachris sent a month ago to a friend, he said that he had no hope of securing a clew to the Petrosino murderers and that the police of Palermo seemed to be absolutely without a clew."

Along with several other newspapers, the *Eagle* said that Vachris was likely to be named to Petrosino's former job as overall head of the Italian Squad. The squad's chief since Petrosino departed for Italy, Lieutenant Arthur Gloster, would get a new assignment, the thinking went. Vachris "is probably better equipped with information concerning the Italian and Sicilian crooks than any other man in the Police Department, and he has in addition a measure of courage so tinctured with intelligence and craft that makes him valued and valuable."

But Vachris was to learn the hard way that neither he nor the documents he secured were valued in the shifting world of New York politics. As he would say: "They just laid there in the desk, in Acting Captain Gloster's desk."[22]

5

"He Got Me Some Clerical Work"

WITH strict instructions not to talk to anyone about his trip to Italy, Anthony Vachris was ordered to Commissioner William F. Baker's office. There, the seventeen-year veteran detective was assigned to work under supervision of the commissioner's twenty-five-year-old personal secretary, Alexander Hart, Jr. "He got me some clerical work to do there," Vachris later explained. "Among other things, why I translated those criminal certificates on special cards that we had in the department." But without Bingham and Woods on the job, there was little interest in the Police Department in pursing the leads Vachris brought back or in cementing the ties he'd made with police in Italy.

Having moved on from careless management of Joseph Petrosino's mission to Italy, the Police Department's leadership was now following through with a slipshod response to the work Vachris and Crowley had done to secure important documents and, even more importantly, to establish a working relationship with Italian authorities. Vachris, itching to make use of all he had learned in Italy, spent three months on clerical duty beneath Hart's eye. Crowley also was deprived of the chance to return to the Brooklyn Italian Squad; he was assigned to plainclothes duty on Saint Nicholas Avenue in upper Manhattan, a neighborhood with few Italians and far from his residence in Brooklyn.[1]

Just four months after Petrosino's murder, his celebrated Italian Squad had landed on the wrong side of the city's politics. McClellan's decision to fire Bingham and install Baker as commissioner was widely interpreted as an attempt to ingratiate himself with the Democratic bosses in Manhattan and Brooklyn. He prided himself on both being a regular-organization Democrat and a gentleman aloof from the bosses' corruption. That was the family tradition; his father, having lost the 1864 presidential election to Abraham Lincoln, went on to serve as governor of New Jersey from 1878 to January 1881. The young man looked on his father as "an aristocrat in the best sense of the word" who, as a gentleman heir to a noble Scottish family, saw it as his obligation to do whatever was right. He lamented that his father had often been cast as the villain to Lincoln's hero, and seemed to view his own career as an opportunity to right the wrongs done to him.[2]

Elected mayor in 1903 with support from the masterful Tammany boss Charles F. Murphy, McClellan led the city as it grew rapidly during the peak years of the great Italian and Jewish migrations. Construction of the city's first subway line was completed in 1904 through tunnels that a mass of poorly paid Italian laborers excavated.

But, as McClellan later bemoaned, New York mayors rarely ever won higher office. A mayor's responsibility for the Police Department had much to do with that. Police corruption was the cutting-edge political issue of the day, the rallying point for an anti-Tammany coalition that fused religiously minded Protestant reformers, Republicans, business leaders, and well-educated progressive activists. The Fusionists' basic charge, amplified in newspapers and New York–based national magazines, was that Tammany exploited its control of the Police Department to sell protection to gambling and bawdy houses. Gentleman or not, McClellan associated with that by accepting Tammany's endorsement. He passed his initial test as mayor by appointing McAdoo as police commissioner—a "really excellent" pick, the *Times* editorialized. The appointment "deliberately affronted 'Big Tim' Sullivan and the gambling element in Tammany Hall," the *Tribune* explained.[3]

But Tammany got one of its own, Thomas F. McAvoy, appointed as McAdoo's first deputy commissioner. McAvoy had resigned as a police inspector after a witness testified before the Lexow Committee's legislative corruption probe in 1894 that he delivered $200 a week in gambling graft to McAvoy's desk. (According to testimony, McAvoy drew the line at taking payoffs from bordellos; he was a "very religious man.")

By cutting ties to Tammany after his 1905 reelection and choosing the independent Bingham as police commissioner, McClellan raised his prospect for building broader support to run for governor, or even president. But he looked to another Democratic boss to sponsor him: State Senator Patrick Henry McCarren of rapidly growing Brooklyn. McCarren fulfilled the traditional role of any leader of a Brooklyn institution, which is to fight against being ruled from its Manhattan counterpart, in this case Tammany Hall. With McCarren's support, the mayor believed he had "better than a sporting chance at landing the governorship, which was the goal I set for myself." This "would have put me in the running for the presidency in 1912."[4]

McCarren had his own political need: he had to hold off a Tammany Hall effort to take over the Brooklyn Democratic organization, a battle being fought in district leadership elections. So it was important to please the influential Democratic leader in Coney Island, hotel owner Kenny Sutherland. And Sutherland's interest was in stopping police vice raids in the seaside resort. "Sodom-by-the-Sea," as the *Times* once called Coney Island, was a favored target of the Progressive, largely Protestant reform movement. This effort of the well-to-do to control the morals of the poor enjoyed considerable support in the press, which pressured the Police Department to cool off the vulgarity and rowdyism that seemed as much a part of Coney Island as the Ferris wheel.

McCarren and Sutherland got their way: the mayor fired Bingham, who insisted on trying to clean up Coney Island. As Vachris discovered, the political chain reaction that led to Bingham's removal was a disaster for the Italian Squad, not to mention his own police career.

The order to recall Vachris from Italy came from the mayor, it turned out. That is known only through an unpublished portion of McClellan's memoir; the mayor wrote that he required that "Vaccris" and Crowley return from Italy after he found out from Ambassador Griscom that Prime Minister Giolitti refused to let the detectives travel to the south. It was an outrageous act of political interference, not noticed at the time; McClellan hadn't gotten the scenario he wanted and was "much dissatisfied" because he'd wanted Bingham to send "his best Italian detective in company with one of his best non-Italians" to Palermo. After learning that they could not get to Palermo, "I took the hint and recalled them," he wrote.[5]

McClellan's dissatisfaction with their journey helps explain why Bingham and Woods pressed so hard for the detectives to go to Sicily when Vachris, no stranger to danger, thought it unnecessary. It also suggests why the Police Department marginalized Vachris and Crowley upon their return—they hadn't provided the mayor with the scenario he wanted. With the departure of Bingham and his deputy Woods, the squad lacked a sponsor in the department's upper echelons and was closely associated in the public eye with a commissioner the mayor and other powerful politicians detested.

* * *

The Italian Squad detectives also had the misfortune that their unit was associated with Bingham's most controversial initiative, his privately funded "secret service." From the start, there was always something separate about the Italian Squad. Its detectives were detached most of all by their ethnicity; the Police Department was a bastion of Irish power, and in the dangerous world of police work—and that included the danger of getting caught taking graft—officers were most comfortable working with members of their own tribe. The squad was created because the regular chain of command was ineffective in fighting crime among Italian immigrants, and Woods supervised it more so than the chief of detectives. Its office wasn't with other detectives in police headquarters, but in a dingy room at 316 Lafayette Street, a few blocks away.

Officially, Bingham's "secret service" was separate from the Italian Squad. But the two were entwined in the minds of elected officials and the general public; Petrosino was put in charge of it. There was a great difference between a shadow team of unknown civilian investigators who were paid through private donors and the Italian Squad detectives, who reported through a chain of command and whose conduct was subject to scrutiny through legislative oversight, civil service procedure, departmental discipline, and courtroom testimony. And Black Hand crime was just part of the "secret service" portfolio; Bingham essentially wanted a local version of a national police intelligence agency, with extremely little public oversight.

Bingham's general obliviousness to civil liberties had helped to ferment demands to rein in police abuse of power. The catalyst was a maverick judge from Brooklyn, William J. Gaynor, whose political prospects were suddenly greater than the mayor's as he emerged as the champion of an aggrieved public. Gaynor had complained for years about police violence and needless arrests. In a 1903 article, "Lawlessness of the Police in New York," he took on the progressives' fixation on vice raids: "The notion that the morals of the community can be reformed and made better, or that government can be purified and lifted up, instead of being debased and demoralized, by the policeman's club and axe, is so pernicious and dangerous," he wrote.[6]

Gaynor became angered by the police practice of photographing and minutely measuring suspects for a "Rogues' Gallery" before they were convicted of a crime. His May 29, 1909, letter calling for McClellan to fire Bingham for this was page-one news. He focused on the unwarranted arrests of George B. Duffy. The nineteen-year-old Brooklynite was held overnight as a "suspicious person" in connection with the theft of some whiskey from a saloon two years before, then released without charges after being photographed, stripped, and measured under the Bertillon system, which gauged 243 categories—skull length and breadth, for example—to create a unique identifier, akin to the fingerprinting just coming into use in New York.[7]

The Rogues' Gallery was posted in headquarters for internal police use, a sort of gang database. Once "marked by the police," Gaynor asserted, Duffy was arrested repeatedly and without cause. Duffy's father insisted that the Police Department remove his mugshot and measurements from its records, then sought Gaynor's help when he was turned down. For Gaynor, the case reflected a larger pattern of abuse. "Many

FIGURE 5.1. The Rogues' Gallery at police headquarters functioned as a sort of gang database. Shown here in July 1909, the month that Commissioner Bingham was fired over its use. Photo credit: Library of Congress, George Grantham Bain Collection.

thousands of false arrests are being made here annually, and many boys begin their downward career from the humiliation and debasement of being locked up in a small cell over night without any cause or for some trifle," he wrote. "The men on the police force do not want to do these and like things, but are forced to by the incompetents, corruptionists, and sometimes buffoons who are put in rulership over them." Gaynor said it was common for Bingham to ignore court rulings and to require his police to disobey them.[8]

McClellan investigated, interviewing dozens of witnesses himself. Within the month, he completed a sixty-page report and issued orders that reined in the Rogues' Gallery postings, required Bingham to remove Duffy's photo, and forced Bingham to fire his closest aide, Daniel Slattery, and a deputy commissioner who was involved in Duffy's case. After Bingham refused to remove Slattery, the mayor fired the commissioner for insubordination.

That's not to say Bingham didn't deserve to be dismissed. In his memoir, McClellan rightly called him "utterly tactless and arrogant," the most troublesome employee on the city payroll. "He was always getting himself and incidentally me into hot water, and I spent much time that might have been more profitably employed in getting him out again."

The chief offense was Bingham's false claim in 1908 that Jewish immigrants were responsible for 50 percent of the crime in New York, which prompted many calls from the Jewish community for him to resign. Mc-Clellan recognized the political damage from this "utterly ridiculous and unsupported charge" but held back from firing him, aware that Bingham remained in good stead with the newspapers and reformers. (The controversy helped lead Jewish leaders to organize the New York Kehillah, an umbrella organization of community groups that promoted Jewish interests.)[9]

With Bingham gone, his "secret service" dissolved. When a reporter asked newly named Commissioner Baker if he would need private investigators, he replied: "I should be sorry to find that necessary. I shall rely on the New York City police. They are the finest body of policemen in the world."

It's difficult to track how large a secret squad Bingham had created since this was a matter he truly kept secret. One clue came from newspaper articles reporting in mid-July that Baker had transferred thirteen "secret service policemen" to serve as patrol officers. Daniel Slattery wrote in the *Boston Evening Transcript* that Bingham had hired three hard-working Sicilians "who had no connection with the police force or any member of it." He added, "These men had little or no detective ability, but they were honest, and that was the main requirement." Their job was to learn names and plans of the members of Black Hand groups, and they "produced results," according to Slattery. Woods later testified that "we were fortunate in being able to get some men who had been on the Carbineers in Italy, who were trained Italian police officers." He added, "These Italians reported to no one but to me personally."

Bingham's annual report for 1908 also provided a glimpse. Noting that the police force had only forty Italian officers in a city with four hundred thousand Italians, he wrote that "there have been, however, during the past year, some outside men available to assist the Department by secret work among the Italians." This was needed, he asserted, because "we are trying to handle mediaeval criminals, men in whose blood runs the spirit of the vendetta, by modern Anglo-Saxon procedure."

But to police officials who remained at headquarters, there was no evidence that the "secret service" had done anything useful. "Nobody at the building to-day seemed to know what they had been doing," the *Eagle* commented on the transfers of the thirteen. "Commissioner Baker said he was unable to find that they had been doing anything whatever."[10]

Gaynor provided a more chilling glimpse. Taking time off from farming chores at his summer home in St. James, Long Island, he told a visiting *Eagle* reporter that Bingham's "secret service" had been spying on him, the mayor, and those who worked on McClellan's Duffy inquiry. "I was unconscious of it until Mr. Crowell, the Assistant Corporation Counsel, informed me of it," he said. (William B. Crowell was the mayor's counsel who led the questioning.)

Comptroller Herman Metz and Patrick McGowan, president of the Board of Aldermen, also said that "Bingham's sleuths" had followed them. Ten days later, the *Tribune* reported that the thirteen investigators moved from the "secret service" to patrol duty were not actually on the "secret" squad, but were regular patrol officers Bingham had pulled temporarily into the Manhattan detective command. Word at police headquarters was that they were the investigators used to spy on Bingham's enemies. City records show they were recent hires.[11] Bingham denied all, but Gaynor's reputation for integrity was such that no one questioned his charges. One newspaper editorialized: "Followed up under the Bingham system, almost any citizen could be led to the inquisition by the illicit use of a secret service investigation into the lives of relatives."[12]

* * *

Politics intervened on both sides of the ocean. At the same time the Italian Squad was blunted, the Italian authorities' probe of Joseph Petrosino's murder fell apart when the Interior Ministry removed the chief investigator, Baldassare Ceola, from his office in Palermo on July 17, 1909. Ceola, a respected, veteran investigator from Italy's far north—he headed the inquiry into the slaying of King Umberto in 1900—had been sent to Palermo eighteen months earlier. Petrosino, Vachris, and Bingham had all underestimated Ceola's integrity: he quickly built the evidence to arrest fifteen defendants for trial. The politically influential Vito Cascio Ferro, the "dreaded criminal" whose name Petrosino jotted in his notes on the last day of his life, was seen as the mastermind of the murder. The polished don looked to be the Sicilian patron for a scheme in which plotters from the Lupo-Morello gang trailed Petrosino.

Ceola fumed over what he saw as a lack of cooperation from Bingham; even though probers on both sides of the ocean thought the assassination plot originated in New York, Ceola could get no useful information from the police commissioner. "With all the detailed, precise particulars this Office provided, it should not be a difficult thing for the New York Police to find and complete the information requested repeatedly and which is of the utmost importance for the investigation," he wrote in a May 16, 1909, report to his superiors. "Especially since the agents on the Petrosino Squad are almost all Italian, and indeed, several Sicilian . . . [and] well know the Sicilian *mala vita* residing in Brooklyn and New York, their habits, their relationships, their meeting places." More precisely than any New York newspaper, Ceola listed the nineteen Italian members of the Manhattan-based squad, reverting anglicized names to Italian (Hugh Cassidy to Ugo Cassidi) and leaving out the Irish, Italian-speaking members (John Crowley, Francis Upton, Thomas McDonough).[13]

Ceola's evidence against many of the defendants was thin, but he had a more solid case against Cascio Ferro and two Lupo-Morello associates from New York, identified as Carlo Costantino and Antonino Passananti. The entire case needed further investigation, as well as full cooperation from police in New York, who knew a great deal about Costantino and Passananti. Instead, the case withered until the Court of Appeals of Palermo dismissed all charges on July 22, 1911, for lack of evidence.[14]

* * *

The true story of the twin missions to Italy—Petrosino's, and then Vachris and Crowley's—differed greatly from their telling at the time. Bingham and Woods planned Petrosino's journey, not Petrosino. He went alone on the first operation of the "secret service" because Bingham didn't have enough private funding to pay for a second detective; the Board of Aldermen would not appropriate money (but was later willing to compensate Petrosino's widow).

Likewise, Vachris didn't want to travel to Palermo to nab his friend's assassins—and did not go there. Bingham and, as it turns out, the mayor pushed for Vachris and Crowley to deliver that politically pleasing scenario. The mayor was the one who unplugged Vachris's mission.

With Bingham gone, the Police Department's personnel moves became transparently political again. The unstated message to police superiors was that they risked their careers if they displeased corrupt local political powers. In this political atmosphere, Baker failed to follow up on the records Vachris and Crowley had obtained, and the much-sought connection with Italian police faded away even though correspondence shows State Department officials were eager to see it through. There were no direct orders, but there was no enthusiasm for pursuing Bingham's initiatives.

"A police department can never be better than the City Hall," the veteran New York police reporter Emanuel Lavine would write in a scathing 1937 book on the secrets of the NYPD. "Nor can a police chief ever be better than the mayor who sits in that City Hall." He wasn't writing here about the Italian Squad, which he'd covered in its later years. But it sums up the political obstacles the detectives faced.[15]

6

"Petrosino Is Dead, but the Black Hand Lives"

No matter the politics coming from City Hall and the commissioner's office, the Italian Squad detectives kept busy confronting a continuous flow of horrendous crimes against Italian victims that the rest of the police force was ill-suited or not exceptionally eager to handle. They had little time for marquee investigations—even to try to solve Petrosino's murder—when they were put on the heartrending stories of crime victims like Maddalena Finizio.

Having rejected the suitor her parents pushed her to marry, she'd arrived in America for a new life with the man of her dreams. Gaetano Finizio had returned to his home town of Ortona, where sloping vineyards framed the western horizon of a fishing village on the Abruzzo coast, to woo his chestnut-haired, twenty-year-old bride. They married in Naples en route to the ship that carried them to New York on a frigid January 19, 1909. With the bride's nineteen-year-old cousin Carminio Scarlato, they caught a train to upstate Middletown, eager to get to nearby Otisville, where Gaetano heard there was a job available. Arriving late in the evening, they stopped in a saloon on Cottage Street to seek a room for the night. Three men offered to help, and took them through town and out to the Erie Railroad tracks. There, the men shot Scarlato, who died on the scene, his body left on the tracks to be run over by a train, and fatally wounded Gaetano. They ran down the fleeing bride, dragged her to a box car, stole her wedding ring, and left her with a man who sexually assaulted her. Though shocked by the attack, Maddalena Finizio was able to give authorities a good description of the assailants. Further, she was determined not to go back to Italy until justice was done.[1]

The sheriff learned that the assailants were visiting New Yorkers with ties to a Brooklyn-based gang, and reached out to New York City police for help. Detective Charles Corrao got a tip on June 22 that one of the suspects was living in a boarding house at 19 President Street in Brooklyn. He showed up there at dawn the next morning. The suspect, variously identified as Alphonse Albanese, Alphonso Albanez, or Frank Perry, was in bed when Corrao arrived. The plainclothes detective tried a ruse: he told his suspect to dress quickly because there was a job he could take in New Jersey. When Albanese insisted, "I don't have to work," Corrao dropped the nickname of a man he heard was helping him hide: "'Pute' says they are on to you. He wants you to join him in Jersey quick. Come on."

Once Albanese dressed, they ferried to Manhattan from the Hamilton Avenue pier, then caught the elevated train to Houston Street. On the way, Albanese talked about the slaying in Middletown and of how he had lured the victims into a trap. As they crossed the Bowery at Houston Street—several minutes' walk from police headquarters—twenty-two-year-old Albanese twisted away, belting Corrao with his suitcase. With blackjack and revolver, Corrao "was forced to beat Albanese insensible before the latter stopped fighting," as one news account put it.[2]

The arrest didn't get much notice in the city, but it typifies the Italian Squad at work, from the tragic situation of the victims to the use of an inside tip to locate the suspect, the ruse, the dangerously thin staffing assigned to the arrest and, yes, to the violent conclusion. Several months earlier, another Italian Squad detective had assisted an enterprising officer from Union Hill, New Jersey, in arresting the murderous gang's ringleader, John Barbuoto, in East Harlem.

Barbuoto was convicted on Maddalena Finizio's testimony and sentenced to die. In the meantime, Maddalena found romance with the man her parents had wanted her to marry, Vincenzo Manginelli, a neighbor's son. He'd come to America and settled into a job at an electric plant in Garfield, New Jersey. After reading a newspaper story about what had happened to Maddalena, her husband, and her cousin, Manginelli went to Middletown to see her, and asked, more than once, for her to marry him. She refused, waiting for her chance to testify against Barbuoto. At his trial, she was the only witness who could testify that she saw Barbuoto shoot her husband. She said it was also Barbuoto who raped her, then stole her gold necklace and two gold rings, one of them her wedding band. On November 9, 1909, the state's highest court upheld Barbuoto's conviction; he was executed in the electric chair at Sing Sing on January 3, 1910. The day after the court ruling, Maddalena Finizio said yes to Vincenzo Manginelli. They married several days later and settled in Passaic County, New Jersey, where they would raise five children.[3]

* * *

The newspapers attributed pretty much any awful crime in the Italian community to the Black Hand. And so it was natural to blame the shadowy "society" for an April 30, 1909, arson fire that killed nine people living in a five-story tenement packed with Italian immigrants at 37 Spring Street. The victims included five children under the age of nine; many more would likely have died had not police from the Mulberry Street station house, a half-block away, responded quickly. One patrolman was said to have caught five babies thrown down from a window, but dropped two who died. A dozen children reportedly survived after being tossed to firefighters and police below.

Landlord Jacob Bruck had received death threats in three letters from the "Black Hand Society." The last, four days before the fire, threatened: "Petrosino is dead, but the Black Hand lives. Give us $1,500 or death, and bring it to the corner of Mulberry Street to-night." Corrao interrogated a young barber whom witnesses had put at the scene, but made no headway. Two weeks later, detectives Peter Dondero and Ralph Micelli arrested a former resident of the building, marble cutter Leopoldo Siano. It turned out that the "Black Hand" letters were a ploy to divert attention from the real motive for the crime: a coroner's jury determined he'd set the blaze in an attempt to collect $500 in insurance on $40 worth of furniture.[4]

News of the grim "Black Hand" fire went national, but once the flames died down, the arrest in this case received startlingly little attention even in New York papers considering that the fire killed nine people—perhaps because it was more of a "Black Hand" hoax than the work of a gang thought to be part of the supposed criminal society. Nor did it have anything to do with Petrosino's death. But the detective work on these cases exemplifies the mission that Petrosino lived for, as US consul Bishop in Palermo wrote in announcing his death: "Dies martyr . . . protecting peaceful Italian[s] in America."

"They Have Those Responsible for the Murder of Detective Petrosino"

J OSEPH PETROSINO never let go of the Barrel Murder case after Giuseppe Morello, Ignazio Lupo, and company were released from jail and the charges dropped in 1903. Unlike most of the "Black Hand" offenders he encountered, they were professional criminals with links to the Sicilian Mafia. They had not arrived dirt poor, as so many others did; they were middle-class criminal-entrepreneurs fleeing murder charges.[1] Morello, instantly recognizable by his deformed right hand but clever at eluding police, operated uptown from East Harlem and from a restaurant and saloon at 8 Prince Street in lower Manhattan's Little Italy. Lupo, an importer who played the mild-mannered gentleman to the street-tough Morello, ran a grocery wholesale business headquartered downtown at 210–214 Mott Street.

Petrosino was vigilant about Mafia or Camorra presence—the real Mafia and Camorra—in New York: In 1907, he tracked down and arrested Camorra leader Enrico Alfano, who had fled Italian charges that he murdered another Neapolitan mob boss and his wife. He was deported and ultimately convicted after a spectacular trial in 1911.

Throughout 1908, Petrosino worked with Bingham and Woods to get criminal records for Morello and Lupo from Italy so they could be deported or extradited to face criminal charges there. Bingham pushed Italy to request Lupo's extradition, as he was not-so-wanted there for his conviction in an 1898 murder. When Italian authorities balked at paying the legal costs, Bingham persuaded Acting Secretary of State Robert Bacon to ask the US Justice Department to undertake the case. Lupo, he wrote, was both a blackmailer "demanding money personally on pain of

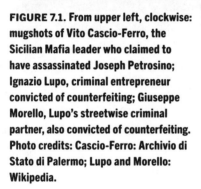

FIGURE 7.1. From upper left, clockwise: mugshots of Vito Cascio-Ferro, the Sicilian Mafia leader who claimed to have assassinated Joseph Petrosino; Ignazio Lupo, criminal entrepreneur convicted of counterfeiting; Giuseppe Morello, Lupo's streetwise criminal partner, also convicted of counterfeiting. Photo credits: Cascio-Ferro: Archivio di Stato di Palermo; Lupo and Morello: Wikipedia.

death" and a commercial swindler. "It would have the most salutary effect upon other blackhanders in this city if we could manage to extradite Lupo." Bacon personally contacted Attorney General Charles Bonaparte to ask that the government appear in court in Italy's behalf. Bingham made a similar inquiry for Morello in a December 17, 1908, letter to the secretary of state, asking at the same time for criminal records of Pietro Inzerillo, the Elizabeth Street coffee shop owner who beat charges in the Barrel Murder. He also pursued Giuseppe De Priemo's records.[2]

Petrosino in the meantime gathered intelligence on a range of Lupo-Morello associates. His targets included mafioso Joseph Fontana; Giovanni Zarcone, a butcher charged in the "barrel" case but not convicted; and Giovanni Pecoraro, a Morello associate whom Italian police would initially suspect in Petrosino's murder. Petrosino's personal papers include a handwritten note to himself: "Gius. Fontana and Giovanni Zarcano Have Fruit market at Danbury Conn." Zarcone had run a butcher shop at 16 Stanton Street in Manhattan where Morello and his gang hung out while planning the 1903 "barrel" slaying. After the case fell apart, Zarcone moved to Danbury, where he prospered as a fruit merchant and farmer. Petrosino did not live to see it, but Zarcone's past caught up with him at 9 p.m. on July 27, 1909, when he became the fourth Barrel Murder suspect to be murdered, shot from ambush. Petrosino had warned Danbury police that Zarcone would either "kill or be killed" because of the Barrel Murder feud.[3]

* * *

Meanwhile, William J. Flynn and his Secret Service agents were conducting exhaustive surveillance of the Lupo-Morello gang, trying to trace counterfeit bills back to its leaders. He maintained cordial relations with the key detectives on the Italian Squad, and in May 1909 Corrao contacted him with an informant's tip about counterfeit money being passed. Corrao used it to track down the individual who passed the money, then arranged to talk to him on the street while agents identified him.

Within a week, Flynn's federal agents started making arrests, first in Newark and Rutherford, New Jersey, then in a violent encounter on June 4 in a saloon at 192 Chrystie Street on the Lower East Side. Flynn and Corrao, accompanied by other agents and Italian Squad detectives, charged through the saloon's swinging wicker doors and into a wave of flying bottles. Within a few minutes, the battle was over and eight were arrested as "suspicious persons." One was held on a counterfeiting charge, Ignazio Provenzano, who was later convicted.[4]

The investigation reached a turning point when a convicted counterfeiter gave up the source of the Morello gang's faked currency, Antonio Cecala. Flynn viewed Cecala as the "third executive bandit" in the enterprise; he put the fake money into the hands of wholesalers, with approval from Morello and Lupo. Flynn found an even better avenue into the operation through another informant he later took credit for developing. In fact, Sam Lucchino's help came as a gift from the chief of police in Pittston, Pennsylvania, James P. Price.

Sam Lucchino's saga is remarkable. He migrated to the United States in 1903 from Montedoro, Sicily, and settled in Pittston, where coal-mining jobs had drawn a large Italian community. In 1907, he was was one of thirteen defendants in the trial of a Black Hand–type gang led by Charles Bufalino, whose four-year-old nephew Rosario would later become famous as Russell Bufalino, leader of the Mafia family known by his name. Lucchino was convicted of extortion conspiracy and sentenced to a year in prison. He emerged as an informant for Pittston's police chief—not secretly, but in full daylight, leading a local group of Italian immigrants who fed information to police. Then he came to New York and secretly posed as a customer of the Lupo-Morello counterfeiting operation; Lucchino made the risky deals needed to complete the investigation.[5]

Now Flynn was ready to make arrests in his counterfeiting case. Looking to act in one swoop so that his suspects couldn't go underground, he called on the Italian Squad for help. On a mild November morning, federal agent John Henry met Corrao and eleven other detectives from the squad at Bowery and Houston Street, where they divided up to hit the suspects' residences. Corrao went with Henry and three Italian Squad colleagues to seek out Morello in his apartment at 207 E. 107th Street, a four-story brick walkup in East Harlem that Secret Service agents had observed for hundreds of hours. When they arrived outside the building, they met seventeen-year-old agent Tom Callaghan, whose boyish looks allowed him to pose as a shoeshine boy as he conducted surveillance.

The investigators found Morello in bed, and his adult son Calogero bedded down in another room, each with a loaded revolver close at hand. Searching the apartment, Callaghan found six letters in an apron pocket. There were two more in Morello's pocket. As the investigators were about to leave Morello's flat, Detective Edward Castano noticed that Morello's wife was fussing with her baby. Castano pulled the child from her arms, then found five more letters hidden in the baby's clothing. All were Black Hand related. People evidently sent them to Morello in hopes he could settle Black Hand threats they'd received—a role that allowed Morello to play the mafioso gallant and also to share in the proceeds of any payoff. "A find which pleased the Italian squad greatly was that of the Black Hand letters," the *Sun* commented.[6]

Flynn knew there was still a serious gap: he lacked the evidence to charge Lupo. Besides that, Lupo was missing, having disappeared a year earlier with creditors looking for him. But on November 12, 1909, Lupo made a surprise appearance in the office of a bankruptcy trustee who was meeting with creditors to divide Lupo's assets. All other matters were set aside as the well-dressed Lupo told his story through a translator, explaining that after moving to Baltimore and Buffalo, he'd been living quietly in Hoboken, working for his brother for twenty-five dollars a week. Lupo claimed that he'd fled because the Black Hand had threatened his life, forcing him to mortgage a property to raise a $10,000 payoff. It seems incredible, but it's possible that rival gangsters tried to muscle the prosperous Lupo.[7]

Six days later, police caught up to Lupo and arrested him on an extortion charge. The larger police strategy was to hold Lupo until he could be extradited to Italy—or even for him to be charged there in the murder of Joseph Petrosino. "There is hardly any doubt that Lupo is a man who had a great deal to do with Petrosino's death," Italian Squad commander Arthur Gloster said. "Of course, there is a difference between suspecting a man of a crime and proving that he did it." *Il Progresso* said as much: "We know from experience that the communications of the police in this city and in America in general, they must be accepted with great reserve."

Sure enough, the extortion charge against Lupo was dismissed after the alleged victim failed to show up in court. "I have met Lupo before," Magistrate Peter Barlow said. "I would be perfectly willing to parole him and don't think he would run away. If he did it would be a good thing for this country."[8]

Early in the new year, Flynn found the witness who would cement a counterfeiting case against Lupo and the rest of the gang. An informant, Charles Mazzeo, had told Flynn about hearing talk of a printer who'd worked for the ring at the farmhouse. As Flynn arrived home from work on the evening of January 4, 1910, he received a phone call from Agent John Henry, who told him he'd just arrested the printer, Antonio Comito, and his companion Caterina Pascuzzo. Flynn headed right back to his office in the castle-like US Customs House on Bowling Green to question Comito, a stocky thirty-year-old man who had arrived in New York from Catanzaro, Calabria, in 1907 with ten dollars to his name. Flynn quickly found there would be some unexpected cooperation: when he showed Comito counterfeit five- and two-dollar bills, Comito responded, "That is my work." And then the story spilled out. Comito said he'd been coerced into this work, albeit paid for it, "but he had to run away as revolvers were pointed at him."[9]

Now the hunt was on for "the Wolf," as newspapers called Lupo, translating his last name into a street name. It took four days of effort from the Secret Service, Italian Squad, Hoboken police, and the manager of the Laude Piano Company to find and arrest him. This was accomplished thanks to a minor charge being investigated in Hoboken: the theft of a piano. The instrument was last seen being hauled away in a wagon that Lupo's brother owned. It was finally located in a home in the Bath Beach section of Brooklyn where Lupo had been hiding.

Secret Service Agent Peter Rubano and Detective Paul Simonetti found Lupo walking toward his Brooklyn hideout around 10 p.m. He denied his identity. In Italian, Rubano responded, "Hello, Ignazio." Lupo surrendered: "Well where do you want to take me?" First, Rubano responded, to his house. "Where is that?" Lupo asked. Rubano: "Why, on the next street."

Then he showed Lupo the house where he'd been hiding, at 8804 Bay Sixteenth Street. While Simonetti watched two men who'd been in the house when they arrived, Rubano took Lupo with him as he conducted a search. When he opened a drawer, both men reached in. Rubano pulled out a revolver first. But Lupo had an offer for Rubano, who wrote it down in his report:

> He said to me, "Don't you need some money? I can give you some, you had better take it and no one will know it." I said for what and he replied, "Let me go." . . . After I completed the search with Simonetti . . . Lupo in the presence of Simonetti repeated the offer of money to me, saying that he could get quite a lot of it, and fix the matter up and for me not to be a baby. I refused to take any money. He then turned to Simonetti and said, "How about you? I cannot do anything with him—will you take it." He also refused the money and then the officer said, "I will take the money from you and then lock you up for giving it to me."[10]

In the meantime, Comito had gleaned some information about Petrosino's murder. He told Flynn:

> I also heard from time to time that they expected news of a certain Calabrian who was sent to Palermo, and that he left before Petrosino did; when news arrived that Petrosino was dead they were all elated, and consumed wine, and had a feast, shooting at a bulls-eye.

Comito indicated that the Morello gang knew about Petrosino's trip before it was revealed in the newspapers. He recounted a February 4, 1909, conversation with Morello, Cecala, and a man identified only as Michele, a Calabrian. "He guards his hide well," he quoted Cecala as saying. "He knows how many he has ruined. He is popular because he ruins so many. Soon he will be dead. I hope it is successfully and cleanly done." Eight or nine days later, Comito said, Lupo denounced Petrosino and spoke of giving Michele the Calabrian money to travel to Italy, posing "as though to see his family who were stricken by the earthquake."

"You have done well," Cecala responded, winking and raising a glass. "Here's a drink to our success here and hope of death to him."

"Sh, sh," Morello responded. "Do not talk so much. Silence is best. Go away and forget what you have heard. The word of success in Palermo will soon come and then we can celebrate." After drinking heartily to that thought, Lupo expressed regret that Petrosino's death had to be quick. "'Tis a pity that it must be done stealthily—that he cannot first be made to suffer as he has made so many others. But he guards his hide so well it will have to be done quickly." A month later, Comito said, Lupo joyfully announced that Petrosino had been murdered. "The way it was planned, it never could have missed in Palermo," Lupo said. "It is well he was fool enough to go there."[11]

* * *

The trial of Lupo, Morello, and six others began on January 26, 1910, at the federal court located in the main post office at what is now the south end of City Hall Park. It quickly became enough of a spectacle that Judge George W. Ray asked the reporters to tone down the sensationalism. But they saw the trial as "the plot for a dime novel," with stock characters straight out of the moving pictures. Lupo was "big and fat and good-natured to all outward appearances, except that his eyes are small and mean, and he has an ugly mouth," the *Times* opined. "Morello, with swarthy complexion, thin-cut features, and long black mustaches, lives up to the picture of a typical Italian counterfeiter."

By the trial's second day, US Marshal William Henkel stepped up security in the courtroom. But Ray was unflappable, even after receiving a "Black Hand" letter at home in upstate Norwich. It threatened: "If the counterfeiters are not liberated you will die like a dog. We have killed better men than you or Smith or Flynn."

The judge permitted friends of the defendants to sit in the small third-floor courtroom; Italian Squad detectives were on hand to scrutinize them, looking for the hand behind the letter. It was a threat to be taken seriously; two years later federal authorities discovered another plot aimed at murdering Ray and Flynn. As the trial progressed, a growing number of Italian Squad detectives joined deputy federal marshals and Secret Service agents in securing the courtroom.[12]

The outcome looked more and more gloomy for the defendants: Flynn had assembled a masterful case. Lupo risked testifying, which meant he had to explain why he had fatally shot a competing grocer in Palermo in 1898, then fled the country and a twenty-one-year prison sentence. He swore that he fired only after the other man drew a gun.[13]

Detectives on the Italian Squad could take heart that the NYPD provided prosecutors with the coup de grâce, delivered in the government's brief rebuttal case just before testimony concluded. Morello's defense had called two doctors who contradicted Comito's testimony by saying that Morello was too sick with inflammatory rheumatism to leave his house in New York during periods the informant said he was at the counterfeiters' farmhouse. Flynn, who had a secret pipeline into the defense through informant Mazzeo, anticipated this and had his agents out on February 8 looking for witnesses who could corroborate Comito's testimony. Predictably, they encountered reluctance. But late that evening, Agent Rubano discovered through a woman who lived in Morello's East Harlem neighborhood that her husband was a police officer who'd "been watching Morello for a long time." That led the agents to discover that the NYPD had conducted long-term surveillance of Morello.

On February 10, Flynn received a welcome dossier from the Italian Squad containing "a number of reports made by six or seven different police officers who shadowed Morello, from July 1908, to April 1909." He noted in his daily report: "The testimony of these officers will be very valuable in rebutting the testimony which I believe will be given in defence of Morrello."[14]

After lunch and another forty-five minutes or so of discussion the afternoon of February 19, 1910, the jury sent word that it had reached a verdict. A few minutes after 3:30 p.m., deputy US marshals opened the courtroom doors so that the defendants, reporters, and some Secret Service agents could enter. The defendants' relatives and supporters were banished; some hundred people congregated outside in City Hall Park. The whole Italian Squad from police headquarters turned out— the detectives couldn't get into the courtroom either, and went outside to monitor the crowd and watch for any possible attempt to rescue the defendants.

Inside the courtroom, the jury foreman announced that all eight defendants were found guilty of all six counts in the indictment. Judge Ray sentenced the defendants immediately. Giuseppe Calicchio, the master printer who supervised Comito's work, was sentenced to seventeen years in prison, a stern penalty for counterfeiting. After the interpreter explained, Calicchio shrieked at the top of his voice, wept, and collapsed into the arms of the marshals, crying out, "Non è giusto, non è giusto" (It's not just).

Morello shook, begging the judge for a suspended sentence so that he could support his family. He promised to return to Italy. Ray imposed a record counterfeiting sentence of twenty-five years in prison; Morello paused, doubled down, and fainted. He was carried out for medical treatment.

Lupo was already crying by the time he stood before the judge. Wiping his eyes with a soggy handkerchief, he said between sobs that the murder charge against him in Italy was unjust and that police in two countries had been hounding him. The judge, a former Republican congressman who'd grown up on an upstate farm, made an effort to show that the sentences did not reflect bias against Italians. The great majority of Italian immigrants were good and loyal Americans, he said, but the evil ones needed to be rooted out, as for any nationality. "Here's Lupo; he's not an ignorant man. He was brought up well and received a good education," the judge said. "He was a merchant. He killed a man in his

FIGURE 7.2. Artist's rendering of convicted counterfeiters Antonio Cecala, Ignazio Lupo, Salvatore Cina, and Giuseppe Morello on their way to the federal prison in Atlanta. Photo credit: *Il Progresso Italo-Americano*, February 22, 1910.

own store at the age of nineteen. I listened to his story of this killing on the stand. I listened with deep interest to determine whether, as he said, he had killed the man in self-defense. I'll not pass judgment on that. His flight from Italy did that." The judge again imposed a record sentence for counterfeiting: thirty years in prison.

When the sentencing was over around 6 p.m., the entire headquarters bureau of the Italian Squad helped escort the now-convicted counterfeiters as they were led out, handcuffed two by two, to the Tombs jail. The scene outside was chaotic as a crowd of relatives and friends massed near the doors. Two of the defendants' wives were said to have fainted as the men were led out. Two mounted police officers hovered, on the watch for a rumored attempt to spirit Lupo away in an automobile. An organ player added the somber tune of the tragic duet "Miserere" from Giuseppe Verdi's opera *Il Trovatore*.

Unstated in all of this, even in the sentencing, was the sense that some of the men responsible for Joseph Petrosino's assassination on that rainy night in Palermo eleven months earlier had been punished. As the *Tribune* put it: "It is believed by those who have been working on the case for the government, and by Headquarters men [Italian Squad detectives], that in Morello and Lupo, and the men who have looked to them for leadership, they have those responsible for the murder of Detective Petrosino in Palermo."[15]

Two months later, Flynn's informant Charles Mazzeo passed along evidence that Lupo set out to murder Petrosino in response to the humiliating beating he suffered at the detective's hands. On the night of April 14, 1910, a frightened Mazzeo sat in on a gang parley in the back room of a Hoboken store that Lupo's brother John ran. The atmosphere was toxic as the gang denounced the convictions and long sentences for Ignazio Lupo and company. Mazzeo was nervous because he knew he was under suspicion as the possible leak to Flynn. A tall man with black hair and mustache—"Don Sebastiane"—closed the tense meeting by saying, "When it is a case of destruction, let it be destruction for a destruction." It was a call to murder Flynn.

Afterward, one of the underlings escorted Mazzeo to the ferry—Mazzeo feared he was done for—and told him a little more. In January 1909, he and another man waited nearly every night near Petrosino's apartment at 233 Lafayette Street with the aim of killing him. They never tried because he always arrived at his doorway with two other detectives. Mazzeo said he was told: "Petrosino was killed because he had slapped Lupo and heaped personal abuse on him (that is how it was termed at the meeting), not because he was a detective and had to do his duty, but because he had no right to strike Lupo."[16]

* * *

On a Sunday afternoon one year and one day after Joseph Petrosino was murdered, hundreds of people gathered on a knoll at Calvary Cemetery in Queens to unveil a monument to the slain lieutenant. Some had waited for hours before Adelina Petrosino and her closest relatives arrived in a carriage from Manhattan for the start of the ceremony. She had been coordinating the project for months, working with the artist Henry A. Bonori, a friend of her husband who owned a monument works near the cemetery's entrance. It called for a bust of her husband to rest upon a twelve-foot shaft of the "Best Barre Vermont Granite," as the contract stated.

The cost was $950, a sum the widow could hardly afford on the half-salary, $1,000-a-year pension she received. An inscription near the base of the monument, contained in a bronze wreath designed by an artist from the Academy of Fine Arts in Naples, explained: "By popular subscription of the Italian newspaper, La Follia, of New York." The satirical, left-wing Italian-language newspaper's commitment was reflected in the role of Luigi Roversi, one of its leading writers, as one of two speakers at the ceremony. The paper needled the powerful businessmen of the Italian community, and especially *Il Progresso*. It was best known for running caricature sketches by the great tenor Enrico Caruso, principal subscriber to the bronze wreath.[17]

Mrs. Petrosino arrived with her mother, her brother Louis Saulino, and her late husband's brothers Antonio and Michele. She surveyed a crowd that included all members of the Italian Squad, twenty men from Brooklyn under Vachris, thirty from Manhattan, led by Gloster. They were there not only to remember their colleague but also to protect against violence—made necessary by continued threats that followed the lieutenant's slaying, starting with a warning that Petrosino's massive April 12, 1909, funeral would be bombed.

Some two hundred lieutenants were present on behalf of a fellow member of the Lieutenants' Benevolent Association. Hundreds more gathered to pay tribute to the slain detective. And then there was the three-foot-tall bust itself, towering above, crafted of Carrara marble. Carefully chiseled—based on close study of photos—it was a precise likeness. Overcome by her emotions, Adelina Petrosino returned to her carriage to compose herself.

Richard Enright, head of the lieutenants' union and a future police commissioner, was the main speaker. He called Petrosino "a perfect public servant," adding that "the man who sleeps here was a true son of the people, a typical policeman, and a typical citizen of New York. Through his veins coursed the blood that gave to this world its discoverer." In death, Petrosino triumphed over the years of discrimination he faced in the Police Department—he was now the quintessential police officer and New Yorker. In declaring that Petrosino shared "the blood that gave to this world its discoverer," Enright touched on the reason that Italian immigrants were so proud of Christopher Columbus: he made them American, too. Enright closed his remarks with a warning to those responsible for Petrosino's murder: "Those who encompassed his death gained but a shallow victory, for Petrosino's death has aroused two nations who are resolved that law and order shall prevail."[18]

PART TWO

1910 to 1914

"The Impotence of the Metropolitan Police"

DURING his frequent stays in New York, the opera star Enrico Caruso resided in his apartment at the elegant Knickerbocker Hotel, Forty-Second Street and Broadway. His generosity to the Italian immigrant community was well known; he handed out alms freely and donated large sums to the St. Raphael's aid society. Fans knew they could write to him in care of the Metropolitan Opera House, and many did—including, on occasion, would-be blackmailers.

This led to one of the Italian Squad's highest-profile cases, carried out in the spotlight even as a newly elected mayor was planning to overhaul the Detective Bureau and do all he could to change the culture of the Police Department. Judge William J. Gaynor had campaigned on a platform of police reform, and not just the usual talk about ending graft. He pledged to end widespread brutality, unnecessary arrests, and other civil liberties abuses that, as it turned out, voters really cared about. With the Detective Bureau under his stern scrutiny, it was the wrong time to foul up a big case.

On Tuesday, March 1, 1910, the mail sorter at the opera house handed Caruso the first of two *Mano Nera* missives demanding the astonishing sum of $15,000. He was ordered to walk on Forty-Second Street until a boy stopped him; he was to hand over the cash. Police arranged to follow along, but the blackmailers didn't take the bait. On March 4, the same mail boy brought Caruso a second letter, "written in the Sicilian dialect which I myself don't understand quite well," he recounted. This time, he was ordered to leave the money that night beneath the steps of a factory at Sackett and Van Brunt Streets, a Brooklyn waterfront district. Italian Squad detectives worked on the hunch that allies of the imprisoned Ignazio Lupo were shaking down Caruso for such a large sum to raise money for Lupo's

FIGURE 8.1. Enrico Caruso at the stage door of the Metropolitan Opera House. The popular tenor testified against suspects accused of trying to extort $15,000 from him. Photo credit: Library of Congress, George Grantham Bain Collection, Flickr Commons.

legal appeals, an early indication that the counterfeiting convictions did not actually destroy the Lupo-Morello gang. They set the trap.

Detective chief James McCafferty assigned Gloster and the Manhattan-based Italian Squad to the Caruso case, a move that stirred up the interborough rivalry that existed even within the Italian Squad. According to the *Brooklyn Eagle*, no one alerted the Brooklyn unit even though the drop was to be in Brooklyn: "The story of the attempt to wring money from Caruso was too good a one, as an advertisement for the Manhattan police, to leave for solution by the Brooklyn detectives. As a matter of fact nothing was said to the members of the Brooklyn Italian force."[1]

Caruso, who grew up in the slums of Naples, was too frightened to go to the Brooklyn waterfront in the dark of night. "I have never been in any portion of Brooklyn save that which it is necessary for me to go . . . to the Academy of Music," he testified. His valet delivered the package.

Gloster handled the case personally, taking detectives Frank Mundo and Eugene Scrivani with him. As it turned out, two of the Brooklyn detectives, Paul Simonetti and Michael Mealli, "chanced" to be in the area when the Manhattan-based detectives arrived around 10 p.m. From that point, they assisted in the surveillance. Also in the neighborhood was a gray-uniformed "special patrolman," one of many the city appointed to vest private security with police powers. There was also the local beat patrolman from the precinct, John McTiernan.

With all that company, the three men checking out the envelope never touched it. They circled around it like finicky fish sniffing a baited hook. A man in a gray overcoat that ran down to his shoe tops "stooped down under this stoop" to peer at the package, Mealli later testified. That was Antonio Misiani, a handsome, upwardly mobile thirty-two-year-old immigrant from Palermo who'd been with his father's wine business back in Sicily and was now an importer, based around the corner on the waterfront block, Columbia Street. But another—Simonetti recognized him as Antonio Cincotta, a stocky saloonkeeper and murder suspect with a jowly, full moon face—saw something that disturbed him. It may have been the special patrolman standing under a bright light in front of a factory diagonally across the street, lighting a cigarette. Or possibly he caught sight of the beat cop on patrol. He told the others in Italian, "run, run." The three men scattered in different directions and the detectives, who hid in a factory, decided to give chase rather than wait to see if the trio returned to the bait. It turned out to be a mistake.

One of the suspects, wearing a peaked newsboy cap, got away. Simonetti followed Misiani. As he turned a corner, he saw the man leave a double-barreled, sawed-off shotgun in a doorway, the side entrance to a saloon. He grabbed the man, reached for a bulge in the right pocket of his overcoat, and pulled out a .32-caliber blue steel Smith & Wesson, all chambers loaded. Meanwhile, the other detectives arrested Cincotta, who'd coolly walked across the street to a saloon.[2]

Cincotta was an especially important suspect; police had been trying to jail him since 1896, when he was arrested and acquitted on a murder charge. Cincotta was arrested on a homicide charge again on March 24, 1909, after a morning shootout with a local bondsman. Cincotta escaped unscathed by either bullets or criminal charges in both cases.[3]

Vachris also believed that Cincotta played a role in a macabre murder in July 1902, the slaying of grocer Joseph Catania. Four teenaged boys going skinny-dipping had found the burly victim's corpse at the foot of Seventy-Third Street at a beach along the Narrows in the Bay Ridge section of Brooklyn, the trussed victim's head nearly severed from his body. The murder frustrated detectives, but Joseph Petrosino told Flynn at the Secret Service that a gang of counterfeiters he was investigating may have slain the grocer, who lived on Columbia Street. Petrosino began working with the feds, who kept the gang under surveillance, eyeing its gathering place in a butcher shop at 16 Stanton Street in lower Manhattan, just east of the Bowery—the place where, eventually, the infamous Barrel Murder would be planned. It turned out that the victim was a familiar face to federal investigators: they had just seen him at the butcher shop.

For a while, Vachris watched Lupo, looking for a link between the Barrel Murder of Benedetto Madonia and the Catania slaying. This became one more reason for police to lean on Lupo; Vachris believed him to be the last person who saw Catania alive. In so doing, Vachris saw that Cincotta was one of Lupo's close associates. Early in 1904, he arrested Lupo "on spec" when he saw him at the Hamilton Ferry pier, a couple of blocks from Cincotta's saloon. He went through his pockets, finding two cans of French peas, religious cards with prayers for saints' feast days, and a loaded revolver.[4] The Italian Squad detectives saw such closeness between Cincotta and Lupo that they evidently believed the two men were brothers. Bingham so argued in his letter asking for Italian authorities to extradite both men and a third supposed brother to face justice for crimes committed in Italy. Italian authorities laid out the parentage of all three; they weren't brothers, and only Lupo faced a pending case in Italy.[5]

The two men resembled each other somewhat, with the same paunchy build and similarly moon-shaped, clean-shaven faces. In their derbies and suit jackets, both presented themselves as successful businessmen; Cincotta "might be taken for a Wall Street broker," one paper said. Lupo often hung out in Cincotta's saloon on Columbia Street, close by the Brooklyn docks. Cincotta was a thirty-four-year-old former longshoreman who owned "a good business, some real estate and many diamonds and good clothing," the *Eagle* said.[6]

The messy police operation had come up with nothing against Cincotta for the Caruso shakedown; he was charged only with "vagrancy." The case quickly disintegrated. When a hearing was held before Magistrate James Tighe on March 8, Simonetti had to appear on his own— neither the district attorney's office nor the Italian Squad officers from Manhattan were present—to plead for a postponement. The *Eagle* blamed Gloster for the "very weak" case. "There was clearly a glaring blunder on the part of the police in the effort to catch the extortioners," it charged. "The Italian squad in Manhattan is in the charge of Arthur Gloster, a good detective, but a man who does not know the ramifications of the Italian criminal mind."

After that poor showing, District Attorney John Clarke announced he'd taken a personal interest in the case and was eager to convict Cincotta. "It is about time that a stop was put to him," he said. Cincotta and Misiani were indicted on charges of attempted extortion on March 25 and jailed. Misiani was convicted in the first trial; Caruso, his golden voice barely audible, was the star witness. Cincotta's case was rescheduled until after Caruso returned from touring. In the meantime, he raised the money to post his $10,000 bail—apparently by putting the arm on merchants he knew. Caruso was reluctant to testify against Cincotta, having told reporters, "He's too big a man." But he testified on March 8, 1913, acknowledging that the Black Hand threats he received had frightened him. Cincotta was convicted and sentenced to two years, six months to seven years in Sing Sing; Misiani had earlier been sentenced to three years, eight months to seven years, eight months.[7]

Ultimately, both men went free. Misiani jumped bail. The state appellate court overturned Cincotta's conviction on April 1, 1914, in a terse 3–2 ruling based on lack of evidence. Cincotta was free on bail when a stranger walked up to him in his old stomping grounds on Union Street at 10:30 p.m. on February 15, 1915, and fired three shots, fatally wounding him. Detective Mealli happened to be in the neighborhood and quickly got to the scene, learning that the gunman had escaped through a backyard. It was appropriate that Mealli, who'd put much effort into convicting Cincotta, would be there: "The police used to insist that the man was the head center of villainy among the local Italians, and whenever there was an Italian crime committed the Italian detectives automatically looked up Antonio and his movements," the *Eagle* said.[8]

The Caruso matter exposed weaknesses in the Italian Squad to public view at just the time a new mayor was planning to overhaul the Detective Bureau. With some fifty detectives in the two branches, it had become a large squad but didn't seem able to accomplish the kind of thorough, detailed major crimes investigations that Flynn had showcased in the Lupo-Morello takedown.

Flynn claimed that he'd destroyed the Black Hand by decapitating its leadership—he looked at it as mostly a single large conspiracy now dismantled at the top. That was not the case, as subsequent waves of bombings showed. But Flynn's success had made the Italian Squad look bad. After the Lupo-Morello guilty verdict, *Il Progresso* commented on "the impotence of the metropolitan police," stating that "for years and years the New York police had tried every way to get their hands on Lupo and Morello, considered the true leaders of the Black Hand. But they always find a way out of the authorities' hands and, furthermore, to act as if persecuted. . . . It took the federal police, based in Washington, to obtain a positive, concrete result."[9]

Flynn did not discourage this. Later, in his book *The Barrel Mystery*, he wrongly stated that after the Barrel Murder defendants were released "the suspects dropped out of sight as far as the police of New York were concerned. The Secret Service kept its eagle eye on them, however." In fact, as we've seen, the Police Department tried quite hard to break up the gang, in part by deporting or extraditing its members. Flynn knew that six or more Italian Squad detectives had conducted valuable surveillance of the gang in 1908 and 1909.[10]

But the Caruso case certainly showed weaknesses in the Italian Squad. Gloster, though respected as a competent police supervisor, was out of his element. That became clear in his testimony at Misiani's trial. The Italian detectives were already familiar with Misiani, Cincotta, their hangouts, and their methods, while Gloster said he didn't know who they were. His outlander status showed through as he testified about the arrest of Cincotta:

> I did not know the man; I didn't know his name . . . I do not speak Italian; I could not qualify in any way to say I do. I am head of the Italian Bureau at this time. I do not speak any Italian. I can say good morning, that's all, yes.[11]

Gloster, age forty, was born in Milltown, County Kerry, and migrated to the United States in 1888. He followed the Irish immigrant path into the Police Department, becoming a patrolman in 1897. Although he was officially reprimanded and his pay docked six times during his first three years on the force, Gloster was promoted to detective first grade on January 14, 1902.[12]

That the Kerryman moved up through the ranks more easily than the Italian detectives could not have gone unnoticed on the squad. He was an Irishman heading an Italian squad, assuming the often contentious role of Irish foreman to Italian laborers. In the tribal politics of the New York Police Department at the time—and long after—these ethnic differences meant a lot. Many decades would pass before ethnicity no longer disadvantaged Italian American police in a department that Irish Americans dominated.[13]

But the Caruso shakedown case, mishandled in full public view, indicated the Italian Squad's need for new leadership. For Gaynor and Commissioner Baker, it was one small piece of a larger effort to reform the nation's biggest municipal police force. From his office in the west wing of City Hall, Gaynor continued to gather information as he prepared to announce his overhaul. Then, in April, he received an unsolicited two-page letter with advice on reorganizing the Detective Bureau from one of the premier law enforcement agents of the day—William J. Flynn. He scheduled a meeting to hear more.[14]

9

"The Policeman's Club"

FROM his first days in office, Mayor William J. Gaynor spent much time personally investigating individual allegations of police misconduct, which arrived in his morning mail. He called the officers before him to respond to the accusations, then directed dismissals from the force. "Let the whole force know once and for all that it will be deemed a greater offense to commit an unlawful battery on a citizen, or to unlawfully enter a house, than to let a criminal escape," Gaynor declared in a letter to Police Commissioner William F. Baker. *Il Progresso* applauded: "These words of the chief of the city are very sensible and reveal once again the spirit of justice and integrity that animates Mayor Gaynor."[1]

None of the excessive-force complaints Gaynor took on were from Italians, however. In the rare instance when an assault on an Italian immigrant caught Gaynor's attention, the complainant was a middle-class woman who'd migrated from Germany. On the morning of June 10, 1910, Tomaso Velone was standing beside his pushcart at Fifth Avenue and 114th Street when Patrolman Samuel Geller shoved him to the ground and kicked him. Thirty-eight-year-old Henrietta Hyman was appalled, and told Geller so. He slapped her across the face hard enough to fell her as well, swore at her, and put her under arrest. On the way to the station house, her brother-in-law Philip Hyman saw them passing his grocery store on Fifth Avenue and asked what had caused the arrest. Geller cursed at him, then slapped his face and arrested him, too. Chief Inspector Max Schmittberger found that two witnesses corroborated the complaint; Geller lost two days' pay for it. The following year, a grocer he arrested on a charge of resisting arrest, Julius Perez, was so bruised and bloody that the magistrate at the arraignment declared, "This is the most unjustifiable assault by a policeman that I have ever seen," and added he

FIGURE 9.1. Mayor William J. Gaynor, a former Brooklyn judge, was a committed civil libertarian who strived to end law enforcement abuses. Photo credit: Library of Congress, Harris & Ewing Collection.

was at a loss as to why the man was arrested. Geller wasn't fired until several months later after he made the mistake of insulting the wife of a stockbroker, telling another cop loud enough for her to hear, "Look at that painted hussy."[2]

The violence Gaynor opposed was engrained in the Police Department that the twenty-three-year-old Joseph Petrosino joined in 1883. One has only to look at the man who introduced him to police work: Inspector Alexander S. "Clubber" Williams, who met Petrosino when he was working on a garbage scow in the days when street cleaning fell into Police Department jurisdiction. Williams's policing is summed up in his dictum: "There's more law in the end of a policeman's night-stick than in a decision of the Supreme Court." He conducted himself accordingly. At the same time, the famed Superintendent Thomas Byrnes, sometimes seen as the creator of the modern Detective Bureau, indoctrinated his sleuths in a grueling interrogation method dubbed the "third degree."

Petrosino learned policing in this school of hard knocks, and passed it on to the men who worked for him. It was well known that he used harassment and extra-legal violence to get his point across. "When Petrosino could not bring about the conviction of these men in New York he made the town too hot for them by a system of police persecution that the circumstances justified in his mind and in the opinion of his superiors," the *Sun* said after his death. It was no secret that the Italian Squad detectives were rough; newspapers winked at it in their coverage. In later years, the squad's chief, Michael Fiaschetti, even celebrated it in his memoir, *You Gotta Be Rough*.

Perhaps those targeted expected no less. "I do not hesitate to say that the Italian here does not receive that even-handed justice which the Constitution guarantees even to him," Gino C. Speranza wrote. "In fact, if there are a few guilty Italians out of prison there are not a few innocent ones behind bars."

Despite Gaynor's civil liberties reforms, there was in effect a carve-out for policing gang activity, especially when it involved Italians. A Manhattan grand jury probe led by First Assistant District Attorney Frank Moss, a Republican with impeccable reform credentials, went on record urging such a policy: "In some parts of the city policemen should have a freer use of their clubs without having to worry about vengeful charges by criminals and the expense and uncertainty of trial on charges."[3]

Through the first seven months of 1910, anticipation grew over what Gaynor would do to transform the Police Department. After working twelve to sixteen hours a day from the beginning of the year, he prepared to depart for a cruise to the North Sea and said he'd announce his plan for the NYPD when he returned. But all else was put aside on the morning of August 9 after a discharged city employee shot him at close range on the deck of the German ocean liner *Kaiser Wilhelm der Gross* as it docked in Hoboken. Fifty-eight-year-old James J. Gallagher fumed as he read about the mayor's luxury voyage in the morning paper; he had lost his two-dollar-a-day city job as a watchman on the docks three weeks earlier, deepening his poverty.

Gaynor's recovery took nearly two months. A bullet lodged in his throat above the pharynx, and doctors determined it was better not to risk removing it. He returned to office on October 3, a shadow of the man he'd been. He had been tyrannically demanding, shouting at subordinates; now he could no longer raise his voice. It felt to him as if his throat would never truly heal.[4]

John Purroy Mitchel, the up-and-coming reformer who was president of the Board of Aldermen, served as acting mayor until Gaynor's return. At age thirty-one, he had already established himself as a skilled investigator of municipal corruption. Mitchel emerged as a rival to Gaynor after the white-bearded mayor returned to office at what now seemed a very old sixty-one. He still had the energy, though, to pursue his passion for changing the Police Department.

Within two weeks of his shaky return, Gaynor acted. On October 20, Baker was out as police commissioner. (Greener fields were ahead for Baker; he became one of the leading figures in major league baseball as president of the Philadelphia Phillies. His team won the National League pennant in 1915, a rarity for the Phillies.)[5]

Gaynor appointed Brooklyn lawyer James C. Cropsey to replace Baker. Descended from an old Brooklyn family (an avenue in the borough already carried the Cropsey name), he was a friend of the mayor from the borough's legal circles. With the job came a long letter from Gaynor directing the reforms he expected. Among them was the directive that all plainclothes officers and detectives report to the new second deputy commissioner: William J. Flynn.

10

"My Boy Will Be Cut to Pieces"

SOON after their son Michael was born in 1907, Dr. Mariano Scimeca and his wife, Leonilda, began receiving *Mano Nera* memos threatening to murder the boy unless a ransom was paid. The doctor brought the letters to his friend Lieutenant Joseph Petrosino, who was from the same town as Leonilda's father, Dr. Michael Petrella. The threats subsided, only to return after Petrosino was murdered. The couple, married on Thanksgiving Day in 1904, had by then moved from Petrella's home on Sands Street in Brooklyn to the Lower East Side, taking a second-floor apartment in a six-story tenement at 2 Prince Street, corner of Bowery. Unlike the Scimecas—he was a respected doctor specializing in ear, nose, and throat maladies, and she the daughter of a doctor—most of the thirty-three families in the building got along on the wages of laborers or perhaps tailors.

The blackmailers' letter displayed alarming familiarity with Leonilda: "Your lady is kind in the building, also benevolent to us. But we have a right to live." The threats intensified, until a final letter dated May 20, 1910, demanded $500: "If not, we will take the blood of yourself and your son and drink it."[1]

Michael went missing the afternoon of June 21. Jennie Yacono, age sixteen, and Millie Micelli, age fifteen, were ambling about after school when they noticed a small boy sitting on the ground at Bleecker and Elizabeth Streets, and a young man picking him up. The boy was dressed in a yellow Buster Brown suit, black shoes, and white stockings and the man—he was little older than Jennie and Millie, handsome, with high cheekbones, a full mouth, a well-cut chin, and wavy brown hair—they had seen him before. "I seen him at the saloon," Jennie later said. And she had chanced to see him walk by her school on Forsythe Street that

FIGURE 10.1. For seventy-nine days, Italian Squad detectives searched for the kidnapped Michael Scimeca, son of Mariano and Leonilda Scimeca. The nation followed the story. Photo credit: *Bisbee (AZ) Daily Review*, July 7, 1910.

morning. The boy, too, was distinctive: he was not another raggedly dressed street kid. The teen friends didn't think much of it until Jennie noticed a story and photo of the boy in the next day's newspaper—for by then, the "Black Hand" kidnapping of three-year-old Michael was front-page news.[2]

From the first hours of the kidnapping, Italian Squad detectives had to do their job in the spotlights of a local press fighting a newspaper war. The pressure was also on because questions were being raised about whether the Italian Squad could function without Petrosino. Four days after the Scimeca boy was lured away with the promise of some candy, the *Eagle* commented: "The most recent of the criticisms of the police of the Italian squad has been its failure to find a trace of Michaele Scimeca. . . . As a matter of fact the children kidnapped by Black Hand gangs have rarely been found by the police. The kidnappers usually abandon their prey somewhere on the street, and there is a suspicion that in most cases money had been paid to them by their parents."

Baker decided on Saturday, June 25, to make Anthony Vachris commander of the Manhattan-based Italian Squad, moving Gloster to another detective command. Vachris had been "aching" for the job while "Gloster did not suit the Italian citizens of the law-abiding class, for they thought the work of rooting out the lawless of their countrymen should be in the hands of one of their own people," according to the *Eagle. Il Progresso* commented that Gloster, "not being Italian and not understanding a word of Italian, doesn't seem capable of fulfilling his mission successfully." The *Times* said the loss of Petrosino had fostered a sharp increase in homicides among Italians.[3]

Following his mission to Italy, Vachris had spent three purgatorial months in headquarters translating the Italian records he'd brought

FIGURE 10.2. Italian Squad detectives Charles Corrao (right) and Edward Castano teamed up on the Scimeca kidnapping case and other notable cases. Photo credit: *New York Times*, September 24, 1911.

back. Passed over for the post many assumed he would get—successor to his friend Petrosino—he was instead restored on November 19, 1909, as commander of the squad's Brooklyn branch. His first order of business as head of the central office's Italian Squad was to sit down with his detectives and hash out the Scimeca kidnapping case; Charles Corrao and Edward Castano were the lead detectives.[4]

The detectives struggled with the Scimecas, who wavered between cooperating with police or paying the kidnappers. Lack of sleep staggered the doctor. His wife wept constantly. They had no idea whom to trust. The couple gave detectives the blackmail letters they'd received, but also began raising ransom money. The Scimecas received new blackmail missives daily. "They all ask for $5,000, but where can I get the money?" Scimeca lamented. "I have pawned my wife's jewelry for $700, but that is all I can get. In the letters the Black Hand men say that my boy will be cut to pieces and his body sent to me section by section unless I pay the money."

The case built pressure for the Italian Squad to be expanded. "Is this an uncivilized country?" the *Eagle* asked, urging that more detectives staff the Italian Squad. "What a pathetic appeal is that made by a broken-hearted father, Dr. Mariano Scimeca, for funds to ransom his little boy. . . . Every resource of the municipality ought to be employed to destroy these 'Black Hand' bandits."[5]

Alberto Pecorini, a journalist and academic who served as editor at the newspaper *Il Cittadino*, organized the Italian-American Civic League to press for better police protection. At age twenty-nine, Pecorini seemed a rising star. An immigrant from Venice, he graduated from the University of Rome at twenty, did graduate work at Columbia, and studied at a divinity school in Springfield, Massachusetts, where he converted to Protestantism and became a professor at American International College. He gathered an impressive roster of non-Italian supporters for his league, including the former ambassador Lloyd C. Griscom. Pecorini traveled the United States, chronicling his impressions in a well-received book. In it, he denounced New York's police as "a corrupt body" fixated on squeezing money from vice purveyors seeking to elude "puritanical" laws. "Meanwhile, under the eyes of the police, strongboxes filled with dynamite are opened, houses are blown up, and children of the Italian ghetto are trafficked."

Pecorini pointed out that the Police Department had made little use of the records Vachris and Crowley brought back from Italy. Of the seven hundred people identified with criminal records in Italy, authorities had moved to deport only those who happened to be arrested for serious crimes, about forty cases. The *Times* published a report Pecorini wrote on this, saying that the failure to use the records Petrosino had died for was "at once as tragic and ridiculous as anything in the history of New York politics."[6]

In the end, Dr. Scimeca gave in. Without telling Vachris, he delivered an envelope containing $1,700 in cash (worth about $47,000 today) to a Brooklyn park on September 8. Twenty-four hours later, Michael's grandmother Giuseppina Petrella received a phone call instructing her to go to East Fifty-Fifth Street in Manhattan. After waiting there for more than an hour with her carriage and its coachman, she found the little one on the dark sidewalk, pale and thinner after nearly three months of captivity. She brought Michael to her home at 181 Sands Street, near the Brooklyn entrance to the new Manhattan Bridge and three blocks from the ransom drop. The relieved Scimecas arrived at the house to see their son for the first time in seventy-nine days.

Vachris was caught off guard. He was zeroing in on an arrest, and had flooded transit points with investigators to catch the suspects. Miffed, he visited the family at the Sands Street home at 1:30 a.m. Dr. Scimeca, meanwhile, falsely told *Il Progresso* that he hadn't paid a cent. His son, he said, would have been rescued much sooner "if the police had not made such a fuss and the American press had not piled up so much nonsense about the kidnapping."[7]

The Scimecas left behind the doctor's medical practice and fled to Palermo in November 1910. Corrao and others on the Italian Squad were still trying to make arrests over Michael's kidnapping, but the Scimecas weren't present to help identify the man detectives suspected.[8]

* * *

After joining the Police Department in October, Flynn quickly got the opportunity to put his skills to work as he supervised the Italian Squad detectives investigating a new round of kidnap cases. Two boys who lived around the corner from each other, Joseph Longo, age eight, and Michael Rizzo, age six, disappeared on the evening of Saturday, November 19, 1910. A stranger lured them to a picture show located across the street from the police station at Fifth Avenue and Sixteenth Street in Brooklyn, about five blocks from where the boys lived.

Joseph Longo's father, a Neapolitan who'd migrated to New York in 1882, could not read or write but was a successful businessman. He established a grocery and was proud to own seven houses on the Brooklyn block, Twenty-First Street between Fourth and Fifth Avenues. When he received "Black Hand" letters that offered a choice between paying $15,000 in ransom or postal delivery of his son's severed head, he needed to have someone else read them to him. "I informed police of the loss of my boy immediately," Francesco Longo later testified. "I telephoned four times to headquarters. I called over immediately that same night. No officer came to my house."[9]

It was a hellish night for the Longos, with anxiety so severe that it was blamed for the death of Joseph's grandmother, eighty-seven-year-old Maria Longo. Her death was "the direct result of the stealing of the Longo child," according to the *Eagle*. The boy was said to be her favorite among his five siblings, and it was she who had given him permission to go out to a picture show, not realizing that a stranger was taking him.[10]

Corrao, who commanded the shrinking Brooklyn unit of the Italian Squad, learned of the case the next morning. He put himself and all four of his detectives on it. Two days later, a former Italian Squad investigator based at the Fifth Avenue station house, Joseph Pucciano, learned from neighbors that Joseph Longo's playmate Michael Rizzo had been kidnapped as well.

Corrao was well schooled in how "Black Hand" kidnap gangs operated. He'd noticed that they worked in groups of five to six, with a married woman to oversee the victim's confinement. She would have children of her own at home, which helped to explain any noise from crying. Though he recognized the pattern, he rejected the suggestion that the Black Hand was an organization. "The Black Hand as an organization is a fiction," he told an *Eagle* reporter.[11]

All roads led uptown to a troubled block of apartment buildings. On December 8, Corrao clambered upstairs to the second floor, rear apartment at 330 East Sixty-Third Street, with detectives Rocco Cavone and Edward Castano. Nicola Rizzo, nine-year-old brother of the missing Michael, accompanied them for identification purposes. After finding that the door was locked, Corrao knocked lightly, then heard a faint voice and some fumbling. He lifted the boy to look over the dusty sill of the transom window.

"That's him, that's him," he said.

"Does your father and mother live here?" Corrao shouted over the transom.

"No."

Corrao realized he was speaking to Joseph Longo. As he kicked in the locked door, Joseph backed away. "Please don't whip me," he exclaimed.

"I won't whip you, boy, I am a policeman," Corrao assured, showing his shield. "What is your name?"

"My name is Longo," Joseph said, both laughing and crying. The only other persons in the apartment were a year-old boy and three-year-old girl. "They belong to the lady that keeps me here," Joseph explained. "A lady makes me mind these kids here."

Outside, a large crowd had formed, coming from a ground-floor grocery where men played cards. After leaving the building, Joseph pointed out a man down the block, walking in their direction. "There is one of them, catch him!" he yelled. Thirty-five-year-old Stanislao Pettanza turned and fled but Corrao hauled down the short, wiry suspect within a few strides.

At the police precinct, little Joseph spotted the woman who supervised his captivity, slightly built Maria Rappa, as she was brought in. "That is her, that is Maria," he shouted. Rappa retorted: "I never seen him in my life."[12]

The following night, Michael Rizzo was found on East 107th Street, crying, cold, and confused, and was brought to an East Harlem precinct. Passers-by had given him pennies. Flynn drove Michael through the streets to look for the place he'd been held. He also bought a bright red sweater for the boy. Meanwhile, Detective John Crowley took the boy's mother and grandfather to the station house to meet Michael. It turned out he had been held next door to where Joseph was confined; the two apartments shared a fire escape.

All told, police arrested fifteen people, most of them as material witnesses. Two were indicted on a kidnapping charge: Pettanza and Rappa. In a flash, they were put on trial, convicted, and sentenced to terms of twenty-five to forty-nine years. In sentencing Pettanza, Judge Lewis Fawcett praised Flynn's detective skills and Corrao's bravery. Newspapers heaped praise on Flynn, saying this was the first Black Hand kidnapping in which police caught defendants with a victim.

The Italian Squad's role did not go unnoticed. At the defendants' arraignment, thirteen detectives from the squad were in the courtroom, eyeing the crowd. Magistrate Tighe called Corrao and Mealli to the bench and told them: "I want to compliment you on the work you have done in this case. It shows that the Italian Detective Bureau is in the right hands and that no change should be made." Flynn took the spotlight, but the Italian Squad detectives had their own access to the press, too. Detective Ralph Micelli noted to the *Eagle* that the squad's detectives brought much experience to the case. "The block on Sixty-third street . . . we have long considered as harboring some of the worst of the criminals with whom we have to deal," he said. "Our attention was first called to the neighborhood back in 1906." He referred to the kidnapping of fourteen-year-old Tony Bozzuffi, whose father John was a banker.

John Bozzuffi, it turned out, was a character witness for Pettanza at his trial. The Italian Squad detectives must have prepared Brooklyn district attorney Clarke well for this, for his questioning quickly showed that Bozzuffi had been plagued with Black Hand threats. Under cross-examination, he acknowledged that he was forced to turn over the East Sixty-Third Street buildings to a man named Salamoni after Bozzuffi's store on the block was bombed. "Since I turned the property over to Salamoni, I have not received any Black Hand letters," he testified. But just the day before, Salamoni had returned the lease, he said.

It was a pathetic scene. Police were on the record as saying they believed Salamoni led the gang that kidnapped the Longo and Rizzo boys. And yet he was doing business, unscathed. For his part, Bozzuffi was obviously pushed into testifying as a defense witness even though he knew the defendants' evils too well. He was grateful to Petrosino for helping to save his son's life in 1906, and with his wife, Mary, had sent an affectionate note to Adelina after the lieutenant was murdered.

"Don't you know that Salamoni has been arrested twenty times and his picture is in the Rogues' Gallery?" Clarke asked him.

"I know that, yes," the banker said.[13]

The questioning highlighted the weakness of the case: only two underlings in a large kidnapping enterprise were convicted. Furthermore, both convictions were reversed based on a March 14, 1913, ruling by the New York Court of Appeals. In a 6–1 decision, the court assailed "an obvious effort by the district attorney to make up for the weaknesses of the People's case by surrounding the defendant with an atmosphere of criminality." The court said banker Bozzuffi's testimony about his troubles with Salamoni would have smeared "any native of Sicily. . . . [T]he atrocity of the crime charged does not justify a disregard of rules of law." Pettanza was acquitted in a new trial on May 23, 1913.

This left thirty-five-year-old Maria Rappa as the only defendant charged. She was a pitiful figure with a grimly drawn face, four feet, ten inches tall, dark-haired. According to the register at Auburn State Prison for Women, she weighed just eighty-five and a half pounds upon entry on January 13, 1911. Although portrayed as Joseph Longo's chief captor, she spent most of her time working in a tobacco factory, testifying that she started at 7 a.m. and made "seventeen cents less than $7.00 per week" if she worked a twelve-hour day—that is, working half the clock for six days a week for the equivalent of about $187 today. On the witness stand, she appeared to be mentally unstable, although she did raise a potential defense about harboring Joseph: "I quarreled with my husband because I did not want him."

Rather than face trial a second time, she pleaded guilty. A sympathetic judge saw her as a victim of the kidnappers and ordered her to retract her plea. She was moved to the Matteawan State Hospital for the Criminally Insane and then deported to Italy on August 1, 1914, as a money-saving measure.[14]

In the meantime, an investigation under Vachris led to the conviction of the man who had walked away with Michael Scimeca. Corrao and two colleagues, disguised once again as scruff-faced laborers, arrested Vito Micelli, a twenty-year-old dandy, on September 29. They thought him to be part of a gang that was coalescing on Chrystie Street on the Lower East Side. With top criminal lawyer Cesare Barra appearing for the defense, Micelli's trial was a tense contest; the prosecution case hinged on the credibility of the two teenaged girls who'd seen him with Michael. (Millie Micelli was not related to the defendant.) Vito Micelli was sentenced to a minimum of twenty-five years (minus a day) to fifty years in prison, on a conviction that stuck. "You are not alone in this plot, and I hope your companions will be brought to justice," the judge told him.[15]

* * *

Win or ultimately lose, these kidnapping cases were presented to the public as great successes that were helping to wipe out the "Black Hand." But in fact, those brought to trial were lackeys, a shortcoming that Flynn was supposed to solve. Rappa's case in particular shows how wealthy criminal entrepreneurs often got off while desperately poor immigrants took the fall.

Outraged editors of the Italian newspapers charged that police failed to protect the Italian community. "There should be a much greater proportion of Italians in the detective bureau and on the police force, and the entire present Italian bureau in the Police Department should be reorganized," said Ercole Cantelmo, editor of *Il Giornale Italiano*. Luigi Roversi, editor of *L'Araldo Italiano*, deplored the general "lack of efficiency" in the Police Department, and said that "a certain bad element in the Italian section is shielded by political influence." The Italian Squad, "though efficient in itself, is from a numerical point of view hopelessly inadequate."

All parties looked for Flynn to transform the Detective Bureau. At age forty-two, he had a formidable reputation. The friendly, easygoing son of immigrants from County Leitrim in Ireland, he lived with his wife, Annie, and their seven children, aged two to fifteen, on City Island in the Bronx. Dark-haired, brown-eyed, and hefty, he looked like someone who could handle the toughest patrol beat. The *Times* called him "the greatest detective in the world" and, in the process of praising Flynn, belittled the rest of the detective force. The Secret Service had true detectives but New York City never had one in its history, the paper asserted. Rather, it had only "policemen dressed differently from other policemen." According to the *Evening Post*, there would be a "weeding out" in the Detective Bureau, fewer arrests, a higher conviction rate, and no publicity after arrests. "In short," it said, "some of Mayor Gaynor's pet theories on the running of a well-organized detective bureau are to be put into effect."[16]

"Where Is Tony Vachris?"

As the temperature edged below freezing on a Sunday night in January 1911, William J. Flynn and Anthony Vachris filled two automobiles with as many Italian Squad detectives as the vehicles could hold and headed uptown from police headquarters. They arrived after 9:30 p.m. at Sixty-Third Street and Second Avenue, the block where the kidnapped Michael Rizzo and Joseph Longo had been hidden. "They held up every Italian man they could find and frisked him for weapons," according to the *Times*. The neighborhood became very quiet.

Coming up with nothing incriminating, Flynn raided 236 East Seventy-Fifth Street, a newly built, four-story brick building with a saloon a few steps below street level. The detectives again frisked every Italian in sight—some fifteen to twenty men—and eventually came to a particularly well dressed young fellow who had a loaded .32-caliber revolver in his pocket. He gave his name as Giuseppe Bellavia, and said he was a cigar maker who lived on MacDougal Street. He was charged with carrying a concealed weapon and held as a "suspicious person" in connection with the Longo kidnapping. "It is not known what evidence leads to the 'suspicious person' entry on the blotter," the *Eagle* noted.

A week before, there was a similar raid on the old haunt of the Lupo-Morello gang, the spaghetti joint at 8 Prince Street, with thirty-four arrested as "suspicious persons" in a kidnapping. Witnesses did not recognize any of them.

Early on February 13, 1911, Flynn flooded Chatham Square at the south end of the Bowery with Italian Squad detectives, who arrested seventeen people on the charge of carrying a concealed weapon. "These detectives will carry their work into the various Italian sections and oth-

FIGURE 11.1. William J. Flynn, shown in 1910, went on to serve as director of the US Secret Service and the federal Bureau of Investigation. His unhappy six-month stint as a deputy commissioner in the NYPD was not one of the high points in his career. Photo credit: Library of Congress, American Press Association.

ers will be assigned to gather up concealed weapons and their carriers in other parts of the city," the *Times* said, adding that, since the start of the year, 150 such arrests had been made.[1]

* * *

Flynn was supposed to engineer bigger, more solid cases; instead, there were dubious arrests of men quickly released. But the mayor and the press had high expectations for Flynn, and he fell into the trap of trying to produce quick and very visible results. Looking to get guns off the streets, he personally led a series of sweeps aimed at Italian immigrants, with favored newspaper reporters riding along to provide on-the-scene flavor.

Flynn had scaled back the Italian Squad, but did not abolish it, as he did all the bureau's other branch units, even the homicide squad.[2] While he viewed the NYPD as dangerously corruption-prone, he was relatively comfortable with the Italian Squad sleuths, having worked well with Petrosino, Corrao, Vachris, and others on counterfeiting cases. Secretly, Flynn arranged for the Italian Squad detectives to launch confidential operations not from police offices, but from his former Secret Service office in the US Customs House. He kept this from Commissioner Cropsey, who was suspicious of Flynn's secret details.[3]

Flynn's take-charge approach was hugely popular in the newspapers, even if his broad sweeps through the Italian community continued a policing practice he had assailed: making arrests first, looking for evidence later. Meanwhile, he was trying to develop a "secret service" of paid informants to probe more deeply. The congenial lawman was popular in the press and on the police force, unlike Cropsey. Reporters couldn't stand Cropsey because he absolutely refused to speak to them, as the mayor preferred. And police detested their lawyerly commissioner for his harsher disciplinary penalties and for humiliating officers with aggressive cross-examining at departmental trials.

Cropsey intended to learn more about Flynn's "secret service." In January 1911, he ordered his supposed deputy to give him a list of all the personnel assigned to "secret" work. Flynn procrastinated, then refused. He insisted that "if the identity of the men was known, one or more of them, working on Italian cases and other police matters in which great secrecy is necessary, would be cut up or shot before they could complete their work," according to the *Brooklyn Standard Union*. Once again, Italian crime was being used to justify more intrusive police tactics.

On Saturday, February 4, Cropsey visited police headquarters near midnight, startling the captain on duty at the Detective Bureau, Thomas H. Murphy. Like an attorney gathering discovery material, Cropsey had the captain show him a log of detectives' phone calls and records of arrests and case dispositions. He wanted to know about secret personnel assignments—the operatives detailed to investigate Black Hand extortions and kidnappings. Cropsey showed up several more evenings, then ordered transfers. They included sending the two captains Flynn had picked as his top aides, Murphy and John F. Linden, to precinct duty in Brooklyn.[4]

FIGURE 11.2. James C. Cropsey served as a police commissioner under Mayor Gaynor, later becoming Brooklyn district attorney and then a judge. Photo credit: Library of Congress, George Grantham Bain Collection.

Flynn was building his "secret service" on the Italian Squad, relying on the model he'd used as a federal agent. It was based on the use of paid informants who infiltrated gangs. At the Secret Service, his agents gathered supporting evidence through long hours of surveillance.

Flynn knew all too well the danger his informants faced. His star undercover man Sam Lucchino was shot twice in the neck in Pittston, Pennsylvania, just a week earlier, on February 6, 1911.[5] Likewise, an Italian Squad operative was shot—for the fifth time, according to newspaper reports—on Stanton Street on the Lower East Side on July 19, 1911. Frank Rosini, age twenty-six, who owned an auto repair shop in East Harlem, had "been doing work off and on for several years for the Italian detective squad of Manhattan," his brother and wife said.[6]

The *Times* was quick to defend Flynn, again noting his cases against Italians:

Nobody knows save Flynn, and possibly Mayor Gaynor, the details of the methods by which Chief Flynn has rounded up the gangs of Italian black-mailers, counterfeiters, and kidnappers. . . . Kidnapped children have ac-tually been recovered, and the kidnappers are serving sentences that will keep them in jail during their natural lives. . . . Mr. Cropsey's jealous inquisition into the methods of the Detective Bureau is uncalled for.[7]

Gaynor backed Flynn. The mayor was proud of the changes he'd in-duced in the Police Department in his fourteen months in office. In a tri-umphant message to the Board of Aldermen on February 21, the mayor asserted that many of the abuses he'd once assailed were sharply dimin-ished: petty, unnecessary arrests; police assaults on civilians; the Rogues' Gallery; and illegal entries into houses. He made national headlines by saying he'd ordered police to respect the civil liberties of socialists. Gaynor himself was no socialist, but he declared, "that their flag is red instead of blue or yellow or green does not annoy or alarm intelligent people." At the same time, he said he was pleased with the progress of his "secret service," ancestor to many a future Red Squad. "The result seems to be good, but we are still watching the change with interest," he said.[8]

* * *

Vachris, Corrao, and their fellow Italian Squad detectives had found a helpful patron in Flynn, but their unit was beginning to draw prominent critics in the city's Italian American community. One of them had the mayor's ear: John J. Freschi, a New York–born son of Italian parents, civic leader, and successful attorney. Gaynor appointed him as a tempo-rary city magistrate at the age of thirty-four in 1910.

Three years before, Freschi had publicly urged city officials to expand the Italian Squad to two hundred detectives; he now considered it un-necessary. He lined up with critics of the squad's existence in a ferocious verbal battle among the Italian community's intelligentsia. In a speech delivered at a banquet in Jamaica, Queens, on December 20, 1910, he assailed the reformist "highbrows" who, he asserted, saw all Italians as criminals. "Your first duty to your race, to your flag, to yourselves, is to protest against the organization of any secret service to ferret out Italian criminals," he declared.[9]

Freschi allied with *Il Progresso* publisher Carlo Barsotti. The paper published an incendiary front-page assault on Alberto Pecorini and his Italian-American Civic League under the three-column headline "Una Stolta Crociata" (A Foolish Crusade). It charged that the League was on a "sad mission to defame" Italian Americans by endorsing the newspapers' insistence that Italians inclined to crime and that "exceptional laws and police personnel are needed to suppress it." The paper noted that the US Immigration Commission had just turned in a key report to Congress recommending restrictions on immigration, and accused Pecorini and his associates of foolishly aiding the nativist movement by focusing public attention on Italian crime.[10]

The Dillingham commission, as it was known, completed its forty-one-volume, three-year investigation on December 5. It concluded that "no satisfactory evidence has been produced to show that immigration has resulted in an increase in crime disproportionate to the increase in adult population," and that in fact "immigrants are less prone to commit crime than are native Americans." Beneath this surface of social-science objectivity, a racist current ran through the twenty-nine-thousand-page report, flowing toward its anti-immigration conclusion. The panel, led by Senator William Dillingham, a Vermont Republican, focused one volume on Italian crime in New York City. There is no question that violent offenses such as bombings and extortion were a problem, but the study made dubious use of data to paint Italians as violent.[11]

Il Progresso's editors were right to be concerned about the Dillingham report; most of its proposed immigration restrictions eventually became law. For *Il Progresso*, it was virtually a crime for Pecorini to aid the enemy, which it saw as the newspapers and elite elements of the Progressive reform movement. "We are all for free immigration; but if we were to wish for restrictions, we would be proponents of one that would provide for the deportation—perhaps to Austria!—of those who, worse than 'Black Handers,' . . . commit the true crime of defaming the Italian colony," it said, with a dig at Pecorini's origins in Venice, which was at points part of the Austrian empire. It concluded: "It is a new kind of crime to be repressed solely with lynching!"[12]

Such a suggestion of violence served *Il Progresso's* cause poorly, but Pecorini, who lived along Washington Square South with his wife and two young children, had touched a nerve at the city's largest Italian-language newspaper. Pecorini, who edited the Italian-language newspaper *Il Cittadino* (The Citizen) while doing graduate study at Columbia University, took a dim view of the city's Italian press, and especially *Il Progresso*. He scorned publisher Barsotti's focus on erecting statues of illustrious Italians such as Christopher Columbus and Giuseppe Verdi, and accused the paper and the *prominenti* who supported it of holding back the Americanization of Italian immigrants to protect their own power. Pecorini implied darkly that those who opposed cracking down on the small number of criminal Italian immigrants were themselves complicit in crime.

It is true that Barsotti, who arrived from Pisa a poor young man of twenty-two in 1872, well ahead of the bulk of the Italian migration, quickly became part of that class of immigrants who would later be suspected of exploiting their fellow Italians. He grew wealthy as a *padrone*, a labor broker who provided workers to the railroads. He further profited through the lodging houses and a savings bank he ran for immigrants.

A friendlier explanation of Barsotti's motive in opposing the Italian Squad is that he was tired of seeing Italians treated as a "problem." The publisher found an interesting ally in his attack on Pecorini and his retinue of American *fannuloni*, or loafers, as *Il Progresso* labeled such high-powered figures as former ambassador Griscom, now leader of the Republican Party in Manhattan, and financier Jacob Schiff. Francis L. Corrao, born in Palermo and formerly an assistant district attorney in Brooklyn—and older brother of Italian Squad mainstay Charles Corrao—pounded Pecorini and his backers. "Atrocious crimes committed in the City of New York by so-called Americans, the Germans, the

Polish and the Irish do not alarm the yellow press, nor the so-called 'Civic League,'" wrote Corrao, the first leader of Italian Democrats in Brooklyn. The league's program, he asserted, "is that we must abandon all our feelings of Italian-ness [*italianità*], all the traditions of our race, as an essential requirement for being good American citizens! The war is against the southerners of our people and against the Sicilians in particular."[13]

Neither side in this verbal battle had a bad word for the detectives on the Italian Squad, whose achievements were seen as bringing credit to their community. But this marked the start of a debate that, surprisingly, had not been fought in public earlier: whether there should be an "Italian" squad, targeted at crime in a single ethnic community. When the squad was created in 1904, the Italian bankers, brokers, merchants, and professionals most at risk of blackmail were its leading advocates. Some, such as Freschi and attorney Corrao, were now so fed up with the newspapers' sensational reporting on Italian crime that they focused more on the perceived insult of having an "Italian" squad.

Pecorini also advocated Italian American empowerment; he viewed the crimes of a small minority as the stumbling block. His well-researched reports on crime in the Italian community were welcomed in prominent magazines and mainstream newspapers. But his movement had an elitist flavor: highly educated and Protestant, he found greater acceptance among Progressive reformers than in the Italian community. A Democratic politician like Gaynor could not but notice that the Democratic political leaders of an immigrant community some five hundred thousand strong—Freschi in Manhattan and Francis L. Corrao in Brooklyn—were now deeply offended by the Italian Squad's existence, as was the publisher of that community's major newspaper.

* * *

By mid-April 1911, Flynn decided he'd had enough of life in the NYPD. He decided to return to the federal government, having taken the precaution of securing a six-month leave of absence. It turned out that reporting to the mayor meant having to address the mayor's political need to clamp down on vice. "I didn't come here to seek evidence of gamblers or to pursue gamblers," he said, puffing a cigar as reporters pressed him on why he resigned. "I was simply to do detective work, ferreting out crimes." He enjoyed going out with Vachris to make arrests with the Italian Squad, which was now losing an important ally.

After dangling for months, Cropsey then resigned on May 23. Gaynor chose his fire commissioner, the socialite Rhinelander Waldo, to serve as police commissioner. His chief attraction seemed to be that he'd amiably do whatever the mayor told him to do.[14]

Within two weeks, Waldo began transferring out Italian Squad detectives; Vachris fretted as he lost three or four a week. He went to the new deputy commissioner for the Detective Bureau, George Dougherty, to find out why. The answer: "I don't know. I couldn't tell you. Too many detectives in headquarters?" By late June, the Brooklyn unit had been closed and Vachris was left with just four detectives in Manhattan; they were working three kidnapping cases.

Vachris called Dougherty at home at night and told him he might as well close the squad because he couldn't handle the cases being referred to him. Dougherty acknowledged it was wrong, adding, "but you know the Mayor has his own ideas about it."

Shortly afterward, Vachris learned that the squad had been abolished; the chief of detectives told him he could continue to do the work himself. As Vachris later recounted, he told the chief, Inspector James Russell: "What are we going to do with all this work? Here is shooting, extortion going on, how are you going to handle it? Your American detectives don't want to handle it; your detectives will tell you, 'I cannot understand these people.'"

"You know this is a funny administration," Russell responded. "We have to do what we are told." Vachris then went up to Waldo's office, taking Dougherty and Russell with him, and renewed his appeal. "I want to tell you it is a serious mistake," he announced. Waldo was already on record in an interview with reporters on why he'd shut down the Italian

FIGURE 11.3. Rhinelander Waldo, Mayor Gaynor's third police commissioner, closed the Italian Squad in 1911. Photo credit: Library of Congress, George Grantham Bain Collection.

Squad: "there wasn't any more need of an Italian Squad than there was of an Irish or German squad," the position that Freschi, attorney Corrao, and *Il Progresso* had urged.

In Brooklyn, a grand jury investigating crime in the Italian community took note of news reports on the squad's demise and opened an inquiry into why it was closed. After Vachris testified, his life changed. "When we got back from the Brooklyn grand jury, I was ordered to remain in the building, and about four o'clock that afternoon Inspector Russell said: 'Vachris, you go up and take charge of the Bronx district.'" It was a long way from his home in what is now called Sunset Park, the neighborhood that was at the time home to the most city police officers. The *World* estimated he would spend four hours a day traveling to and from work, summed up in a headline: "Vachris Talked and Now He Takes Long Rides." After learning that Vachris had been moved to the Bronx, the Brooklyn grand jury asked to be extended for ten days so that it could investigate. The panel called in both Vachris and Waldo, and Waldo did not appreciate being grilled over reassigning the lieutenant.

Vachris was further isolated, put on nighttime uniform duty on City Island, the Bronx's maritime province. Vachris, so popular in the Italian community that he was chosen to be grand marshal of the Columbus Day Parade in Brooklyn that year, was booted from the Detective Bureau. The trip from Thirty-Ninth Street in Brooklyn to City Island took close to four hours *each* way when he worked at night, involving five transfers: trolley, horse car, shuttle train, railroad, subway. When he was on the shift ending at 1 a.m., he would have had to wait until 8 a.m. to get transit home; he stayed at the precinct, cooking his own meal.[15]

Six months earlier, Vachris played a starring role beside Flynn. He had a national reputation as successor to Joseph Petrosino. Now, his squad's work had come to a halt. But the heart-wrenching kidnappings, the bombings, the vicious blackmail threats: they went on. The *Eagle* editorialized: "Abolition of the Italian Bureau of the Police Department will not abolish kidnapping or Black Hand activities. 'Forget it' is about the worst of the bad police mottoes."[16]

* * *

Anthony Vachris took his cases one at a time; what mattered to him was the the family terrorized by kidnappers, the grocer threatened with a bomb, and catching anyone connected to the murder of Joseph Petrosino. It was a hard-nosed but community-oriented form of policing; his contacts were the small-time merchants, the owners of grocery stores, fledgling macaroni factories, and tenements. Flynn would not be the last federal law enforcement official to try to federalize local policing, and the results would often be mixed. Eight decades later, Mayor Rudolph Giuliani, a former US attorney, and Police Commissioner Howard Safir, formerly a high official in the Drug Enforcement Administration and US Marshals Service, flooded high-crime neighborhoods with task forces of officers who stopped and frisked Black and Latino boys and men, looking especially for guns. Crime rates plunged but resistance and resentment toward police grew in neighborhoods that once cried out for more policing. Calls for the department to hire more Black and Latino officers intensified.[17]

The dispute between Alberto Pecorini and *Il Progresso* captured the dilemma for the leaders of minority groups stereotyped as criminal. Public safety required a call for better policing and greater responsibility within their own community, but self-respect made it necessary to fight back against those who exaggerated crime for their own political or business interests. The Italian Squad was caught in the middle of a larger battle among the city's Italian immigrants over assimilation; the Italian detectives, as Vachris's diary in Italy reveals, favored speedy Americanization, helped along by ridding the Italian community of its bad apples. The law enforcement reasons for maintaining a squad of Italian-speaking detectives who specialized in Black Hand–branded crimes remained, but the politics involved in targeting one ethnicity had become much more complicated as Italians made their voices heard in City Hall.

Nonetheless, it was not long before Vachris and his squad were missed. "Where is Tony Vachris, the best Black Hand expert we've had since Joe Petrosino died?" the *Evening Post*, then owned by civil liberties advocate and NAACP co-founder Oswald Garrison Villard, asked in a front-page column on rising crime. "He's at City Island."[18]

12

"The Temperament of Your Race"

STATE Senator "Big Tim" Sullivan's motive for pushing passage of New York State's landmark gun-control law in 1911 defies easy explanation. On one hand, he was tied up in underworld intrigues through his gambling interests and gangland alliances. On the other, his political success owed much to his keen awareness of his immigrant constituents' needs. His push for what is still called the Sullivan Law has been viewed through both these lenses. The forces behind the law were still being debated as it became the focus of a major case before the US Supreme Court in 2022. Was it, as pro-gun advocates argue, targeted at foreigners—especially Italian immigrants?

* * *

After the Sullivan Law took effect on September 1, 1911, Detective Charles Corrao was quick to apply it to an old nemesis—for it was now a felony to carry an unlicensed, concealed weapon. The target was a much-feared but slightly built and benign-looking Calabrian immigrant, twenty-eight-year-old Giuseppe Costabile. Corrao had been gathering intelligence on Costabile since the days when he partnered with Joseph Petrosino. The detectives believed the dapper young olive oil salesman was behind many a bombing, the enforcement mechanism used to coerce merchants into paying twenty to fifty dollars a month in "protection" money. The Italian Squad had collected scores of complaints about these payoffs, but no victim was willing to testify.

Corrao and Petrosino had arrested Costabile in 1908 after nabbing an underling in the act of lighting a dynamite bomb. The detectives acted on a complaint from Francesco Spinella, an immigrant businessman who had worked his way up from stevedoring on the Brooklyn docks to owning his own cabinet-making shop and a pair of recently built five-story brick tenements at 314–316 East Eleventh Street in Manhattan. Spinella had spurned a series of blackmail missives before the first bombing shattered the windows fronting his property. When he asked for protection at a local police precinct, he was shaken down for thirty-two dollars, he said. Rather than pay up the $7,000 the extortionists demanded, he went to Petrosino, who put Corrao on the case. Disguised—the husky Corrao passed easily for a "pick and shovel man," as he put it—he infiltrated the Chrystie Street gang on the Lower East Side. He theorized that the bombers were the weaklings in the gang, and that led him to pick out and follow twenty-one-year-old Bonaventura Pinzolo.

Corrao and Petrosino trailed him into the East Eleventh Street tenement's dark hallway, crouching as they watched him stoop, light a fuse, and straighten. Petrosino sprang up and jammed his gun into the man's cheek while Corrao defused the dynamite.

Corrao had seen Pinzolo with Costabile, suspected leader of the gang; Pinzolo refused to talk about it and pleaded guilty. But just before leaving for Sing Sing, Pinzolo—who would become a major organized crime figure in the 1920s—allegedly told Petrosino he'd been working for Costabile. Pinzolo still refused to testify, though, and went upriver to do two years and eight months. "That is the truth," he reportedly said. "Watch Costabile and you will get him sooner or later."[1]

That "sooner or later" came four days after the Sullivan Law went into effect. Late in the morning of September 5, 1911, Corrao saw Costabile walking toward him near the corner of Elizabeth and Prince Streets. Costabile looked up, apparently spotting Corrao and two other detectives, Peter Dondero and Edward Castano, from fifty yards away. He reversed direction. Corrao caught up, put his hand on Costabile's shoulder and asked, "Where are you going, Giuseppe?"

"Home," he answered. "I forgot something."

Corrao caught the bulge in Costabile's jacket and tapped it. "What've you got there?"

"Fruit for my wife and babies," he answered. "Let me alone, will you?" As his two fellow detectives held back Costabile's arms, Corrao opened his coat and caught a bundle that fell out, wrapped in a front page of *Il Bolletino della Sera* that pictured a bomb exploding. Inside the paper was a grapefruit-sized bomb with a thick six-inch fuse, already lit once as an apparent test.

"I think that's the kind of fruit you've been eating for years," Corrao later said he remarked, adding, "we've got something on you that would have pleased Petrosino."

Costabile staged a scene, weeping, then crying out that he was being framed, and finally, according to the police, telling Corrao, "If you send me to prison I will kill you when I come out. I'll kill every man who helps put me in prison."

Costabile was a slender five-foot, four-inch, blue-eyed swell. When arrested, his curly brown hair was groomed slick with pomade and his short mustache was waxed. He sported a flannel suit, dark green with faint vertical stripes, and a red tie accompanied by a colorful handkerchief. His shoes were a shiny patent leather. He was "something of a dude and as innocent looking as a lamb," the *Sun* commented.

As would often occur after a gangster's arrest, police and the press inflated the defendant's underworld status. "In many ways, Costabile is the most important prisoner we have ever entertained," Inspector Edward Hughes, the chief of detectives, told reporters. The *Washington Post*, which led its front page with the arrest, editorialized that Costabile was "the real leader of the Black Hand Society" in New York and that the case was "the first genuine victory of the powers of the law in its long but unsuccessful attempts to cope with the greatest menace presented by any organization of crime in this country."[2]

Costabile claimed from the outset that he'd been framed. His lawyer, former assistant district attorney James E. Brande, contended that the three detectives had planted the bomb on Costabile to save the Italian Squad and their careers. Brande, who migrated to New York from Italy as a child and represented a number of men accused in Black Hand crimes, had been spreading this conspiracy theory in newspaper interviews. "Why the so-called Italian Squad should be so active just now in trumping up charges against the Italians may be understood by a consideration of the recent history of the so-called Italian Squad itself," he told the *Times*. "When Police Commissioner Waldo was first appointed he abolished the squad, because, he said, it wasn't doing any good and that its members could be better employed on less comfortable but more necessary work. The members of the squad didn't like this and a great number of mysterious 'bomb explosions,' most of which did no damage to speak of, began breaking out."

Costabile testified at his trial that police had harassed him. "Corrao has been hounding me for years," he said. "He drove me out of the [olive] oil business in Elizabeth Street. When I moved uptown he followed me and drove me out. I had to go to Pennsylvania. When I came back Corrao lost me for a while, but when he heard I was here he hunted me up and said he would put me out of business because he didn't like my face."

Brande's accusations went nowhere with the jury, which convicted Costabile after eight minutes of deliberation. Costabile was sentenced on October 17 to three and a half to seven years at Sing Sing.[3]

Bombings continued. Targets included the Siragusa brothers, milk merchants who lived and worked in Manhattan's new dynamite district between East Eleventh and Thirteenth Streets. Early on July 12, 1911, a bomb placed at the front door of twenty-five-year-old Salvatore Siragusa's apartment at 349 East Twelfth Street blew a hole in the floor, smashed the door, and shattered plaster on the three-generation household. On July 24, a bomb exploded in one of the family's Prudential Milk Co. wagons on board a ferry to Hoboken. Another bomb detonated in front of a family member's door at 314 East Twelfth Street—and, unknown to the bomber, one of the relatives caught a glimpse of him as he fled: a driver who'd been fired and gone to work for a rival milk company.

Corrao, Dondero, and Castano were summoned in the wee hours, and before the morning was gone were able to identify the driver as he went about his route delivering bottles of milk and, as it turned out, bombs to the Siragusa family. They followed him to a tenement at 356 East Thirteenth Street, a five-story building where the Siragusas and thirteen other families lived. Giovanni Rizzo, a boyish-looking nineteen-year-old, turned down a hallway, shut the door, and knelt to light the fuse on a bomb hidden amid his milk bottles. The three detectives barged in, practically falling over Rizzo, who extricated himself and ran up the stairs. Corrao stayed behind to stamp out the sputtering fuse while the other two detectives ran Rizzo down and beat him with the butts of their guns.

By the time the detectives brought the battered Rizzo outside, hundreds of people had come from the tenements to jeer the captured bomber and, for some, to try to lynch him. The "boy dynamiter," as the *World* called Rizzo, pleaded guilty on October 23 and was sentenced to two to seven years in Sing Sing.[4]

* * *

The incidents that helped build support for the Sullivan Law had no tie to immigrants or minority groups: the shooting that seriously wounded Mayor Gaynor, and the murder of novelist David Graham Phillips in Gramercy Park. But the remarks of the first judge to impose sentence under the law and a good deal of the news coverage gave the impression that the measure was passed to go after Italians.

"It was the intent of this beneficent law that hot-headed and impulsive people of the temperament of your race should be restrained from carrying a weapon," Judge Warren Foster told twenty-eight-year-old laborer Marino Rossi, whom he sentenced to a year in prison. Rossi had pleaded guilty to carrying a gun with the explanation that he didn't know about the law, and was passing through Manhattan from his home in Newark on the way to New Haven to seek work. He was armed to protect himself against the Black Hand, he said.

The *Times* editorialized: "The judge's warning to the Italian community was timely and exemplary."[5]

FIGURE 12.1. Timothy D. "Big Tim" Sullivan, powerful Tammany Hall leader on the Lower East Side, was known for his connections to the gambling underworld and for his keen understanding of his immigrant constituents' needs. He won passage of a landmark gun-control law in 1911. Photo credit: Library of Congress, George Grantham Bain Collection.

Judge Foster's remark was cited 110 years later in a brief submitted to the US Supreme Court in a closely watched gun-law case, *New York State Rifle & Pistol Association v. Bruen*.[6] The rifle association used it as evidence that the gun-control law was designed to discriminate against minorities, arguing that the statute was passed "to disarm newly arrived immigrants, particularly those with Italian surnames." The court didn't mention Italian immigrants in its ruling that struck down the Sullivan Law, but picked up on the anti-minority theme. In the majority opinion, Justice Clarence Thomas wrote that gun restrictions had been used to prevent Black people from possessing firearms in the post–Civil War South.

The plaintiffs' brief asserts that some 70 percent of those prosecuted under the Sullivan Law in its first three years were Italians. But that figure, based only on a "close perusal" of *New York Times* coverage from that period, is an unreliable yardstick; it proves only that the *Times* published a lot on crime among Italians.[7]

More precise data can be found in a New York State report on convictions during the year ending October 31, 1912. It shows that 35 percent of the 381 people convicted in New York City for carrying a concealed weapon were born in Italy.[8]

Additional data can be found in the registry at Sing Sing, where those sentenced to more than a year were initially sent. For the year ending October 31, 1912, there were 1,170 admissions. Of these, forty-five had been convicted in New York City of carrying a concealed weapon; eighteen were either born in Italy or American-born of Italian ancestry—40 percent of the weapons convictions with sentences of more than a year.

It's not the 70 percent figure placed before the US Supreme Court, but it is still high—partly due to the fact that the adult Italian population in New York skewed young and male.[9] Pro-gun parties exaggerated how often the Sullivan Law was directed against Italians, and there is a certain irony that groups fusing with the anti-immigration movement complained about anti-immigrant bias a century ago. But they are correct that, at least in the newspapers, the law was viewed as a weapon against the "Black Hand." It's another instance in which fear of Italian crime was used to justify tougher criminal laws.

13

"Arrested by One of His Own Countrymen"

O N May 18, 1912, Charles Corrao marched up Broadway and Fifth Avenue in an honored place at what the newspapers called (annually) the largest police parade ever. Some 7,784 officers, three-quarters of the force, stepped to the cheers of immense crowds. From the packed steps of the New York Public Library's central branch, a top-hatted Mayor Gaynor pinned the Medal of Honor to Corrao's suit jacket as he stood square-shouldered and bare-headed before him, first in a line of seven officers—the others all in uniform—to receive the Police Department's highest honor on the first occasion it was awarded. Commissioner Waldo added a second honor for him, the Rhinelander Award.

Perhaps Corrao's greatest honor was that, with the arrests of Costabile and Rizzo, the *Times* anointed him as "Petrosino's successor." Even though Petrosino's Italian Squad had been abolished, a remnant continued to exist unofficially under Corrao's leadership, doubling as the NYPD's Bomb Squad, which had not yet been created. Newspapers still referred to an Italian Squad, contributing to its shadow existence.

Even without a squad to command, the spotlight was Corrao's. "Many stories have been written about Flynn, when he was head of the Detective Bureau," the *Times* noted in a Sunday profile of Corrao. ". . . [B]ut Corrao, Castano, Dondero, and the others of the Italian squad have seldom figured in the press reports except as the men who did the arresting." The *Washington Post* saw Corrao as a credit to all Italians. "Not the least interesting and hopeful phase of the matter is to be found in the fact that Costabile was arrested by one of his own countrymen," the paper editorialized. "All praise is due."[1]

While Petrosino, Vachris, Corrao, and later Michael Fiaschetti were all celebrated in New York and across the country as star detectives,

FIGURE 13.1. Charles S. Corrao was the first to win the NYPD's
highest award, the Medal of Honor. Courtesy of Heather Barr.

rising through the ranks did not come easily for any of them. It was a
particular triumph for Corrao, who had to overcome anti-Italian (and
anti-Sicilian) bias to advance in the department.

He was hired on the City of Brooklyn force on January 8, 1896, and
assigned to work under the politically connected Captain Thomas J. Cullen in a hot-spot waterfront precinct based on Hamilton Avenue. Corrao
played a role in one of the year's big arrests, the case against Antonio Cincotta and three others in the shooting of Giacchino Cocchiara, a pros-

ecution witness at a Boston murder trial, and the slaying of his friend Salvatore Serrio. Cullen and Detective Sergeant Daniel J. Farrell went with Corrao and Patrolman John Crowley (the future Italian Squad detective) in plainclothes to get shaves from a barber who was one of the suspects, allowing them to snoop on the conversation. Later, Farrell and Corrao went to East New York to arrest Cincotta, accomplished after a fight.[2]

Several days after the arrest, the *Eagle* ran a feature spread on the case with one section headlined, "Why Italians Are Useless in Police Work." The article quoted Cullen extensively and featured a sketch of his mustachioed visage, then shifted into quoting an unnamed police captain who complained that Italian officers were afraid to investigate the Mafia. The captain referred to what the paper called "a singular case of Italian murder," telling the reporter about an Italian officer who worked for him: "I asked my man for some information on this case and he said: 'Captain, I dare not act as an informer. They may be would not all attack me because of my uniform, but some member of my family would suffer. . . . I'd be a marked man if I was to act as a spy among them.'"

Though the "singular" murder and the captain were not identified, it had to be clear to any insider that the speaker was Cullen—the only Brooklyn captain to handle such a major Italian murder case that year—and that he was referring to Corrao, the only Italian officer in his precinct, and one of three on the Brooklyn police force. The unnamed captain was quoted as saying, "Give me an Irishman or an American to work up such a case, but none of your dagoes."[3]

The article prompted an angry letter to the editor from Corrao's older brother, attorney Francis L. Corrao:

A police captain capable of uttering such false and outrageous language is not fit to be such and is a disgrace to the police department. He is not intent with arrogating to himself and to his Irish detective all the glory of an inglorious arrest . . . but puts the badge of cowardice and incompetence upon every Italian police officer and citizen and gratuitously casts a slur upon the Italian race.

Attorney Corrao was evidently referring to Farrell, the lead detective in the case and, like Cullen, a son of Irish immigrants. As for the lawyer's dig that police had arrested innocent men, that reflects his own unmentioned role: he represented the defendants at their initial court appearance.[4]

Charles Corrao's early experience contrasts with a story Farrell liked to tell. Farrell compiled a strong record, eventually as a lieutenant. But he got a pass to get on the police force, as he told the *Daily News* in an interview marking his hundredth birthday in 1964. An exasperated inspector asked him why he didn't know the answers for many of the questions on the test: "Is there anything you do know that a policeman should know?"

"Yes, keep my uniform neat and my mustache trimmed," replied Farrell, who would indeed have needed to invest some effort to keep his expansive handlebar groomed.

"You're in," the inspector said.[5]

Vachris also had to overcome obstacles to advance. "Vachris has tasted of the bitter cup of disappointment so often that he is getting used to it," the *Eagle* commented in 1902. "He has been at the head of two eligible lists for promotion, but the lists were done away with before he could be reached." He started on the Brooklyn police force on March 30, 1892, and soon proved himself invaluable in policing Coney Island (where he made national headlines for his courtroom demonstration of a belly dancer's act). He was promoted to roundsman—a street supervisor—and did the job of detective sergeant without the pay. By law, he should have qualified automatically to be a detective sergeant after the Brooklyn and New York police merged. He was being sworn in—his hand on the Bible—on January 1, 1902, when a new police commissioner, John Partridge, arrived at headquarters to take over. All else was dropped and Vachris, last on line, was left hanging after everyone else had been sworn. Ultimately, he had to go to court to win the promotion.

Ten years later, he had to go to court against the Police Department again, this time to be able to retire. Marooned on City Island patrol duty, he filed for retirement; with twenty years on the job, and a finding from the Board of Police Surgeons that he had lost hearing in one ear, he was entitled to retire with a pension at half pay. But Waldo would not act; Vachris was so blackballed that he couldn't even resign. A judge ruled for Vachris, noting there were no charges against Vachris, or even any criticisms of his record.[6]

Vachris was able to enjoy a victory lap as grand marshal of Brooklyn's 1911 Columbus Day parade, in which ten thousand marchers strutted the length of Eastern Parkway to Grand Army Plaza. Vachris's transfer to City Island was "a change that angered the Brooklyn Italians, with whom he is very popular, against his superiors in office," the *Eagle* explained.[7]

As a result of politicking within the Brooklyn Italian community, there were two rival lines of march. This was largely due to Francis L. Corrao, who had wanted Brooklynites to give up their local parade in favor of the larger one in Manhattan ("larger and more pretentious," the *Eagle* crowed). Corrao, pursuing a political and personal feud with the chairman of the Brooklyn parade, former judge John Palmieri, then decided to muster a contingency to march in Brooklyn. He appointed his famous brother Charlie as the "real" grand marshal.

The two detective colleagues avoided friction when the rival contingents merged along the route; they marched side by side. That the two competing parade factions both looked to former leaders of the borough's Italian Squad to be their standard-bearers for Columbus Day indicates how popular the detectives remained in the Italian immigrant community—perhaps because people understood that it wasn't so easy for one of their number to advance in the Police Department.[8]

14

"This Is Another Administration"

IT had been a year since Commissioner Waldo reduced Frank Upton from detective first grade on the Italian Squad to patrolman in Harlem, cutting his pay nearly 40 percent. No one criticized Upton's work; he'd been ensnared in Waldo's mass transfers—in the sixteen months after Waldo took over, he transferred out 294 of the approximately four hundred detectives, and moved in 254. Now, someone in headquarters remembered Upton for his methodical sleuthing, his network of informers, and the Irishman's ability to speak Italian. He was summoned to headquarters to help find the gunmen who killed gambler Herman Rosenthal, a crime that set off the biggest scandal in New York policing history.[1]

Four men gunned the gambler down at 2 a.m. on July 16, 1912, outside the Hotel Metropole on Forty-Third Street beneath the bright lights of Broadway, six hours before he was to meet with Manhattan district attorney Charles Whitman. Rosenthal wanted to tell all he knew—which was plenty—about police graft, and especially about one Lieutenant Charles Becker, Waldo's handpicked commander of the Strong Arm Squad.

Whitman, a forty-four-year-old former judge from the Republican-Progressive movement, got out of bed and raced to the scene eager to take charge before a police coverup could ensue. He lambasted the police investigation, releasing a letter to Waldo complaining that the five or six officers who were nearby the shooting allowed the gunmen to escape "with little more than a pretence of pursuit." The press overlooked the colossal error Whitman had made in announcing his coming meeting with Rosenthal beforehand.[2]

Waldo was not one to admit mistakes. He was a Social Register type; his mother was one of the Rhinelanders, a family with New York roots dating to the seventeenth century. He'd been a captain in the US Army's Philippines occupation force, then served as Bingham's first deputy police commissioner. The press and the rank and file derided him as a blue blood with no police experience. Nonetheless, Gaynor moved him from his post as fire commissioner to lead the Police Department.[3]

"Ye Gods!" Waldo exclaimed when he learned of the Rosenthal slaying in an early-morning call in his suite at the Ritz-Carlton.[4] A week later, frustrated with the pace of the investigation and DA Whitman's insinuations, he was forced to admit error by sending for some of the former detectives he'd reduced to patrol duty a year earlier. Whitman, meanwhile, had so little confidence in the police that he hired a private detective with Scotland Yard experience to work on the investigation.[5]

There is no record of what Frank Upton said when he was called in to help rescue Waldo from the press. Whatever it was, he undoubtedly had the ability to swear in many languages; he spoke Italian, Yiddish, German, and French fluently, and was picking up an additional language under instruction from his local laundry man, a Chinese immigrant. He spent his spare time with grammar and vocabulary books. Upton liked to tell the story of an Irishman who came up to him on the street to ask directions while he was in uniform. He responded in Italian. "An' sure, since when are they a-puttin' Dagoes in the perlice?" the Irishman answered, then walked away.

Upton migrated with his parents from Ardagh, County Limerick, in 1882 at the age of six. He showed himself to be one of those uncommon officers who easily crossed the barriers that divided Italian-born police from the the Irish-dominated ranks of the NYPD. Promoted to detective first grade exactly seven years after his 1901 start date, he was assigned to work under Petrosino.[6]

Waldo and his second deputy commissioner, George Dougherty, had learned the identities, more or less, of the four gunmen who murdered Herman Rosenthal. The real question, of course, was who put them up to it. But first, the shooters had to be arrested: Jacob Seidenschner, a.k.a. Whitey Lewis; Harry Horowitz, nicknamed Nick the Blood; "Lefty

FIGURE 14.1. Editorial cartoon mocks Police Commissioner Waldo as a well-coiffed lamb surrounded by predators, especially the "System," the term for organized payoffs to police. Photo credit: Library of Congress, *New York Herald*, September 16, 1912.

FIGURE 14.2. George S. Dougherty had headed the Pinkerton agency's New York office before becoming second deputy police commissioner in charge of the Detective Bureau in 1911. He had a national reputation as a sleuth. Photo credit: Library of Congress, George Grantham Bain Collection, Flickr Commons.

Louie" Rosenberg; and "Dago Frank" Cirofici. Upton didn't have much to work with. Dougherty, a former Pinkerton man who replaced Flynn, was sending out alarms to police departments nationwide to search for the foursome.

Upton suspected that "Dago Frank"—authorities didn't have his full name yet—was hiding out locally. He snooped around Cafe Dante, a saloon at 163 West Thirty-Fourth Street in the Tenderloin. There was a "Dago Frank" who haunted the place, a well known tough in those parts and close friend of the proprietor, James Verrella. Soon after, Upton and two other officers arrested twenty-seven-year-old steamfitter Frank Cirofici in an apartment at 523 West 134th Street, where they found him dazed from smoking opium. He had two suitcases packed, but wasn't in any condition to travel.

Upton and two fellow detectives quietly brought Cirofici and a lady friend held as a witness into headquarters through a back way. Two hours later, Inspector Edward Hughes came out to tell reporters his detectives had caught one of Rosenthal's killers. He praised the three officers who brought the suspect in.[7]

The announcement was aimed at telling a very skeptical city that the NYPD could indeed police this scandal itself. Some reports credited Dougherty—who had a formidable reputation as a sleuth—with getting the tip on where to find Cirofici. The *Herald* corrected that: "The real capturer of 'Dago Frank' . . . was a policeman named Upton, who was formerly attached to the Central Detective Office, with the rank of detective." The paper noted that he came back from patrol duty willingly "and helped materially to clear up the case."[8]

Since the other suspected shooters and the victim were all Jewish, the controversy especially shocked the city's Jewish community, contradicting its self-image as peaceful. Amid much soul-searching, the New York Kehillah community organization created a "Bureau of Public Morals" to fight Jewish organized crime. Sometimes called the "Jewish police station," its investigators compiled hundreds of files on suspected Jewish gangsters, sharing the information with police.[9]

* * *

In short order, the roof caved in for Waldo and Gaynor. Their method for ridding the Police Department of graft backfired. In a force of more than ten thousand, Waldo limited the number of police enforcing vice laws to under two hundred. But the unintended consequence was the creation of a centralized shakedown system under Lieutenant Becker's command. Waldo and the mayor stood by Becker and the big, aggressive cops on the Strong Arm Squad despite many complaints that Becker was corrupt and his unit abusive. They wrote this off as an effort by criminals to tarnish police, but the complaints were much broader. For example, the *Eagle* expressed alarm at a raid in an African American neighborhood, calling it a "reign of terror"; the headline was "Innocent Negroes in Police Dragnet: 'Strong Arm' Squad Arrests and Batters Luckless Colored Men on Street." The squad "from Manhattan"— that is, officers unfamiliar with the Brooklyn neighborhood and its residents—"cut a wide swath in the way of arrests on Saturday and Sunday and as a result there were fifty-seven prisoners all told in the Adams street court on Sunday morning." Local police who normally worked the area criticized Becker for arresting respectable people.[10]

As the *Eagle* editorialized, the Becker case had proven that graft was systemic in the Police Department. "It is a fact . . . which has put the Mayor and the Police Commissioner upon a defensive so difficult that their worst enemies could hardly have wished them in a more embarrassing plight."

As the scandal grew, a special Board of Aldermen committee under Republican-Fusion alderman Henry Curran scrutinized the Police Department. Waldo was defiant: "There is nothing wrong with the Police Department except public clamor," he testified on September 20, 1912.[11] Meanwhile, Whitman investigated the ties between police and gamblers. By the spring, there were graft indictments against eight inspectors, a captain, a sergeant, and eight patrolmen.

The former Italian Squad was untainted in the investigations, and a number of prominent witnesses before the Curran Committee called for the unit to be reinstated. "Since the Italian squad was abolished, we don't get many of these bomb throwing and extortion cases," Judge Edward Swann testified on February 13, 1913. "But bomb throwing and extortion is still going on. The complainants in these cases are afraid to tell the facts, but the squad was usually able to coax the necessary information out of them."

Judge Norman S. Dike likewise urged a return of the squad, albeit with some other name. "We have the necessity, among our detectives, of being able to cope with very many languages, and an Italian squad is an excellent thing," he told the committee. As a Brooklyn-based judge, he'd presided over many trials in which the "fearless" Vachris testified. Noting that Vachris was posted "to the far distant part of our city," he testified, "I regarded him as one of the most splendid and efficient officers and detectives, a splendid successor to that great detective, Petrosino."

Former Deputy Commissioner Arthur Woods also spoke about the need for the squad. "I do not see how you could handle this blackmailing crime among the Italians without a special squad," he testified, explaining that although extortion was no more common among Italians than other residents of the city, it had taken a "peculiar form" in which Italian immigrants preyed on their own. He continued to be convinced that most of the extortionists had criminal records in Italy; the solution was to deport them. John Purroy Mitchel also called for the Italian Squad to be reinstated when he testified before a joint state legislative committee.

Alberto Pecorini testified before the Curran Committee, jabbing at those in the Italian community who opposed a special squad, saying they "are such people as would not be in favor of the suppression of crime." He noted that the Police Department hadn't made use of the records Vachris and Crowley brought back from Italy in 1909.[12]

Vachris, now freed from working for the city, finally got to tell his story. Sworn in on the afternoon of February 21, 1913, he spoke for the first time in public about the trip he and Crowley took to Italy four years earlier. He said that after he took command of the Manhattan-based Italian Squad on July 1, 1910, he found that the records he obtained in Italy for more than seven hundred cases had been left a mess in Gloster's desk, with no action taken on them. In his one year as head of the squad, two hundred were deported, but in many other cases, it was too late to act within the three-year-window in US immigration law, he said.

Vachris also described the efforts he made to save the Italian Squad after Waldo dismantled it. He told Waldo about the large number of deportations done in coordination with the Italian government and US immigration authorities. But Waldo responded: "Vachris, I understand that, but you know this is another administration. Now that is all." To which Vachris added for the committee: "and that was all."

Vachris also had the chance to detail Waldo's retaliation against him for testifying before a Brooklyn grand jury in 1911. He gave a vivid description of his commute to City Island. "Was there any reason given why you were sent up there?" the committee's lawyer asked. "No, sir," Vachris responded. "No charges."

It was a friendly forum for Vachris, with the Republican-Progressive alliance known as the Fusionists in control of the committee. After Vachris's retirement, he became involved in the Progressive Party, serving as president of the Bull Moose club in Brooklyn's Seventh Assembly District. Pledged to an anti-boss platform, he ran for Assembly in 1913, coming within 203 votes of defeating the Democratic incumbent.[13]

The Curran Committee opened a window on corruption in the NYPD: promotions bought and sold; officers carrying out robberies and thefts; payoffs taken to lie on the witness stand; detectives allied with criminals; arrests staged for shakedown purposes; extortion of women who ran bordellos. Its report called Waldo "incompetent and unfit to perform the duties of his office," and documented how the commissioner and mayor had failed to respond properly to repeated warnings about Lieutenant Becker.

And tucked inside it was a call for the Police Department to bring back the Italian Squad, saying its loss was "detrimental."[14]

Tammany Hall's floor manager, Alderman Frank Dowling, ably rallied the votes to reject the report (even though Democrats were in the minority), but the reformers made their point through eighty public hearings; 224 witnesses, many with damning testimony; indictments; and convictions. Waldo would dangle in office a few more months.

A physically weak Gaynor blasted the "miserable little political grafters" at Tammany Hall as he left New York to rest during an extended cruise on September 4, 1913, before what promised to be a tough campaign for reelection. He died at sea six days later. The acting mayor,

Ardolph Kline, angrily fired Waldo on the administration's last day in office, refusing to accept his resignation.[15]

Becker was convicted of murder, twice—the first verdict was thrown out on appeal on grounds that the judge, anti-Tammany reformer John Goff, was biased. He was executed in the electric chair in Sing Sing on July 30, 1915, sentenced by Justice Samuel Seabury, another anti-Tammany reformer. Becker made a last appeal to the governor—it was by then Charles Whitman—who refused. Becker went to his death with his wife's photo pinned over his heart; his execution required three shocks over six minutes. His case—the verdict is still a matter of dispute—had many consequences besides amplifying calls for the Italian Squad to return.[16]

"The murder made District Attorney Whitman governor of New York and an active candidate for the presidency of the United States," the journalist Andy Logan wrote in her well-received 1971 book *Against the Evidence*, which questioned the verdict. "It helped bring to an end the political career—and, many thought, caused the death in office—of Mayor Gaynor. . . . And it led the political bosses and outlaw elements of the city to conclude that the financial arrangements between their two groups would have to be put on a more businesslike basis, a resolution that caused them to install a ruthless and wily gambler named Arnold Rothstein as the czar of the New York underworld."[17]

In the first week of the new year, with a new mayor and new commissioner, it was reported that the Italian Squad had been restored. Details were scant; there was no announcement of who headed the squad. But Dougherty, still the second deputy commissioner, met with the squad's thirty members and told them to "get busy."[18]

15

"That Is the Stuff"

CHARLES CORRAO reached into a manger in the stable at 341 East Eleventh Street, felt his way through the straw and finally found what he'd been looking for: two sticks, eight inches long, each an inch round. They were wrapped in yellowish paper, like a pair of sausages. Corrao pulled the package out slowly, unwrapped it, and confronted Angelo Settimana with the contents. The twenty-two-year-old milk wagon driver acknowledged: "That is the stuff."

"The stuff" was two three-quarter-pound sticks of dynamite, hidden in the stable by a gang responsible for dozens of bombings that shook New York and northern New Jersey in 1913. Settimana had shown up at the stable in the wee hours of October 11, 1913, to hitch a horse and wagon for the milk route he drove for the Prudential Milk Company, unaware that three associates in the bomb gang had fingered him after they were caught.[1]

With a big case in the works, Deputy Commissioner Dougherty called out the Italian detectives to make the arrest—if he had actually reinstituted the Italian Squad, as reported, it was on an ad hoc basis. Corrao, assigned to detective duty in the Twelfth Precinct at 205 Mulberry Street, was sent to find the milk man. He went with two of his former Italian Squad colleagues, Edward Castano and Frank Upton.

Settimana was an underling of the underlings in a well organized bombers-for-hire operation. He was of so little consequence that, in court and in news accounts, he was misidentified as "Angelino Sylvestro." At his trial, Settimana testified that detectives "were all excited themselves and could not get my right name." No one corrected the record.

When it came to the act he was convicted of—placing a bomb outside an apartment at 170 East Houston Street on the evening of August

31, 1913—he was so nervous that he couldn't actually light the three-inch fuse, which functioned as a timer set to perhaps twenty minutes. "Angelino was smoking a cigar, and he took it and started to light the cord, and while he started, he started to get shaky and cold feet, and so I took it from him and lit it myself," his associate Alfred Lehman, or "Schmitty," testified.[2] Settimana, who spoke proudly from the witness stand of the seventeen dollars a week he earned as a delivery man for the Siragusa brothers' milk company, did not seem a hardened criminal. But Schmitty and two fellow conspirators who cooperated with police were, and the story they casually unwrapped at Settimana's trial shook the city.

Of the 130 bombings police had recorded in the city during the first nine months of 1913, the witnesses, known mainly by their street names of "Zump," "Burke," and "Schmitty," admitted to at least thirty-five in their testimony, a number that multiplied in news accounts. ("Zump," Rocco Puccielli, said that he couldn't remember all the bombings, but when pressed insisted "it ain't over 40.")[3] Their clientele consisted of two Black Hand–style gangs that serviced schemers looking to destroy rival businesses, tilt a labor dispute, blackmail for profit, or just exercise spite. Settimana's bomb, targeted at a tenement at 170 East Houston Street, fell into the last category.

Gang leader Joe Fay had taken a liking to a neighborhood girl, seventeen-year-old Nellie Pecoraro. Nellie, a pretty young woman with dark, flashing eyes and a lighthearted manner, was also taken with Fay, "a dashing young man, handsome and engaging, who dressed in the latest fashion and though no one could tell what his trade was . . . always had plenty of money, which he spent lavishly," journalist William C. Hudson wrote.[4]

Joe Fay—his real name was Giuseppe Ferrara or Ferrari—wanted to marry Nellie, but her father, Ciro Pecoraro, and her uncle, Carmelo Calderone, objected. So Fay visited Pecoraro once more. "He said he wants my daughter," the father recalled. ". . . [H]e said if you don't give me your daughter, then I will fix you."[5]

The blackmail machine, headquartered in a saloon at Elizabeth and Houston Streets, went to work. Giuseppe Polari made bombs in the saloon's cellar; Antonio Levatino, nicknamed "Scapponi," did the same downstairs in his grocery at 187 Chrystie Street. Dynamite was available from construction sites; at that point, the bombers were using a cache of thirty-eight sticks that "Burke"—Polish immigrant Anthony Sadaitys—cadged from a project in upstate Sullivan County. Pietro Giambruno, known as Petrino, wrote the threatening letters. A skull-and-crossbones stamper was inked and applied; that was more efficient than drawing the design. Fay made sure the letter was delivered. The "mechanics," who did the actual bombing, got as much as $150 to $200 of the capital extorted from the victim.

The bomb placed at the Pecoraro family's door never exploded. Next-door neighbor Isidor Neshek, a tailor, stepped on the burning fuse, doused the device with water, and deposited it on the desk of a startled Lieutenant Francis McCarrick just after midnight in the station house at Fifth Street and First Avenue.[6] But the Settimana case had exposed to public view what Italian Squad detectives had feared from the early days of fighting crude "Black Hand" crimes—that some of these groups would coalesce into more fearsome criminal enterprises. Nor were these "Black Hand" attacks entirely the work of Italian immigrants.

The case had developed thanks to two police chiefs in New Jersey. One recognized three "suspicious characters" after a bomb wrecked a small clothing factory in Lyndhurst. The other pressured one of the trio, a sixteen-year-old suspect from Houston Street, to inform on the ring. That led to arrests in the Lyndhurst bombing; "Schmitty" turned informant after the ring refused to put up bail money for him. "Burke" and "Zump" followed suit; their spectacular story cemented New York's reputation as the nation's bomb capital.[7]

The real success of the investigation was that some of the ringleaders pleaded guilty. Antonio Levatino stepped down from the witness stand after testifying in his own defense and admitted his role. He was sentenced to five to nine and a half years. Pietro Giambruno was sentenced to three and a half to nine and a half years.[8]

Settimana's lawyer, James E. Brande, urged leniency after jurors convicted following two minutes' deliberation, telling Judge Otto Rosalsky that the young man had "strayed into becoming one of this crowd," and that "they tried to get him in line by putting him in fear."

"Why did he not testify against those men?" the judge demanded. ". . . Instead of that he contested the issue and committed perjury."

"Well," Brande responded, "he said to me that the lives of his family were at stake."

Settimana had in fact met with the prosecutor after his conviction and told him a bit about the gang, but then suddenly lost memory of what he'd divulged. In any case, the judge, who grew up seven blocks from the Houston Street bomb site, was not moved. "You showed absolutely no regard for human life," he told Settimana, sentencing him to three and a half to six and a half years in prison and a $1,000 fine.[9]

Rosalsky had experienced a bombing himself: a package mailed to his Riverside Drive apartment exploded two years earlier, taking a finger from city inspector Owen Eagan as he examined it. At the time, police officials dismissed the bombing as the work of a crank—and then two more bombs arrived at the judge's home.[10]

What Corrao saw in the bomb barrage was something bigger—the beginnings of an American Mafia. "The problem that confronts us in New York today is the eradication of a band of criminals who after all are legitimate successors to what was, and is still known, in parts of Italy as the Mafia," he declared.[11]

* * *

Restoring the Italian Squad was part of the policing agenda that thirty-four-year-old Mayor John Purroy Mitchel adopted before taking office on January 1, 1914. "The sequel to the abolition of the Italian squad is the rampant condition of Italian crime throughout the city," the Fusion Campaign Committee argued in a briefing paper. ". . . To-day the squad is disbanded and men who do not understand the language are investigating Italian crime." The Italian detectives "proceeded with vim" and were "not men who looked upon a case with apathy because it 'was only a 'Wop' anyhow.'" The former squad members were part of the Italian community and thus "heard the gossip of the saloon, the café and other congregating places of the Italians." Unconfined to precincts, they could travel as needed.

The report took umbrage at the Police Department's shabby treatment of Vachris, contrasting that with the Italian government's presentation of a gold watch to him in recognition of his crime-fighting work. It noted other injustices to Italian Squad detectives. Ralph Micelli, one of the squad's original members, dispatched to Coney Island for the summer, "was kept watching the barkers and hawkers." Frank Upton—the report pointed out his role in making a key arrest in the Herman Rosenthal murder—was chasing down small-time thieves in Manhattan. Sergeants Joseph DiGilio and Peter Dondero, two original members of the squad, were also demoted unfairly, it was said.

Arthur Woods, one of Mitchel's campaign managers, wrote the report.[12] After Mitchel named him police commissioner in April 1914, he sought to bring the Progressive spirit of well-ordered, on-the-merits governance to the chaotic world of police headquarters. The police force, demoralized from the corruption disclosed in the Becker scandal and from the often imperious discipline of the Gaynor administration, was in bad shape. Woods aimed to fix that. He increased vacation time; expanded the "Training School" for recruits; installed gyms in some precincts; ordered health inspections for station houses; and announced he'd be available to meet with any officer who wanted to see him.

Woods brought to bear the the growing field of social work, which was important to the Progressive agenda. "It is my conception of my job that corrective work in criminal problems should not be left entirely to the prisons," he said.[13]

All of this bode well for the Italian Squad; its detectives were the best channel the NYPD had to broker relations with an immigrant commu-

FIGURE 15.1. Arthur H. Woods, innovative police commissioner in the Mitchel administration, had worked closely with Joseph Petrosino and the Italian Squad during an earlier
stint as a deputy police commissioner. Photo credit: Library of Congress, George
Grantham Bain Collection.

nity that distrusted the police. Joseph Petrosino was so much the student
of the causes of crime that the *Times* once headlined him as "Detective
and Sociologist." He told a *Times* reporter: "We need a missionary more
than a detective in the Italian quarters of New York . . . a missionary
who would go among the newcomers and impart to them a reasonable
amount of knowledge concerning our Government."[14]

When Woods announced that the Detective Bureau would be re-
structured into nine districts as of August 1, 1914, he told reporters that
he had brought back squads to investigate homicides, pickpockets, truck
and loft thieves, and pawnshops. Woods added that he expected shortly
to add an Italian Squad, to be called the "Bomb Throwers Squad."[15]

As Woods met with reporters near the end of July 1914, the Great War
was breaking out. Priorities were about to change in a big way. Even before the US gave up on neutrality, it was apparent that there was bound
to be a home front on New York's waterfront, a key supply point. The

federal government was ill positioned to fight that war. And political passions—nationalist, anarchist, socialist—were inflamed.

Times changed in 1914. The scandal surrounding the Herman Rosenthal murder reminded the newspapers that crime wasn't exclusively or even mostly the work of Italian immigrants. The papers published much more coverage of violent, non-Italian gangs that had been overlooked in favor of the upstart foreigners of the Black Hand. They called on Woods to produce results; Pulitzer's *World* identified the city's most serious criminal activity as the "bomb industry" and the "system of contract crime."

Woods defended his work, releasing a list of 178 hoodlums who'd been convicted since the beginning of the year. The names of their gangs read like an index for the book newspaperman Herbert Asbury would publish in 1928, *The Gangs of New York*: the Gophers, the Hudson Dusters, the Gas House Gang, the Owney Maddens, the Dopey Benny Fein Gang, the Cherry Hill Gang, the Dock Rats, the Marginals. Woods talked tough. "We are prepared to use force, and our nightsticks won't be fragile," he told a business association luncheon. "The gangster must go. Public opinion won't stand for him any longer. There is only one way to wipe him out, and that is by force."[16]

Meanwhile, the Italian Squad existed during this period in a bureaucratic half-light, its investigators parceled out to nine detective districts but gathered together when the commissioner needed them. Often, it seemed as if they were called out in desperation.

* * *

A trial held early in 1914 delved into one such case. A dispute between Italian gangs led to the fatal shooting of gunman John Rizzo on May 3, 1913. Rizzo's business activities included terrorizing and shooting strikers—he had been charged two weeks earlier with wounding a striking shirt presser and was free on bail when he met his death.

Once Rizzo was gunned down outside 237 Mulberry Street, his assailant fired on two uniformed police officers who had hurried over. Patrolman William Heaney was killed instantly and Charles J. Teare was fatally wounded. Once again, a crackdown was announced: "Acting under director orders from Commissioner Waldo all Italians doing detective duty in the department were assigned to the case," the *Tribune* reported.[17]

Two former Italian Squad detectives, Liborio "Leo" Gambardella and Joseph DiGilio, found the key witness in the case. Sixteen-year-old Nellie De Carlo knew Gambardella, who was twenty-nine at the time, from around the neighborhood. She also knew twenty-one-year-old tailor Oresto Shilitano, who lived on the block and whom, she told the detectives, she saw shoot Patrolman Heaney as she looked out the window of her family's two-room apartment. Furthermore, she said, she saw Oresto's father, Michael Shilitano, hand his son a shiny object, presumably a gun.[18]

Gambardella spent the next month living in an apartment across the street from the Shilitanos, on the lookout seven nights a week for Oresto to come home. Finally, Shilitano's mother, Angelene, told him she wanted him to arrange for her son to surrender to police. "I know you a good many years, Leo," she said, telling him that Oresto was innocent but hiding out of fear police would kill him. "Now if I give him to you will you guarantee me that they won't hit him?"[19]

Nellie testified for the prosecution at Shilitano's trial but her father, Joseph De Carlo, appeared for the defense in an attempt to negate his daughter's crucial testimony. For Shilitano's father was an influential man—the Republican county chairman, Samuel Koenig, was one of his son's lawyers—and the De Carlos' landlord at 243 Mulberry Street. Due in large part to Nellie's testimony, Oresto Shillitano was convicted and sentenced to die in the electric chair at Sing Sing.

Oresto's older brother Johnny, who operated his father's poolroom on Mulberry Street, rounded up statements from four prosecution witnesses who recanted, including Nellie. The witnesses told their story to the *World*, and hearings were soon scheduled on whether to overturn the verdict. Nellie testified that Gambardella and DiGilio forced her to lie—that they put her in a room in police headquarters, lifted her chair to the ceiling, and dropped it. "I came down all of a sudden and I fell unconscious," she claimed. "I fell unconscious for almost a few hours and I had pains all over my body." She decided to come forward now, she said, because a priest at Old St. Patrick's Cathedral had told her to do so in confession, and refused to give her communion until she did.

Her story unraveled a bit when the prosecutor cross-examined her, but after the Rosenthal-Becker scandal, confidence in police integrity was very low. Testimony from Acting Detective Sergeant First Grade Isabella Goodwin, the NYPD's first woman detective, helped save the conviction. For nine months after the shooting, Nellie had lived with Goodwin and her daughter Margaret. Goodwin, a widow, had been a police matron for sixteen years before her promotion to detective.

As Nellie acknowledged, she developed a close relationship with the Goodwins. They went to Mass weekly and confession at St. Charles Borromeo Catholic Church, near Goodwin's home at 136 Montague Street in Brooklyn Heights. Nellie confided in Goodwin and her daughter, and both testified she made clear that she had witnessed the murder. "The first night she was with me she screamed in the middle of the night and she awakened me and I asked her what was the matter and she said that the thought of that murder made her very nervous," the sergeant testified. "She imagined she was still looking at it."[20]

The state's highest court upheld the conviction and Oresto Shilitano was executed on June 30, 1916—but not before he fatally shot a prison guard in a brief escape a week earlier.[21]

* * *

The Police Department's underlying problem in fighting "Black Hand" activity continued to be its disconnect with the Italian community. Caesar Conti, a prominent businessman, complained that police officials were indifferent even when Italians presented detectives with incriminating evidence. According to Alberto Pecorini, the NYPD had not been able to overcome the distrust Italians had for police in their homeland: "I am sorry to say, that they have not been given protection . . . or, at least enough protection to take away that prejudice from their minds."[22]

Woods would claim that he incorporated the anti–"Black Hand" tasks of the old Italian Squad into the Bomb Squad. Perhaps he intended that, but as it turned out the new squad had few Italian investigators, and none with experience. Its commander, Acting Captain Thomas J. Tunney, listed its original thirty-three officers in a memoir he published after the Great War—three with Italian surnames. All three were rookies— and Tunney needed to select one of them for a groundbreaking undercover assignment.[23]

PART THREE

1915 to 1919

"Framed for Something He Did"

A DELINA PETROSINO held to the memories, even the most har-
rowing. The pain of her husband's final undercover operation was
renewed six years later as she read of the exploits of the rookie officer
Amedeo Polignani, a Calabrian native who infiltrated a circle of Italian
and Jewish immigrant anarchists. He went to their lectures, took in their
fiery debates, cleaned the meeting room, and helpfully acquired the
ingredients for bombs brought into St. Patrick's Cathedral as the 7 a.m.
Mass was celebrated on March 2, 1915. Polignani's ruse came to a climax
when detectives disguised as scrubwomen and bewhiskered old men
swooped in to arrest Frank Abarno and seize two crude bombs before
they could be detonated. The detectives chained him to Polignani, still
in his undercover role as anarchist. They then arrested another suspect
who was charged with making the bomb, eighteen-year-old Carmine
Carbone, at his apartment. The story was on front pages everywhere. So
were Polignani's name (in many spellings) and photo. And this worried
Adelina Petrosino, deeply enough for her to speak her mind when a *New
York Tribune* reporter visited her at home.

"You remember, after the newspapers said that my husband was going
to Italy to fight the Black Hand, only two months later he was dead. My
husband was angry with that story; he said it should never have been
made public," she told the reporter.

The same was true for "this boy" Polignani, she continued. "His name
should never have been given out, nor his picture, nor anything about
him. Now he is a marked man, and sooner or later they will kill him. It
is too bad, for he was very brave."

At age forty-three, Adelina Petrosino was a formidable woman: blunt,
authoritative, twice-widowed, always dressed in black. She lived quietly

with her seven-year-old daughter in a home she shared with her younger brother Louis Saulino and his family at 623 Fiftieth Street in Brooklyn.

The reporter asked her whether the publicity surrounding the bomb case—especially the release of Polignani's photo—would hamper his future detective work.

"How can I tell?" she answered, shrugging her shoulders. "The police do something foolish and then you expect me to tell you. But I think they are like everyone else and want credit, and always more credit, for anything they do; so right away they rush to the newspapers and tell them. All this talk will make everything much harder for them in the future. My husband used to say that if he was known outside he would be no more use, and he would not let us, even, his family, recognize him on the street."

This lesson was lost on the police brass: On the same day Adelina Petrosino was interviewed, the *Tribune* carried a photo of Polignani "in the bosom of his family," beside his wife, Lucy, and his mother-in-law, Lucy Madden. Eleanor Booth Simmons, an accomplished newspaperwoman and suffragist, focused her article on the women in the star undercover's life. "People ask me if I'm not afraid the anarchists will get him, as they got Petrosino," his wife, twenty-one-year-old Lucy Polignani, told the reporter. "No, I am not afraid." But, she said, "I prayed my beads every night."

With dark hair and big brown eyes, Lucy might have looked Italian, but her ancestry was largely Irish—their Hibernian-Italian union was an unlikely one in that era. Her parents ran a candy shop; she met Amedeo in his mother's dressmaking shop. The reporter observed that Mrs. Madden, of all those present, felt some dread, although she would not admit it. "I'm a suffragette, and suffragettes are not afraid of anything," Mrs. Madden declared. Amedeo bounded over from the piano to agree. "I'm a suffragist, too," he added.

"No use advertising where we live, is there?" Lucy Madden asked the reporter, who later wrote: "But when I said the address had been given out from Police Headquarters already she nodded resignedly." The address was published: 147 Eighth Avenue at Seventeenth Street.[1]

FIGURE 16.1. Amedeo Polignani (center) emerged from an undercover assignment posing as an anarchist bomb conspirator and posed for a news photo with his wife, Lucy (right), and mother-in-law, Lucy Madden. Photo credit: *New York Tribune*, March 4, 1915.

* * *

There was indeed danger to Polignani and his family: "One thing to be guarded against is that Detective Polignani does not meet the fate of Lieutenant Petrosino," the *Telegram* editorialized. It is astonishing that the lessons from Joseph Petrosino's death were so soon forgotten in the Police Department—one more instance of careless management that endangered Italian Squad detectives. The case became a battleground for the political passions of the day, raising important questions about how far undercover police should go to facilitate a crime.[2]

From the start, defendants Abarno and Carbone charged there was a "frame-up," a cry amplified in the anarchist press and amply covered in mainstream media. The counterattack was personal, portraying Polignani as a rogue operator who fabricated the bombing attempt to impress his superiors and win a promotion with a pay raise. A leading anarchist newspaper, the *Cronaca Sovversiva*, ran a front-page headshot of him with a caption suggesting he was a traitor to his people, a Judas who sold out for thirty "*denari*" from the police. In another issue, the paper called him "filthy, dirty carrion," a "louse," a "pig."

Polignani, five feet, ten inches tall and slender at age twenty-five, walked confidently into this maelstrom when he arrived at the court-house on March 30, 1915, to testify as the first witness. "He encounters only hostile faces in the corridors of the Court," the *Cronaca Sovversiva* asserted, adding that his presence induced nausea and provoked one woman to spit on him.[3] The prosecutor, Arthur C. Train, started with a curious question:

Q: Is the final vowel of your name an "i" or an "o"?
A: "i."
Q: Polignani?
A. Yes, sir.

In his opening argument, Train drew on his narrative skill—he was an accomplished novelist—to describe how Polignani used a bit of cha-risma and some elbow grease to become a hanger-on in the Bresci Circle. Named for Gaetano Bresci, who assassinated Italy's King Umberto in 1900, the group met in the basement at 301 East 106th Street in East Harlem.

This name recalled an important chapter in Petrosino's career. Italian authorities were convinced that Tuscan-born Bresci, who'd lived in Pat-erson, New Jersey, had co-conspirators; they pressed President William McKinley to investigate. Vice President Theodore Roosevelt suggested Petrosino could help. Posing as a laborer, Petrosino resided for three months in a Paterson hotel the anarchists frequented.

Petrosino reported personally to McKinley and Roosevelt that the Italian king was slain as part of a broader anarchist campaign to kill heads of state—and that McKinley was himself a target. The president made light of that, and failed to insist on the stricter security that Petrosino urged. There is no evidence that the Polish-born man who fatally shot McKinley in Buffalo on December 6, 1901, Leo Czolgosz, was tied to Bresci. Nonetheless, he was carrying a newspaper clipping about Bresci's attack on the Italian king.[4]

Anarchists and other political radicals were never a major target of the Italian Squad after Petrosino formed it in 1904, however. It was a Black Hand squad—the Bomb Squad was created ten years later for the often controversial work of investigating political radicals. It was a Radical Squad, not a hybrid Italian Squad. Even Polignani spoke only broken Italian. He grew up in Rossano, an old cathedral town in the Cosenza province, but forgot much of the Italian he spoke as a boy. "I could not speak good Italian," he testified, explaining why he had little to say at the Bresci Circle meetings. "I could only have a little conversation like saying 'Hello, how are you?' That is all."[5] Lacking Italian expertise, Tunney's team was hard-pressed to investigate suspected anarchist bombings. Then on the morning of July 4, 1914, a powerful dynamite bomb exploded in an East Harlem apartment, killing four people, injuring seven, and tearing up the top three floors of a six-story building at 1626 Lexington Avenue, between 102nd and 103rd Streets. It had exploded in the apartment of Industrial Workers of the World organizer Arthur Caron, one of the dead. Police believed it was intended for the home of John D. Rockefeller, Jr., in Tarrytown. That same day, a demonstration was held there in response to the Ludlow Massacre, in which the Colorado National Guard opened fire on striking workers at a mine Rockefeller owned, resulting in a pitched battle that killed twenty-five people, including eleven children and two women who burned and suffocated.[6]

Emotions were high and Tunney's bench was thin; he wanted to infiltrate the Bresci Circle, which he considered the source of the bombings, but had no one who could pass as Italian. He resorted to a detective who spoke only English. "Whenever the agitators had a really important matter to discuss they used the Italian tongue, and it was impossible for

our man to eavesdrop," Tunney was to discover. "Perhaps he was over-
eager, for twice he was brought to trial by the Circle charged with spying.
Twice he was acquitted. But when his enemies had him formally charged
a third time with treachery, the anarchists decided that although they
had no evidence against him beyond a powerful suspicion, he would be
better outside. Outside he went."[7]

The pressure on Tunney's unit grew after a small bomb exploded inside the Fifth Avenue entrance of St. Patrick's Cathedral shortly after 5
p.m. on October 13, 1914, panicking churchgoers. The message became
clearer when a more powerful bomb was thrown near the rectory of St.
Alphonsus Liguori Church just after midnight at 310 West Broadway.
The twin bombings seemed to respond to police handling of an earlier
IWW demonstration inside St. Alphonsus that led to 190 arrests. The
IWW's church invasion protests prompted police into a frenzy of club-
bing at anarchist and IWW events.[8]

Publicly, police and church officials blamed the St. Patrick's bomb on
a "crank."[9] No one actually believed that, however, and Woods told Tunney he needed to get a detective inside the Bresci Circle. An anarchist
attack on St. Patrick's Cathedral went to the heart of the Irish Catholic
culture that prevailed in the Police Department, Tammany Hall, and the
church itself. Mayor Mitchel, who ran against Tammany, was a devout
Irish Catholic as well. The Irish in New York remained bound to their
church, a centuries-old response to British oppression in their homeland. But there was a strong anti-clerical streak among southern Italian
immigrants, especially men, and certainly not limited to anarchist circles. The church was among the institutions that failed southern Italians.
Conflicting attitudes to clerical authority caused no end of Irish-Italian
conflict within New York's Catholic Church for decades—and the status
of Italians in the New York Catholic Church was echoed by their shaky
status in the NYPD.

Tunney, a Catholic who migrated from Ireland at the age of sixteen
in 1890, searched for an Italian undercover. After reviewing five or six
candidates the department sent, he settled on Polignani, who was a few

months out of police training school. Though he was later acclaimed for his undercover work, it was never noted that it had been difficult for him to even get hired.

He applied to be a patrolman early in 1912. A year later, the Municipal Civil Service Commission moved to disqualify him on grounds that he had failed to disclose an arrest on his application. On March 5, 1913, he appeared before the three-member panel to explain himself; he was thrown off the eligible list. It's not clear from available records what, if anything, he'd been arrested for in the past. It was likely nothing serious, since the board reversed the decision at its November 19 meeting. Having scored in the top 4 percent on the civil service eligibility list—number 26 of 656 candidates—he was appointed a probationary patrolman on December 1, 1913. He'd been unemployed for the previous year. Two months later, he married Lucy Madden.[10]

Tunney liked that Polignani was "strong, mild-mannered and unobtrusive. And he knew Italian." But not really, as noted earlier. Polignani said good-bye to his wife and moved to his own apartment. As a cover, he worked days at the Brewster automobile factory in Long Island City. He spent evenings with the anarchists under the name Frank Baldo.[11]

The more experienced anarchists such as the colorful labor organizer Carlo Tresca were not about to fall for an outsider who spoke broken Italian, but Polignani ingratiated himself by sweeping and washing the floors. His stock rose when he got the goat the anarchists raffled off shortly before Christmas to pay an associate's legal bill. Gradually, the undercover man befriended two peripheral members of the group, Carbone and Abarno. By his account, they thought other members of the Bresci Circle were all talk; they wanted to carry out bombings. Polignani was there to help.[12]

The great controversy in the case was over how far Polignani went to encourage them. He acknowledged paying for the chemicals used to construct the bomb, important since the defendants lacked the money to carry out the plot. He also admitted holding the key for the furnished apartment the trio rented to plan the bombing. Abarno and Carbone

FIGURE 16.2. Frank Abarno and Carmine Carbone, shown in court in 1915, charged that an undercover police detective set them up in a plot to bomb St. Patrick's Cathedral. Photo credit: Library of Congress, George Grantham Bain Collection.

accused Polignani of conceiving the crime, egging them on, and bully-
ing them into it. They claimed he told them he was a Black Hander and
would retaliate if they backed out. But in the end, there was no avoiding
that Abarno was caught in the cathedral with a bomb at hand (although
he said he'd decided not to detonate it). Then he made matters worse
for the defense by trying, moments after his arrest, to blame it all on
Carbone; it would take another day before he realized that Polignani
was the informer.

Their case became a cause for the anarchist movement, which charged
that police had created the crime. Carlo Tresca "was active with the lawyers for these men in preparing their defense," an FBI report on Tresca
said.[13] But despite the evils that the charge of "entrapment" suggested to
the general public, the term was understood very narrowly in the law.
The US Supreme Court wouldn't deliver a major decision on the entrapment defense until 1932. New York law took a dim view of the entrapment claim. It was a difficult defense to win on.[14]

Based on that, Judge Charles C. Nott, Jr., instructed jurors that a defendant would have to demonstrate a "reasonable apprehension on his
part of instant death or grievous bodily harm" to show he acted under
duress—and that was not the case for Abarno and Carbone. Further,
the judge instructed, if there was no more than "mere persuasion" from
Polignani—which *does* seem to be what happened—the entrapment defense had to fail.[15]

The jury went out at 6 p.m. on April 12 and deliberated late into the
night, lingering even though one man on the panel had just learned that
his father died. Police blocked off access to the courtroom, but did allow
entry to some of the anarchists, including Emma Goldman and women
from her circle. At 11:20 p.m., the jury sent a note: "We request to be
informed whether Detective Polignani was justified as an agent of the
police in co-operating with the defendants to the extent of purchasing
bomb materials."

The judge answered that Polignani was not committing a crime because he lacked criminal intent. The question signaled, though, that ju-

rors were troubled even if the undercover tactics were legal. "The matter of Detective Polignani's interest in the case seemed to bother the jurors more than any other item of the testimony," the *Times* noted.

At 11:45 p.m., the jury foreman read the verdict: "We find the defendants both guilty, with a recommendation for mercy."

* * *

The outcome of the case brings to mind a courthouse press room quip from the late newspaper columnist Murray Kempton, who would write brilliant commentary on trials of political radicals and mobsters in New York in future decades. "They framed him for something he did!" he liked to exclaim.[16]

Abarno said as much the day after his conviction to a *World* reporter visiting him in the Tombs. "On the evidence submitted, I don't see how the jury could do anything else but convict me," he said, adding that he still claimed "that the case was a police frame-up, and that Detective Polignani was more of an instigation than a silent partner. I think it is an injustice, and I think that men far higher up than Polignani are responsible for it. I will go so far as to say that Polignani may have thought he did right, but I think any fair-minded man will see that he did more than merely follow us in what we did. He suggested it and urged us on."[17]

At sentencing, Nott said he had no doubt that Abarno and Carbone "were the leading parties in the conspiracy. It is true a policeman cooperated with them, but I do not think Polignani was the instigator of the crime." Still, the judge said he was perplexed at how severe to be. He sentenced the two young men to six to twelve years, less than half the maximum.

As for Polignani, the claim that he was to be awarded a pay raise was simply false.

He remained a patrolman earning $1,000 a year, or $27,836 in 2022 dollars, and advanced with the civil-service pay steps. In 1927, he was still a detective second grade in the Headquarters Division, at $2,700. Heroics aside, he was not among the eighty-six first-grade detectives in that division, making $3,300. Just two of them had Italian names. It took until 1928 for the Police Department to promote him to detective first grade. Four years later, Police Commissioner Edward Mulrooney visited Polignani at his death bed to promote him to acting lieutenant. He died on July 13, 1932, at the age of forty-three.[18]

Tunney wrote that the greatest result of Polignani's undercover work was to decrease bombings in New York and disorganize the Bresci Circle. "The group was frightened, and the members began to suspect each other of espionage," he wrote in his memoir. It was published shortly before bombs were set in eight cities on June 3, 1919, including the Washington, DC, home of Attorney General A. Mitchell Palmer, touching off the infamous "Palmer Raids."

Among them was a shockingly powerful bomb that destroyed the front of Judge Nott's four-story brownstone at 151 East Sixty-First Street, killing a night watchman and passerby. The judge rushed home from the Connecticut shore and found his wife, who'd been thrown from her bed by the blast, otherwise unhurt and lucky to have gotten out on a fire escape. Standing in front of his home's wreckage, the judge told a reporter: "Of course this may be the work of friends of the two anarchists who attempted to place a bomb in St. Patrick's Cathedral and were sentenced to prison by me."[19]

* * *

Italian defendants were again at the leading edge of a more aggressive law enforcement strategy, and an Italian immigrant detective took the heat for making it succeed. The undercover methods that Tunney used to catch a suspect in the act of a crime may have been somewhat shocking in 1915, but they would become common. The targets would no longer be limited to political radicals or gangsters. The tactics of persuasion used on Abarno and Carbone could also work on members of Congress, as in the FBI's "Abscam" probe of political corruption in 1979 and 1980.

In the post-9/11 period, the question of how far police can go to facilitate a crime to prevent one became especially important, since a terrorist attack with modern weaponry could be so, so deadly. "Can law enforcement officials exploit an individual's mere desire to kill tens of thousands of innocent people and even facilitate the commission of the crime right up until the last second, controlling the unfolding events to ensure that the perpetrators remain unaware they are dealing with undercover agents?" FBI assistant general counsel David J. Gottfried asked. "Where is the line between an individual's thoughts and desires and criminal activity?"[20]

Just 9 percent of the 580 post-9/11 federal terrorism prosecutions represented "a genuine threat of terrorist attack," two scholars found in a 2015 study, suggesting that "the government should rethink its focus on targeting law-abiding Muslims for inducement."[21]

That's not to say it's easy to make the decision on if and when to arrest; misjudgment could be catastrophic. But in 1915 and now, it would be a lot of weight to put on the shoulders of a rookie patrolman. The undercover work Amedeo Polignani did was indeed similar to tasks that Joseph Petrosino undertook, but only after many years of policing experience. There was one key difference between the Italian Squad and the Bomb Squad: under Petrosino, Vachris, and Corrao, an important part of the mission was to connect with the Italian community so that crime victims might feel comfortable in seeking help from police. Lacking that, Tunney's Bomb Squad was no replacement for the old squad of Italian immigrant detectives. And that was beginning to show in the intensifying gangland warfare that the veteran Italian detectives, now dispersed around the city, were encountering.

17

"They'll Get Theirs"

MICHAEL FIASCHETTI was working the evening shift at the East Harlem station house when the call came in from an officer on foot patrol: shots fired on 109th Street; send reinforcements. With other cops, Fiaschetti hustled to the familiar block where Giosue Gallucci, "the King of Little Italy," headquartered his realm. He ran into a saloon that the don's twenty-year-old son Luca owned: empty but for a trail of blood. It led him to a room in the rear where a bloodied Luca Gallucci sprawled on the floor. Hearing shouts from a bakery cafe that the father owned, Fiaschetti hurried down the block and found an older man on the floor, surrounded by henchmen, blood covering his face. "It was the King," he later wrote.

Both men were taken to Bellevue Hospital. The younger man died first. His father lingered, giving Fiaschetti the opportunity to go to his bedside. He could see Giosue Gallucci's dark eyes, but his oval-shaped face was covered with bandages. He'd been a stout and vital fifty-year-old, a five-foot, three-inch bulldog of a man with a mustache that bristled authority, waxed into sharp points at either end. Fiaschetti wanted him to identify his assailants. As far as Gallucci was concerned, that was as good as done: "They'll get theirs," he replied. He died on May 21, 1915.[1]

Gallucci, who migrated from Naples to New York in 1892, had become both powerful and a marked man as he moved in on business that Giuseppe Morello and his brother-in-law Ignazio Lupo commanded until their counterfeiting conviction in 1910. Morello's Sicilian siblings continued his criminal enterprise, but Gallucci took over the numbers racket, made loans, built a feared "protection" business, and pushed toward controlling the sale of such commodities as coal, ice, artichokes, and hay for the area's stables.

He also built an alliance with Tammany Hall by rallying East Harlem's Italians to vote. New York's first Italian immigrant elected official, Salvatore A. Cotillo, an assemblyman in 1915 and later a state senator and judge, recalled: "To Gallucci, all people were either hirelings or payers of tribute. It was a matter of concern in the neighborhood if you were looked down upon by Gallucci."[2]

By 1915, police were well aware that a gang war was being fought— and that it was beyond their control. "I have never known the police to be left in such darkness about so widespread and important a criminal affair," Fiaschetti recalled.[3]

Gallucci illustrated Petrosino's fear that the neighborhood toughs he encountered would eventually organize into more powerful gangs. The decision to break up all centralized detective squads hampered the Police Department's ability to take on criminal combines that were spreading beyond their neighborhood origins in the 1910s. Meanwhile, the gangs were increasingly sophisticated: they had top-notch lawyers on call, seemingly legitimate businesses, and connections to police and politicians. Their biggest obstacle was each other, and a war ensued as a reviving Morello gang locked into competition with two Neapolitan gangs from Brooklyn. The Gallucci hit was the result of a very temporary cooperation between the Morellos and the Neapolitans.[4]

The NYPD's response was piecemeal. In a July 1913 roundup aimed at stopping the dozens of bombing that afflicted Italian districts, police brought in suspects with any charge they could come up with; one of the easiest solutions was to arrest people for selling tickets to the lottery. Gallucci, his nephew Russomano, and lackey Generoso "Joe Chuck" Nazzaro were among the forty-three arrested. It didn't seem to accomplish much other than to anger Nazzaro, who lingered in jail after Gallucci and his nephew made bail. He defected to Brooklyn's Navy Street gang and became part of the team that gunned down the two Galluccis.[5]

* * *

A remnant of Anthony Vachris's Brooklyn-based Italian Squad continued to investigate crimes in northern Brooklyn's Italian sections. Detectives Joseph Pucciano, Bernardino Grottano, and Michael Mealli often worked together, along with Mealli's brother Andrew. Trying to connect the mob hits that dotted their district, they were able to bring in an informer who broke open that era's version of Murder, Inc.—but also accused the detectives who'd investigated him of corruption.[6]

Under Captain John Coughlin, who would become inspector in charge of the Detective Bureau in 1920, the Italian detectives kept poking and probing a gang of Neapolitans headquartered in a coffeehouse at 113 Navy Street, under the Brooklyn side of the Manhattan Bridge. The Italian detectives were familiar with this turf—especially the Mealli brothers, who lived at 11 Navy Street. The detectives spotted a weak link in the chain that bound the gang's secrets: a particularly loathsome hoodlum named Ralph Daniello.

A barber by trade, Daniello was a thirty-one-year-old father of four living in a tidy three-story brick building at 143 Douglass Street in Brooklyn, a man with both a past and a present to hide. Born Alfonso Pepe in Pagani, Campania, in 1886, he had escaped prison in Italy in 1906 while held on suspicion of murder. He fled to New York. Daniello was arrested on suspicion of murdering a man in Brooklyn over six dollars' worth of cocaine in May 1916. The charge didn't stick; he was released a week later. But the detectives learned that Daniello was wanted in Italy—as Alfonso Pepe—and Coughlin began the process of getting his Italian criminal record, first step toward deportation.[7]

Meanwhile, Daniello hung out with the gang at Leopoldo Lauritano's coffeehouse. As an underling paid twenty dollars a week, he was in on secret meetings held with the Navy Street gang's leaders, Lauritano and Alessandro Vollero, and a Coney Island–based gang led by Pellegrino Morano. The topic was whether, and then how, to murder the leaders of the Morello gang.

On September 7, 1916, gunmen murdered Giuseppe Morello's half-brother Nick Terranova (a.k.a. Nick Morello) and Charles Ubriaco after

FIGURE 17.1. Brooklyn's Navy Street gang in 1918 in photo admitted into evidence in the *Vollero* trial. Ralph Daniello is identified as No. 2, Leopoldo Lauritano as No. 3, and Alessandro Vollero, No 4. Photo credit: Wikimedia Commons. For further details on who is depicted: *Vollero*, fols. 3211–12.

they were lured to a meeting on Navy Street. Five days later, Daniello sent his wife and children to Italy for their safety. He had gotten the money for their passage from Teresa Giordano, a friend he had known as a boy in Pagani.[8]

Not long afterward, Daniello visited Giordano's home at 462 Sackett Street, Brooklyn, to push forward the Navy Street gang's plan to control the artichoke trade, another incursion on the Morellos. He arranged for Teresa's husband, produce man James Giordano, to open an artichoke distributorship at the Wallabout Market, the city's largest, located on the eastern side of the Brooklyn Navy Yard.

Giordano, godfather to two of Daniello's children, initially agreed. Then he came to his senses and realized he shouldn't do business deal with

Daniello and his gang; he wanted out. "You had better tell to them yourself, what you have told me, because they don't believe me, on account of the fact that we are *compares*," Daniello told him. So Daniello brought his boss, the feared Alessandro Vollero, to the Giordano home. It was a family affair: in addition to Teresa Giordano, her pretty teenage daughter from a previous relationship, Amelia Valvo, was present. Daniello, who had known Amelia since she was about ten years old, took note of her.

FIGURE 17.2. Ralph Daniello (top) provided detectives with information on twenty-three murders. He informed on Alessandro Vollero (below), a leader of the murderous Navy Street gang. Photo credit: Wikipedia.

With his wife and children conveniently sent to Italy, Daniello began an affair with Amelia, who was at least thirteen years his junior. "Any time that I wanted her I would let her come over," he boasted. That arrangement continued for six or seven months until, as Daniello boasted, "I took her away from her mother's house." They went to Philadelphia, where Daniello arranged a sham marriage with Amelia Valvo.[9]

Teresa Giordano was enraged, and her ire proved to be Daniello's undoing. She filed a complaint with police accusing Daniello of abducting her daughter, and eventually passed along the tip that he had bragged about the murder he'd committed in May 1916—the charge he'd already beaten. News accounts said her daughter was fifteen or sixteen years old, although, if Amelia's birth certificate is correct, she was eighteen, born in Jersey City on January 15, 1898.[10]

The Brooklyn detectives got to work and Daniello was brought to trial in February 1917 in Brooklyn. To his rescue came Giacomo Damico, a Philadelphian who resembled Daniello. He testified that he was the one who married Valvo. She went along with the ruse, and once again, Daniello beat a criminal charge.

Brooklyn's district attorney, Harry Lewis, would not let go. The next month, he won a perjury conviction of Damico; the Philadelphia judge who married Daniello and Valvo, Maxwell Stevenson, came to court to identify Daniello as the groom. "The identification was made easy through the presence of a long, deep scar on the side of Daniello's face," the Brooklyn Standard Union noted.[11]

Other efforts followed. On one occasion, Detective Grottano thought he spotted Daniello with a revolver. He chased him into the Navy Street coffeehouse, where Daniello tossed the gun before he could be caught with it. The next move was to try Daniello on a robbery charge, a drug-related shakedown. He was acquitted on April 20, 1917. In the meantime, Pucciano and Michael Mealli arrested gang boss Leopoldo Lauritano at his coffeehouse on March 22 on a charge of possessing a weapon, a weighted pipe they found while searching for cocaine. He was convicted and sentenced on May 7 to three months to three years in prison.

Daniello was called to trial in May, this time on a grand larceny charge. Damico was back in court, too, charged with abduction. Damico was convicted on June 1 and sentenced to one to ten years at Sing Sing.

Daniello did not show up for his trial. Amelia Valvo had been subpoenaed before a Brooklyn grand jury, then told Daniello what the panel asked her about. That's when they fled to California, and on to Reno, Nevada.[12]

It's not clear exactly how the Brooklyn-based detectives located Daniello and Valvo in Reno. Daniello made it sound almost as if he turned himself in and cooperated with police because he was so angry that the gang wouldn't send money—his cut of the proceeds—to help him or his (real) wife in Italy after he wrote numerous letters. Years later, Michael Fiaschetti would take credit in his memoir for the tip that located Daniello. After Joseph Pucciano died at the age of forty-nine in 1928 as a celebrated detective, the New York Daily News reported that he was the one who'd stumbled on the information. In questioning gang members in their coffeehouse quarters, he accidentally—or perhaps on purpose—knocked a picture off the wall and noticed an address written there. "Pucciano apologized humbly for being so clumsy," and memorized what turned out to be Daniello's address, the News said. Another report said Valvo had written to a Brooklyn friend from California; that helped put police on the trail. Yet another newspaper credited Michael Mealli with tracking down Daniello.[13]

Reno police chief John D. Hillhouse was able to arrest Daniello and Valvo on October 10, 1917, from information the NYPD sent—he had such a knack for criminal identification that he became known as "the man with the photographic eye." Pucciano and Grottano were sent to Reno, arriving on November 2.[14]

Daniello would claim he confessed his crimes to the Reno police chief right after his arrest. But from the glimpse given in the Reno newspaper, it seems he was mainly bent on going after the police officers who'd been investigating him. Once in Brooklyn, he hit the ground with his mouth running. Assistant District Attorney Herbert Warbasse debriefed him, then dispatched detectives to corroborate the details of the twenty-three murders Daniello recounted. In addition to the slayings, Daniello emphasized that the gang was paying off police—leading prosecutors to send him to Deputy Commissioner Leon Godley in Manhattan.

Daniello, who functioned as a bookkeeper for the Navy Street gang, didn't actually pay any bribe himself. But he said he heard talk from gang leaders about, for example, an unnamed police captain who took graft to protect the gang's gambling operations—no surprise at the time. Where Daniello named names, his targets were Italian detectives: Charles Corrao, the Mealli brothers, "Bennie" Grottano, and an unidentified "Castagnia." Of those Daniello accused, Corrao was the biggest surprise, given his good reputation. After the slaying of the two Morello family figures in his bailiwick, Navy Street gang leader Vollero expected to be arrested, questioned, and then released for lack of evidence—a tried and true formula, since he could be confident that no one in the neighborhood would testify against him. Daniello told investigators that before turning himself in, Vollero wanted the gang to check in with its fixer, Tony Ferrara, who owned the thriving pastry shop at 195 Grand Street, corner of Mulberry. "He was the man who used to fix our cases, either in New York or in Brooklyn," Daniello asserted. The pastry shop would grow into a nationwide business; Ferrara, an important opera impresario, founded it in 1892. Vollero denied knowing him. According to Daniello, Vollero said: "Let Ferrara speak to Corrao, and Castagnia, so that if they take me to New York, they will not strike me, and to fix everything."[15]

Daniello didn't know Corrao himself, but it was true that after Vollero turned himself in, Pucciano and Michael Mealli brought him to the First Branch Detective Division, where Corrao coordinated the probe of Vollero. In his straightforward way, Corrao made short work of Daniello's allegation when he testified at Vollero's trial. Under cross-examination, he explained that after witness Ike Cutter, a card dealer, failed to identify Vollero in a lineup, the suspect had to be released.[16]

Bernardino Grottano, who was "Bennie" in the Italian neighborhoods and "Barney" in the Police Department, also testified uneventfully. During the trials he played a behind-the-scenes role for the DA with Pucciano and another former Italian Squad detective, Felix DeMartini. They escorted Daniello and others to court, and tracked down reluctant witnesses. Had Grottano been suspect, the district attorney would not have included him in the prosecution team.

The same cannot be said for Michael Mealli, however. Despite his expertise in Italian gangs and his important role in the Navy Street case, he was not involved in the trials. He was demoted to patrol duty "for the good of the force."[17]

Mealli was born in New York to parents who migrated from Sala Consilina, a town in the province of Salerno that bordered on Petrosino's home town, Padula. He joined the police force in 1903 at the age of twenty-seven, leaving behind a job in the Fire Department, and advanced quickly as an integral part of the Italian Squad.[18]

Daniello's allegations against Michael Mealli were more detailed than those against other officers he named, although still hearsay. "Mealli never arrested any of us," he scoffed. "He would come down there with a superior officer and wallop some of us. But that was only a bluff."

Daniello and the hoodlums he testified against spoke with familiarity about the Mealli brothers, whom they evidently knew from the neighborhood. Daniello said he heard the gang's bosses, Vollero and Lauritano, agree to chip in fifty dollars each "to make a present to Mike Mealli" before one of the gang members was surrendered, for example. On another occasion, he understood that Vollero had arranged a $200 payoff to "fix up the case" against Daniello and gang member Andrew Ricci; they were to turn themselves in to the Mealli brothers. If so, it's hard to see how the alleged bribe paid off; both men were released only after a trial in which they were acquitted.

Beatings were common, and the wallops Daniello casually dismissed may have left more of a mark on him than he could admit. Vollero testified without contradiction that Daniello fled because Mealli was looking for him. "Ralph told me that Mike Mealli had been up to his house, and that is the reason why he didn't go back there," he said.

There were never any formal charges against the detectives Daniello accused of taking payoffs. Under Woods, it is safe to say that there was not enough evidence to support even a disciplinary charge. Moreover, Michael Mealli's demotion to patrol duty was not the result of any charge Daniello made; it came about three months before the gangster began informing.[19]

* * *

This was the closest that the Italian Squad came to a corruption scandal during its on-and-off existence. Gangsters themselves seemed convinced that Italian detectives were on the take. But in an era when there was much proof of systemic corruption in the NYPD, cases involving the Italian detectives were few.

One former Italian Squad detective, Liborio Gambardella, was arrested in November 1914, on a charge of attempted extortion for allegedly taking twenty-five marked dollars from the owner of a pastry cafe at 201 Grand Street. The charge was dismissed in exchange for his testimony against a patrolman, Agidia Damico, whom authorities said solicited the payoff. Gambardella contended that the patrolman had stuffed what turned out to be marked money into his pocket. Damico was convicted and sentenced to one year, eight months to three years, four months in Sing Sing.[20]

Joseph Petrosino had started the Italian Squad on a high ethical note, reflecting the sense of mission that drove him and other early members of the unit. Mealli may have slipped from that, as did a detective he often partnered with, Paul Simonetti.

Reduced to patrolman, Simonetti retired from the Police Department in 1917. His downhill slide seems to have started in 1912, around the time his father, a successful wholesale grocer and civic leader from Chiavari in Liguria, died of a lung disease. Simonetti underwent a department trial on charges that he beat a Brooklyn undertaker and held a gun to his head. By the time Simonetti was cleared, he'd been reduced to patrolman, with a large pay cut. The following year, he lost three days' pay for being absent from his patrol post. After retiring from the NYPD,

Simonetti opened a detective agency. In 1921, he was sentenced to two to five years in Sing Sing for committing perjury in a divorce case; he lied to create the appearance that his client's wife was unfaithful. "For a long time he was capable and fearless and rose in the Police Department and then something happened," Judge Norman Dike, a keen observer of the Italian Squad's work in Brooklyn, said in sentencing him. ". . . He began to slip. He was reduced in the department, finally resigned and organized this detective agency which stood ready, it seems, to furnish perjured testimony."[21]

As ethnic outsiders within the department, the Italian detectives were cut off from the methodical graft rendered to police to permit gambling, prostitution, and liquor law violations. One of the squad's strengths was that many of the detectives lived or grew up in the city's Italian immigrant neighborhoods, but—as may have been the case for the Mealli brothers and Gambardella—that could lead to questionable associations and the temptation to take graft. In the big picture, though, the corruption record of the Italian Squad members was comparatively clean.

18

"The Man with a Hole in His Hand"

THE letter from Akron, Ohio, intrigued Detective Michael Fiaschetti. A suspect wanted in the murders of four police officers was believed to be in New York, with an identifying mark: "Look for the man with a hole in his hand," Akron chief of detectives Harry Welch wrote in the spring of 1918.

The four Akron officers were slain in three separate attacks, starting the night of December 23, 1917, when twenty-eight-year-old Patrolman Guy Norris was shot in the chest from three feet away as he searched three men for weapons. After "putting every suspicious looking foreigner they find through the third degree," police could not find the killers. Seventeen days later, gunmen ambushed and killed two more officers. Patrolman Edward J. Costigan, a tall, hefty man who aggressively patrolled Akron's version of the Tenderloin District, was shot four times in the back. Rookie Patrolman Joseph Hunt, a thirty-three-year-old father of three, was hit five times.

On March 12, 1918, Patrolman Gethin Richards was shot just after midnight; he died less than twelve hours later. But this attack differed: after a chase, police captured Frank Mazzano, an eighteen-year-old Sicilian immigrant who'd lived a year in New York before coming to Akron, and Paul Chiavaro, age twenty-four. Richards identified both in the local hospital's surgery room. But, Richards told police, there was a third man.

That was Rosario Borgia, a twenty-four-year-old pimp. He was enraged with Costigan and other police who patrolled his turf; they searched him constantly—he'd already been convicted of unlawful weapons possession. He was further enraged that police arrested him—and his wife, Filomena—in a vice roundup for "keeping a questionable place."[1]

He'd been on the way with lackeys Mazzano and Chiavaro to murder a rival gang boss when Patrolman Richards encountered him, prompting the gangsters to open fire. Akron detectives later found him hiding out in a hotel room. Welch soon learned that one of the assailants had fled to New York with a telltale wound to his hand, and contacted the NYPD.

At the time, thirty-six-year-old Fiaschetti was an acting detective sergeant second grade. It was entry level in the Detective Bureau: the NYPD had designated *all* detectives as at least acting sergeants to exempt them from a state law requiring a monthly change in tour of duty. At second grade, Fiaschetti earned the same pay as a patrolman. But: he was getting the attention that can lead to a promotion.[2]

In 1913, Fiaschetti received a department commendation for breaking up a Black Hand ring in Williamsburg, Brooklyn, with the arrest of Cosimino Casanova, who tried to extort $1,000 from a shoe dealer with a blackmail letter written in blood. In 1914, Fiaschetti was credited with defusing a lit bomb, stopping olive-oil dealer John Iannone from blowing up a macaroni store at 192 Humboldt Street, Brooklyn. It won Fiaschetti a department award.[3]

In 1916, Fiaschetti arrested a Bronx carpenter who admitted to selling dozens of bombs. Forty-five-year-old Calabrian immigrant John Attanasio stowed an amazing cache of explosives in the apartment he shared with his wife and five children at 212 East 212th Street. Fiaschetti showed off the seventy-eight bombs police to reporters. Commissioner Woods took note of the arrest.[4]

A big man with expansive ambitions and a gift for self-promotion, Fiaschetti took on the Akron case with typical energy. He put out word to his informants and, in three weeks or so, a contact from a Williamsburg poolroom called to say he'd seen the man with the wounded hand.[5] Newspapers, the official account in the NYPD's annual report, and Fiaschetti's own versions in his memoir, a magazine article, and a newspaper column all conflict on what followed—and Fiaschetti's memoir is so unreliable that it even describes the events as occurring in 1919, rather than

READ DECTECTIVE STORIES AS A BOY

SNUFFED OUT BOMB FUSE WHILE SPUTTERING

FIGURE 18.1. Michael Fiaschetti was celebrated in newspapers and magazines across the country for his exploits as a detective. His achievements were many, but he exaggerated them. Photo credit: *Santa Ana (CA) Register*, September 11, 1922.

1918. The bottom line is that Anthony Manfriedo and a partner in crime, Lorenzo Biondo, had been hiding out in a three-story brick apartment building at 176 Graham Avenue in the industrial Williamsburg section. By 3 a.m. on May 6, 1918, they were both under arrest; Detective Welch arrived the same day from Ohio to bring them back, and Fiaschetti went with him.

Fiaschetti worked some detective magic on the train to Akron. He knew that the Borgia gang had nearly killed Tony Manfriedo, leaving him with a psychological scar as well as the tell-tale mark on his hand. With a handsome face, resolute jaw line, wavy brown hair, and easy-going manner, Manfriedo seemed more like a college student than a street-hardened criminal. Lorenzo Biondo, still under his alias James Palmieri—"Jimmy the Bulldog"—had the dour, puffy-faced look of a street tough. Fiaschetti guessed that he accompanied Manfriedo to make sure he didn't squeal and, when the chance arose, to murder him. He separated the two men on the train, broke this news to the apparently naive Manfriedo, and convinced the twenty-one-year-old to confess to save himself from the electric chair. Once in Akron, Fiaschetti and local police persuaded Lorenzo Biondo to confess as well, although Biondo maintained his defense that Borgia coerced him into shooting officers Costigan and Hunt.[6]

These confessions gave Fiaschetti a bead on another suspect. Shortly after arriving in Akron, he rushed to Sandusky, Ohio, about ninety miles northwest on Lake Erie. Sheriff James Corey took him by car to Cleveland with detectives Welch and Edward McDonnell. The tires on the Rubber City car blew out repeatedly, slowing them up. In Cleveland, they caught a train—Fiaschetti convinced the railroad to make a special stop in Sandusky. Once inside a house on McDonough Street, Fiaschetti found his man in the bedroom. Pasquale Biondo, a twenty-one-year-old with a dark mustache that didn't quite meet at the center and eyebrows that did, denied he'd ever been in Akron. He gave a phony name.

Fiaschetti confirmed his identity quickly. "Whose bag is that over there?" he asked, gesturing at a leather satchel on the floor. "Mine," Biondo said. Fiaschetti then noted it was stamped with Biondo's correct name. A search found a .38-caliber revolver. Once back in Akron, Biondo confessed to the authorities there, with Fiaschetti serving as the translator. Biondo's admissions typed up to twenty-three pages. When brought before a judge, Biondo proceeded to enter a plea of "Not guilty! I was forced to do it."[7]

Cletus Roetzel, the twenty-eight-year-old chief prosecutor for Summit County, Ohio, was amazed at Fiaschetti's ability, as he recounted for a local newspaper:

> "He is the cleverest man at securing confessions I have ever known," Roetzel said Monday afternoon. He is never rough, never tries to overawe or frighten the man he is talking to, but he gets a confession with much speed. Why, can you believe, he had James Palmieri crying?
>
> Fiaschetti, Roetzel continued, "is my idea of a high-class detective. Always the gentleman, he never seems annoyed. But if he is on a case he won't rest. For example, yesterday he insisted that he could get 'Patsy' Biondi in Sandusky. Some told him that he was on the wrong track. He went to Sandusky, however."[8]

Roetzel called Fiaschetti the "chief witness" in the trial of Pasquale Biondo, which began June 10. The detective's role was to affirm that the defendant's confession was valid. Attorney Seney A. Decker, who accepted the court's assignment to defend the accused cop killer with much reluctance, didn't challenge it, however. He acknowledged that Biondo had committed the murder and pleaded that he be spared the death penalty. In seventeen minutes, the jury convicted Pasquale Biondo of first-degree murder in Costigan's death. There was no recommendation of mercy.[9]

When Lorenzo Biondo's trial began on August 10, Fiaschetti was again at the center of the action. Biondo, not known to be related to Pasquale Biondo, was represented by Cleveland's first Italian-born attorney, Benjamin D. Nicola, who put up a spirited defense. Nicola challenged the confession Fiaschetti obtained. He accused Fiaschetti of trickery, charging that the detective falsely promised a light sentence to Biondo if he testified against Borgia, sparing him the death penalty. Nicola brought in Anthony Manfriedo to testify; he flatly contradicted Fiaschetti's testimony.

Fiaschetti spent an afternoon on the witness stand denying that he'd promised leniency to Lorenzo Biondo. All he told him, he said, was that Manfriedo had already spoken to him truthfully, and that he also had information on Biondo from another member of the gang, Frank Mazzano, who turned state's evidence after being sentenced to death. "It would be better for him to tell the truth," Fiaschetti said he told the hoodlum.

Biondo insisted that he confessed only because of Fiaschetti's promises. He testified he heard Fiaschetti tell prosecutor Roetzel, in English, that he'd promised a light sentence. After Fiaschetti returned to the witness stand to deny it, Judge William Ahern admitted the confession into evidence and allowed it to be read to the jury. In closing arguments, the prosecutor urged a verdict without mercy—that is, one leading to execution. Nicola asked for mercy, arguing that Borgia had forced his client to murder Patrolman Joseph Hunt.[10]

A decade later, Fiaschetti wrote in a magazine article that he had gotten Manfriedo to testify by telling him he would avoid the electric chair, essentially confirming Manfriedo's testimony for Biondo. "'Come through, Manfredi [sic],' said I, 'and you won't burn. Do the right thing and you'll get off with a prison sentence.' Strong argument, that. I don't know whether he would have fallen for it if he had kept kept intact his faith in his dear friend Biondo."[11]

This jury found Lorenzo Biondo guilty of murder in the first degree, with a recommendation of mercy. Manfriedo pleaded guilty the following day, although he continued to maintain that he was not at the scene of the slaying. The Beacon Journal said that "reports of witnesses substantiate this allegation." He was sentenced to life in prison, as was Lorenzo Biondo. Judge Ahern specified that Biondo be held in solitary confinement between January 10 and 14 every year to remind him of the four days it took for Joseph Hunt to die from his wounds.[12]

Pasquale Biondo was less fortunate: he was executed in the electric chair on October 4, 1918, even though an appeals court in Cleveland had granted him a stay nine hours earlier. Borgia, Mazzano, and Chiavaro also died in the electric chair.[13] Lorenzo Biondo managed to be paroled and was deported to Italy in 1934. After forty-seven years in prison, Tony Manfriedo, the man shot in the hand, received a pardon from Ohio governor Jim Rhodes in 1965. The governor recognized he'd been a marginal figure in the Borgia gang. No one challenged Manfriedo's contention that while he knew of the murder plans, he was not involved in the slayings, even as a lookout. Cletus Roetzel said that Manfriedo should have been released sooner.[14]

* * *

The Akron murder case marked a turning point in Fiaschetti's career. On September 13, 1918, Mayor John F. Hylan honored him at City Hall, pinning a pair of gold medals sent by Akron's mayor and Chamber of Commerce. Most significant for Fiaschetti was his promotion that day to detective first grade, which meant a pay increase of 50 percent. Given his earlier successes, it was overdue. But Italian detectives seemed to have a particularly hard time landing one of the coveted first-grade slots; they just didn't have the pull needed for that within the Irish-dominated NYPD.[15]

As great as his achievement was, Fiaschetti started spreading the story that that he had nabbed all six of the cop killers on his own. A week after the medal ceremony, the *Akron Beacon Journal* made fun of one New York newspaper account that said Fiaschetti arrested Rosario Borgia, who had been jailed for two months by the time the New York detective arrived in Ohio. Fiaschetti used his access to the press to further embroider the story in the next few years, then authored his own articles that had little resemblance to what actually happened.[16] His actual achievement was great enough without being inflated. "The information which we had was very meagre and was given to Mr. Fiaschetti with the result that he not only succeeded in apprehending the criminals, but also succeeded in getting confessions from them, and later arrested the third murderer in Sandusky, Ohio," Prosecutor Roetzel wrote to Commissioner Richard Enright. "Without the confessions, we would have been unable to secure convictions."[17]

And Fiaschetti had many headlines ahead of him before he would begin publishing the tales himself.

"Appreciation and Thanks"

MICHAEL FIASCHETTI'S Associated Press obituary would erroneously credit him with arrests that led to "scores" of executions.[1] There were at least six, however—and he very much regretted one of them.

It was the case that boosted him toward detective superstardom. Fiaschetti unraveled a plot that began when a neighborhood hoodlum known as "Little Joe" ordered Michael Casalino to come up with a hundred dollars—money he certainly did not have from his job digging sewers. "I'm married and I work night and day to support my wife and two little children," Casalino said he replied. "Little Joe" shot back: "Find someone who can get it."

That someone was Joseph Holbach, the sixty-ish owner of Holbach's Hall, a popular spot for dinner and dancing on Rockaway Boulevard in Queens. Casalino told Paul Ricci, whom he'd met while working on a sewer job, about his dilemma. Ricci, who worked on a truck farm in the area, knew that Holbach had money because he lent it to help out the farm workers. After checking it out, Casalino went to the roadhouse one night with "Little Joe" and two associates. By the 1 a.m. closing time, everyone else had left. That is when Little Joe demanded the cash from Holbach, who fought back. Little Joe shot him. Holbach's wife, fifty-something Helen, rushed in and, amid the tumult, Casalino shot her dead. The robbers fled without any cash, leaving behind a black plush fedora. Joseph Holbach died less than twelve hours later, but not before giving detectives a detailed description of his assailants from his hospital bed.[2]

The double slaying of an older married couple was a national story, and Michael Fiaschetti was soon called in from the Bronx Detective Bureau to help the investigation. There are several stories of how Fiaschetti cracked the code to find Casalino. His memoir's version is that a week after the slaying, he found a well-worn black slouch hat in the woods near the Holbachs' roadhouse, the type Italian laborers wore. He looked around the truck farms in the area, pretending that he wanted work, and then sat himself down for lunch with a group of sewer workers. That's where he discovered that Casalino went missing from the job after the Holbach murders.

It may be, though, that the hat trick is a Sherlock Holmes touch that Fiaschetti's creative writing partner, Prosper Buranelli, dreamed up. There was a black hat, but newspapers reported the day of the shooting that police found it at the scene of the crime. It's more likely that Fiaschetti was able to identify Casalino through the details Joseph Holbach gave on his death bed. Either way, it was a good start.[3]

Fiaschetti and Detective Louis Dardis visited Casalino's anxious wife, Rosina, in their apartment at 146 Classon Avenue, Brooklyn. Then they traced him through letters he wrote to his wife. "They trailed Casalino to Bayonne, to Staten Island, to Philadelphia, back to Bayonne and then to Philadelphia again," according to the *Sun*. "They always arrived a few hours after he had left." When they tracked Casalino to a farm ten miles east of Rochester, Fiaschetti arranged to be hired there, then mingled with Casalino as a fellow laborer.

According to Fiaschetti, he got Casalino to pour out his heart as they sat in the barn drinking hard cider. The next morning, April 9, 1919, he informed Casalino that he was under arrest. The official version in the Police Department's 1919 annual report differs, saying that Casalino at first denied knowing about the Holbach murders, but that Fiaschetti secured a confession and the names of other participants from him on the way to New York. Fiaschetti and other detectives rounded up all but one of the six suspects in two weeks, and then "Little Joe" Zambelli was caught in New Haven on July 1.[4]

The trial of a highly agitated Michael Casalino in Long Island City, Queens, was stopped because he appeared to have a mental breakdown in the courtroom. After doctors ruled him competent for trial, a new jury was picked on June 12. Nicholas Chiusano and Anthony Bruno, two of his confederates, testified for the prosecution, describing how the plot was planned in a saloon at Franklin and Flushing Avenues, a Brooklyn hangout that happened to be seven blocks from the cold-water flat where Fiaschetti resided at 67 Grand Avenue.

"Detective Michael Fiaschetti, who solved the murder mystery, testified that he had had many conversations with Casalino and that it was through Casalino's aid that the gunmen who raided the Holbach Hotel were located," the *Eagle* reported. On June 14, Casalino's weeping wife Rosina nodded to him as he left the courtroom, convicted of murder in the first degree, the first such verdict in Queens in twenty-two years. On June 17, he was sentenced to be executed in the electric chair at Sing Sing prison the week of July 27.

Fiaschetti was celebrated once again. "The solution of this double murder is one of the most commendable cases in the history of the Police Department, there being no one on the premises other than the assailants and their victims," the Police Department's annual report declared.[5]

But Fiaschetti became uneasy about the death sentence imposed on Casalino.

* * *

Fiaschetti's success was rewarded shortly after. On July 8, 1919, Police Commissioner Richard Enright reinstituted the department's Italian Squad, appointing Fiaschetti to lead it. Yet again, the newspapers celebrated "Big Mike." In the *Brooklyn Times Union*, he was the detective "whose exploits almost compare with the adventures of the mythical Sherlock Holmes." The *Telegram* enthused:

> Fiaschetti is an athlete, standing just six feet in his stockings and weighing 190 pounds. . . . He dresses in the most up-to-date fashion, without being extreme, and is incidentally one of the most popular men in the

Detective Bureau. It is said of Fiaschetti that he never employs the third degree on men suspected of a crime. "If a man is guilty a detective has a seventy-five per cent start on him," he said. "Use your wits against his, and it is only a matter of hours, or perhaps a day, when your man breaks down and pleads for mercy."

The squad was reinstated to clear a large backlog of bombings and murders. It went unstated that this long list of unsolved violent crimes was the result of years of neglecting the rise of organized crime combines that gripped the Italian immigrant community.[6]

Enright, a son of Irish immigrants, started in the department in 1896. He knew the Italian Squad's story well: in 1910, he delivered the stirring memorial address at the gravesite of Joseph Petrosino in his role as president of the Lieutenants' Benevolent Association. During Enright's long years in the department, he stood out because of his leadership ability. He developed a reputation as a silver-tongued orator, the ideal toastmaster, and "the brainiest man in the department," as the *Brooklyn Citizen* said.[7]

He was also a friend of Mayor Hylan. A Brooklyn judge known as "Red Mike" for his thinning red hair, Hylan took office on January 1, 1918, drawing on the support of a strange-bedfellow pact between publisher William Randolph Hearst and Tammany Hall. He ran a populist campaign, attacking the private companies that ran the subway. With less than half the vote, Hylan defeated Mayor John Purroy Mitchel, whose single term, in the words of historian Terry Golway, "featured first-rate efficiency and third-rate politics." (Mitchel's career was cut short when he died on July 6, 1918, after falling five hundred feet from a single-seat plane he flew during Army flight training.)[8]

The non-Hearst press viewed the Hearst-Tammany alliance with great skepticism and scrutinized the new mayor's handling of the Police Department.[9] "Lieutenant Enright's appointment is looked on with anxiety by those who remember the days of a political police force under Tammany administration," the *Outlook* magazine warned. When Enright demoted Inspector "Honest Dan" Costigan from head of the vice squad, the message received was that Tammany once again had its "wide open" town. As gangs flourished with Prohibition, which took effect on January 17, 1920, the press held Enright responsible. He assailed the newspapers bitterly. "The press of this city has always employed the Police Department as a weapon with which to destroy the city administration," he rumbled in one of his annual reports.[10]

Enright knew policing in ways that no previous commissioner could, but some of his appointments played into his critics' hands. When Enright hired the mayor's sister-in-law Mamie O'Hara as an executive clerk, a reporter asked Hylan if she was related to the mayor's brother-in-law Detective Irving O'Hara. Hylan, a big man with a thin mustache, answered: "Not that I know of." When the reporter asked Irving O'Hara, he said, "Yes, she is my sister. What of it?"[11]

Irving O'Hara quickly became a power in the Police Department, Hylan's ears and eyes. Hylan's first commissioner, Frederick Bugher, resigned almost immediately, complaining that O'Hara was trying to give him personnel orders. When Hylan took office, O'Hara was an acting detective sergeant second grade, earning a patrolman's salary after sixteen years on the job and working from the Bronx. Soon enough, he was appointed to detective first grade, with the 50 percent pay hike, and assigned to the headquarters detective squad.[12]

When Bugher resigned on January 23, 1918, the mayor called in Enright from desk lieutenant duty in Williamsburg to lead the department. Looking older than his forty-five years, a stocky man with a full face, wavy, whitening hair, and a salt-and-pepper mustache, Enright went directly to City Hall to be sworn in, still in uniform. He arrived in the job with unparalleled experience, but also the burden of twenty-one years' worth of bruising in-house political battles and the resentment of constantly being passed over for promotion to captain, even when at the top of the eligibility list.[13]

While Enright warred with the press, Fiaschetti and his Italian Squad received nothing but positive notices. Fiaschetti stepped into the shoes of his late mentor, Joseph Petrosino. News coverage made it appear, however, that he was the first Italian Squad commander since Petrosino was murdered, ignoring the work that Anthony Vachris, Charles Corrao, and Arthur Gloster had done. Fiaschetti's squad had ten investigators, according to Police Department records—not 150, as his memoir would claim.[14]

* * *

As Fiaschetti tackled his new assignment, Michael Casalino's death sentence troubled him. Casalino turned state's evidence—no promises in return, according to prosecutors—and helped convict "Little Joe" and other accomplices. Fiaschetti felt the usual practice would be to commute his death sentence, even if there was no promise for leniency. Horrid as Casalino's crime was, Fiaschetti could see that he was not a professional criminal. He wanted the chance to plead with Governor Nathan Miller for Casalino's life.

Fiaschetti reached out to the former DA who oversaw the Holbach murder prosecutions, Denis O'Leary. They met with Miller, a Republican from upstate Cortland County who'd temporarily unseated Democratic governor Alfred E. Smith. Fiaschetti begged the governor to spare Casalino, but Miller insisted there was no need for him to intervene.

Casalino maintained to the end that he'd been promised a reprieve in return for cooperation. But he went to his death with a calm that surprised a Queens newspaper reporter who witnessed the double-jolt execution in the final hour of May 5, 1921. Frederick R. Curran recalled how fidgety and downcast Casalino had been on the witness stand. Now, he wrote, "Casalino was as one who had passed through a wonderful transformation. He showed emotion, but it was not fear, and he carried his head high and he accepted death at the hands of the state without protest."

On the night before his death, Casalino penned a thank-you letter to Fiaschetti, the person most responsible for his doom. Curran noted that "the letters in English were well worded and in neat hand"—another transformation for the Italian-born Casalino, who became fluent in English during his months on Death Row.

Perhaps there was a touch of transformation as well in Fiaschetti, who wrote that for a while after Casalino's execution he couldn't sleep nights and that, for years afterward, he occasionally brought money to Casalino's wife and children.[15]

PART FOUR

1920 to 1922

20

A "Vast and Complex" Mission to Naples

O N February 1, 1920, the joint book section of the *Sun* and *Herald* touted William J. Flynn's new book *The Barrel Mystery*, which recounted the 1903 murder of Benedetto Madonia and the Lupo-Morello counterfeiting case. "Only through eternal watchfulness on the part of the authorities can the characteristic activities of malefactors from southern Italy and Sicily be controlled in New York city," the reviewer advised.[1]

That was also the day that the book's chief villain, Giuseppe Morello, was paroled from the federal prison in Atlanta after serving ten years of his twenty-five-year sentence for counterfeiting. Flynn's book received national attention, and many newspapers published excerpts. Morello's release went unnoticed, but it was a sign of the times.

He soon became the right-hand man to Joe Masseria, a five-foot, three-and-a-half-inch tall, barrel-bellied thirty-four-year-old who'd compiled a long criminal record since he migrated from Marsala in western Sicily in 1901. With Morello's counsel, his Chrystie Street gang was poised to cash in on Prohibition, aided by proximity to an outdoor market where illicit liquor deals were brokered. It moved from corner to corner in an area with Prince Street to the north, the Bowery to the east, Canal Street to the south, and Mulberry Street to the west—police headquarters was just one block further west. The *Times* likened it to the old "curb exchange" where securities were traded outdoors, informally, downtown on Broad Street. As the mob power in this domain, Masseria attracted other talent in addition to Morello: Frank Costello, the Calabrian immigrant who'd be renowned for his political influence; and Salvatore Lucania, later known as "Lucky" Luciano. Masseria was ready to go to war—and with this Prohibition-era battle, a powerful American Mafia would emerge.[2]

The Italian Squad could have been a much-needed counterweight, but the detectives' time was devoted to other Detective Bureau priorities: low-level Prohibition enforcement, clearing homicide cases that grew out of petty squabbles, and taking part in giant "Red Scare" raids to arrest political radicals. Fiaschetti was a dynamo, but the NYPD was not wired for the extended surveillance and long-term probing needed to break up the growing crime syndicate in Little Italy as it drew strength from bootlegging profits. And always, there was the question of how much the department leadership wanted to during a Tammany administration.

* * *

The entire unit was thrown into the gargantuan raids that Attorney General A. Mitchell Palmer mobilized in November 1919 in response to a series of terrorist bombings, including one at his home. Political radicals were arrested with little regard for whether they had committed crimes; that was the case for four men Italian Squad detectives arrested outside a meeting hall on St. Marks Place for distributing circulars for a meeting to celebrate the Russian revolution. They were quickly freed in the magistrate's court on Essex Street.[3]

William J. Flynn, now director of the federal Bureau of Investigation, returned to New York to lead federal agents and hundreds of police in raids. "This breaks the backbone of the radical movement," he declared after mass arrests. Times had changed since Flynn worked for Mayor Gaynor, who insisted that police respect the civil liberties of socialists.[4]

Meanwhile, Enright and Hylan battled with the newspapers about whether there was a crime "wave." Enright called it a lie. Nonetheless, newspapers published long lists of unsolved murders and robberies. In Brooklyn, a grand jury issued a report blaming homicides and other violent crime on "foreigners who have no understanding of the genesis or genius of American institutions," and urged curbs on immigration. The city's crime wave was national news: "New York has thrown away the nickel novel of 1920, to begin reading the 1921 thriller of Dead Man's Gulch moved into Broadway," the Associated Press exclaimed.[5]

FIGURE 20.1. Richard Enright (right) was promoted from desk lieutenant to police commissioner under Mayor John F. Hylan (center). They are pictured with department store businessman Rodman Wanamaker, who held the title special deputy police commissioner. Photo credit: Library of Congress, George Grantham Bain Collection, Flickr Commons.

The *Herald* listed 338 murders that "left Enright baffled." The *Tribune* did its own list and published a similar take on the rising number of thefts. With the "crime wave" a hot political issue, the mayor and commissioner urged businesses to retaliate by boycotting newspapers that hyped crime.[6]

Many of the victims in unsolved cases were Italians, particularly in Brooklyn.[7] The *Eagle* tried to find out why:

A subordinate officer who did not want to be quoted—for there is a vey strict order forbidding subordinates to talk for publication—asserted that most of the murders on the Brooklyn list were of Italians and declared that the Italian murderer was hard to catch. In the first place, he said, the victim if conscious before death almost invariably declines to talk, or denies that he knows his assailant. Then the fear of assassination deters the eyewitness from giving information to the police. Italian murders are, therefore, he contended, rarely cleared up.[8]

This was the same defeatist viewpoint that Petrosino had fought. Its persistence signals that forty years into the great Italian migration, in a city with 390,832 residents born in Italy, relations between the police and Italian community were still broken.[9] The "subordinate officer" spoke for many in the Police Department. But a fairer assessment comes from a respected Manhattan prosecutor, Arthur C. Train. "The 'Omertà' is not confined to Italians. It is a common attribute of all who are opposed to authority of any kind, including small boys and criminals," he wrote. ". . . Thus may be accounted for much of the supposed 'romantic, if misguided, chivalry' of the south Italian. It is common both to him and the Bowery tough."[10]

* * *

In the early evening bustle of Mulberry Street on March 7, 1920, a gunman looking to settle a personal feud opened fire on a man leaving the Caffe degli Artisti, a few doors off Kenmare Street. Looking to avenge an insult to his girlfriend, he shot Joseph de Cesare, a thirty-six-year-old barbers' union delegate. But as he sprayed bullets over the busy street corner, he also struck two young women who were on the way to the theater. De Cesare survived, but Lena Spinelli, age nineteen, who stood next to him, and eighteen-year-old Josephine Gentile, hit by a stray bullet as she fled, did not.[11]

Fiaschetti quickly learned that the shooting stemmed from a quarrel between the two men's girlfriends, who were prostitutes. De Cesare's woman, Carrie Coppola, slashed Lizzie Marino's face with a pocket knife—ten stitches needed—after she took a client from her, or, as Coppola testified, "because she took bread out of my mouth."

The gunman, twenty-three-year-old Vincenzo Papaccio, eluded police. But Fiaschetti unearthed evidence that Papaccio, who lived in Long

FIGURE 20.2 and FIGURE 20.3. Teenaged friends Josephine Gentile (left) and Lena Spinelli (right) were on their way to catch a show when they were fatally shot on Mulberry Street, innocent bystanders to the result of a sordid dispute. In a request to Italian authorities for help in arresting the gunman, a police official called them "beautiful and good girls." Photo credit: Courtesy of the Archivio di Stato di Napoli and the Ministero della Cultura.

Island City, Queens, was in effect a US citizen because his father had naturalized. After Italian authorities indicated he would be turned over, President Woodrow Wilson signed a document authorizing Fiaschetti to bring him back.[12]

Fiaschetti sailed from New York on October 28, accompanied by Detective Irving O'Hara, a blue-eyed, five-foot, ten-inch man whose chestnut hair was starting to gray at age forty-six. If Fiaschetti objected to taking the mayor's brother-in-law instead of one of the Italian-speaking detectives on his own squad, there is no record of it. But in his memoir, he limited O'Hara's role to "he had some business or other in France or Rome." Then again, the memoir describes his trip as a secret mission "to hunt down and get" Papaccio. In fact, Papaccio was already in Italian

FIGURE 20.4. The NYPD wanted poster for murder suspect Vincenzo Papaccio (identified as "James Papcaccio") describes him as a cocaine addict with a criminal record and a five-pointed star tattooed on his right arm. By the time the poster was released, he'd fled New York for his hometown near Naples. Photo credit: Courtesy of the Archivio di Stato di Napoli and the Ministero della Cultura.

custody and the "secret" mission was high-profile enough to be reported in detail in the *Eagle* on the day the detectives departed.[13]

Fiaschetti enjoyed a restful voyage to Le Havre, then traveled by train with O'Hara to Rome. He had the pleasure of returning to a city he recalled from his boyhood; his family passed through while migrating to the United States from their hometown of Morolo, forty-three miles to the southeast, when he was ten years old in 1892. Following the same path as Petrosino and Vachris, he met with Italy's chief police official.

Fiaschetti's superiors in New York, eager to clear homicide cases, had sent him with a list of thirty-two murder suspects believed to be in Italy. And according to Fiaschetti, he also hoped to solve Joseph Petrosino's murder. It's disconcerting that the Police Department sent Fiaschetti on such an assignment without keeping it quiet. Unlike Petrosino and Vachris, Fiaschetti was single; he had not yet remarried after the untimely death of his wife, Eugenia, his beloved "Jennie." He still had his thirteen-year-old daughter, Anna, to care for, however.[14] Whatever secrecy existed ended on December 15 when the Italian newspaper *Giornale d'Italia* reported from Naples that Fiaschetti was there with his list and looking to arrest suspects wanted in New York homicides. Fiaschetti reportedly arrested one man, identified as Vincenzo or Rafaello Granito, in connection with a Brooklyn slaying. Fiaschetti was quoted in the *Times* as saying his mission "is a very vast and complex one." It was, he said, "connected with the new campaign for the extermination of that tremendous network of dangerous criminals who constitute the Black Hand gang." Italian authorities later arrested two more of his murder suspects, including one wanted for slaying a woman in Somerville, Massachusetts.[15]

In his memoir, Fiaschetti told a fascinating tale of how he disguised himself and infiltrated the Neapolitan underworld. Given his Roman dialect, he posed as a Roman who was fleeing police. He sought the help of a Camorra associate who lived in Rome, "Don Gennaro." Fiaschetti wrote that he stayed with Don Gennaro, paid him well for the room, and enjoyed the plates the don brought of macaroni and garlicky salad, "which is the way salad should be." Fiaschetti posed as "Don Pasquale," and said he sipped Frascati with his host. After a week, according to Fiaschetti, he intervened to stop two intruders from murdering Don Gennaro, who now owed his visitor a big favor for saving his life. When his innkeeper brought him coffee and brandy in the morning, Fiaschetti claimed he was running from a robbery charge and needed to leave the country.

Don Gennaro sent him to an oyster vendor in Naples whose husband would help him board a ship. More spaghetti and good wine followed and, according to Fiaschetti, he worked his way into meeting high-level members of the Camorra—and even to getting a lead on Petrosino's slayer. But the gentlemen of the Camorra began discussing the news that Detective Fiaschetti was in town, and decided to locate his picture. After that, Fiaschetti ended his undercover mission, only to be hunted by the Camorra.[16]

"Once I was shot at," he wrote in a newspaper column the year after his return. But forty-one-year-old Homer M. Byington, the "American consul, with whom I was walking, saw the leveled revolver and made me duck just in time."[17]

Fiaschetti's story of infiltrating the Camorra was colorful and just right for the "golden age of detective fiction," as the 1920s have been called. Some parts of it may be true. But the premise for the tale—that he went undercover to find Papaccio—is fabricated; court records in New York and Naples show he was already in custody.[18]

On January 1, 1921, Italian authorities rejected the request to extradite Papaccio, finding that he was in fact an Italian citizen; he would be tried in Naples under Italian law. Fiaschetti remained to testify at the trial and to act as District Attorney Edward Swann's representative. O'Hara left Naples for New York on January 9.

Back home, Detective Silvio Repetto, a member of the Italian Squad who'd also served under Petrosino, worried about Fiaschetti. "Don't relax your vigilance and don't get careless," he wrote, telling him to "leave the wine alone" so he didn't become an easy target. Further, he advised, using underlined capital letters, "write to your daughter." Anna was "very much hurt" at not receiving letters from her father, he wrote. And, the veteran detective added, "write to us here too. We don't know a thing you're doing." When the Papaccio trial was delayed again, Fiaschetti returned home.[19]

When he got off the boat in Philadelphia late on the evening of February 18, Fiaschetti learned from a reporter that Ignazio Lupo—still suspected of having Petrosino killed—had been paroled from his thirty-year counterfeiting sentence after serving ten years. Lupo's parole on June 30, 1920, went largely unnoticed until he was stopped when entering New York on return from a trip to Italy in 1922; federal agents thought his overseas travel violated his parole terms. But the trip was legitimate because, as it was discovered, President Warren Harding had commuted Lupo's sentence. "The order amazed the Secret Service officials and local police," the *Times* said.[20]

Fiaschetti would return to Italy twice more for the continually delayed case. Papaccio was finally convicted in Naples and sentenced on February 7, 1923, to eight years, nine months, and sixteen days in prison, far less severe than any penalty he would face in New York for the double murder of the two young women. Two months after his release from San Gimignano Prison in March 1931, he was caught trying to slip into New York—and charged with the double murder. In a significant decision, Judge Freschi ruled it was not double jeopardy for him to be tried in New York for the same murders he faced trial for in Italy. But ultimately, authorities moved to deport Papaccio.[21]

* * *

That Morello and Lupo could slip back into New York unnoticed a decade after they were sent to prison—and in the midst of much ado over Flynn's book on their case—illustrates how little scrutiny the police were giving to the growing threat of truly organized crime. In retrospect, the Italian Squad's attention needed to be on the Masseria gang down the street from police headquarters. Soon enough, there would be no way to ignore the problem.

"Cunning, Effective Detective Work"

LIKE everyone else in town, Rae Nicoletti was moved by newspaper accounts of the kidnapping of five-year-old Joseph Varotta, a seraphic-looking child pictured with big brown eyes, a Buster Brown haircut, and a cute sailor outfit. Like no one else in town, she was in a position to do something about it; she was the the city's only policewoman of Italian origin, and she was aching to help the boy and his parents, Antoinette and Salvatore Varotta.

Italian Squad commander Michael Fiaschetti had a similar idea. He knew the kidnappers would watch the Varottas' building on East Thirteenth Street, but thought a female officer might be able to slip through their surveillance. He called Deputy Commissioner Elizabeth Loft (Mrs. George W. Loft, wife of the candy manufacturer, as the society pages called her). Nicoletti had already come to her about the case; she was sent to meet Fiaschetti at the Italian Squad office.

The famous detective told the twenty-three-year-old patrolwoman of his plan to insert her into the Varotta family, warning it could be dangerous: the assignment was a request, not an order. He promised she would be protected to the extent possible, but added, "you may be in someplace where you will have to protect yourself. Can you?"

Patrolwomen had the option of carrying a revolver, but it was not mandatory. Nicoletti pulled one from her handbag, and said she had a place to carry it in her skirt. She scored high at the shooting range, she added.

The case that unfolded riveted the city's attention. It would show the Italian detectives at their best, reflecting their deep passion for protecting vulnerable immigrants from the *malavita*. It displayed their understanding of the Italian street, of its family life and neighborhood ways.

But it would also become Exhibit A for their use of extra-legal violence. For Fiaschetti, it yielded what he said was his biggest mistake.

* * *

When Nicoletti arrived with two suitcases at the Varottas' at 8 p.m. on May 29, 1921, the Sunday before Decoration Day, there were several women in the four-room apartment. Nicoletti, who had given birth to her daughter, Marie, nineteen months earlier, knew in an instant which one was Mrs. Varotta. "There was no mistaking that look of grief," she said. "I ran to her and threw my arms about her neck and kissed her." Antoinette Varotta, who was eight months pregnant, knew what to do: she told the visitors that this was her cousin from Detroit who'd come to help her.

Nicoletti cooked, helped with the wash, embroidered a dress for the couple's daughter, looked after the three children. She entertained visitors; she sang the folk songs of Naples, fluently. After 10 p.m., she sneaked out to spend the night at home with her husband, Tom, and daughter Marie in their apartment at 2212 Second Avenue, in the Italian enclave in East Harlem. But most of all, she spent long days with the Varottas, watching and listening.

She observed a wiry man with jug-handle ears spending long periods watching from a window across the street. The Varottas told her this was Anthony Marino; they considered him and his wife good friends. She suggested they invite him over. She was scrubbing clothes in a tub when he arrived, and was again introduced as a cousin visiting from Detroit.

"Well, say, what do you think about my cousin's boy. Isn't that awful?" Nicoletti said. Marino, a thirty-five-year-old bricklayer assistant, agreed. He then slid into a role familiar to investigators of "Black Hand" crimes—the family friend who could serve as mediator. He advised Salvatore Varotta to come up with more money than he had offered to get his boy back from the kidnappers, who had demanded $2,500, far more than the truck driver had. That's when Nicoletti announced that she had $600 to offer. Varotta noticed a tear in her eye as she lamented, "My poor cousin, my poor cousin got no money."

Marino was hooked. He spoke of how he once ran with a gang when he lived in Waterbury, Connecticut, and said he knew how to talk to such people. But, he told Varotta, there was a problem: "You people reported to the police." Nicoletti turned on her "cousin." "You keep away from the police," she warned. "Do not let the police know know anything about this."

"Well," Marino replied, "I will go out and speak to them and come back and let you know."[1]

Nicoletti slipped out at night to brief Fiaschetti, who saw she had already pushed the investigation a giant step forward. Part of the mystery was why kidnappers targeted an impoverished family. The reason had to do with a used car the Varottas bought on May 23, 1921, something of an event on the block. Neighbors thought the Varottas were suddenly rich.

There was reason to suspect as much. Their nine-year-old son, Adolfo, had been burned on his face and arms in a traffic accident, left disfigured and maimed after six months in Bellevue Hospital. Social workers at the hospital took pity on the Varotta family. Mrs. A. J. Biddle, Jr., a Fifth Avenue socialite, helped out and had her Wall Street lawyer represent the Varottas in a $50,000 personal injury lawsuit.

Antoinette Varotta, a twenty-eight-year-old native of French Tunisia, was rather proud of this distinction. When Mrs. Marino visited her on May 23 and asked why the family had bought a used car instead of a new one, Antoinette assured her that her husband could have afforded a much more expensive one. It was a gossipy boast—the lawsuit was unresolved—but on the street, it confirmed that the Varottas had struck it rich.[2]

At three the next afternoon, Mrs. Varotta tossed a penny from the window to her little boy, whose sailor outfit was a hand-me-down from a social worker at Bellevue. He was a precocious child who could speak in the Italian he picked up from his father, his mother's French, and English. That was the last she saw of him. For two days, the family prayed that he'd just walked off, and that he'd be found. Then the mail brought a Black Hand threat warning that Joseph would be drowned unless the family turned over $2,500. The Varottas had no hope of raising such money; Salvatore brought the matter to Fiaschetti.

On June 1, Marino's stepson James Ruggieri recruited Roberto Raffaele, a down-and-out former serviceman, into the scheme. Raffaele, age twenty-four, worked as a five-dollar-a-week dishwasher and lived in Bowery lodging houses. For fifty dollars, "I decided to go wrong, even at the risk of getting arrested," he later said.

He knocked on the Varottas' door at 11:30 p.m. that night to tell the couple that the gang wanted to be paid. Salvatore Varotta sank to his knees and kissed Raffaele's shoes, begging that his son be spared. He promised to get the money.[3]

The next day, Fiaschetti sent Detective James Pellegrino to the apartment, disguised as a plumber dressed in worn overalls; he hid in the bedroom. Another down-and-outer brought into the gang showed up at the door at 10 p.m. to collect the ransom money. That was John Melchionne, a friend of Raffaele from the Bowery. Pellegrino hauled Melchionne into the apartment from the hallway, took the cash from his pocket, sat him down, and told Salvatore Varotta to put a white rag in the window. Meanwhile, detectives arrested Marino and Raffaele as they waited outside. At the same time, detectives arrested another family "friend" who'd plotted the kidnapping, Santo Cusamano, a forty-six-year-old baker who was working the overnight shift. Ruggieri, age twenty-four, was also arrested.[4]

The suspects were rushed to police headquarters for a grueling night. Fiaschetti bet that he could get the suspects to give up the Varotta boy's location—the alternative would have been to let them walk off with the ransom money so they could be followed. Using three adjacent interrogation rooms, Fiaschetti and his team, including Nicoletti, desperately tried to get their prisoners to tell them where Joseph Varotta was hidden. No one was more desperate than Salvatore Varotta. The thirty-eight-year-old immigrant from San Fratello in Messina, Sicily, went from tearful begging to pounding the suspects furiously, without being held back. Emanuel H. Lavine, a New York American reporter who covered the story and later wrote about it in a noted book on police brutality, said the prisoners would not fall for various tricks, and that the detectives, aware that they probably only had a few hours to find Joseph, "decided to drag out every device they possessed to make unwilling people talk. This included rubber hose, automobile tires cut into convenient lengths, blackjacks, revolvers loaded with blank cartridges, discolored water which is supposed to represent a highly corrosive acid, a few chairs and a baseball bat." At his trial, Raffaele testified that Fiaschetti and a second detective beat him "with a rubber hose, sticks and with their hands." They forced him to sign a confession.[5]

The confession was so obviously coerced that prosecutors did not submit it as evidence at Raffaele's trial. Therefore, they were able to persuade the judge to bar a doctor in the city jail from testifying about the marks he saw on Raffaele's body when he examined him the next day. Under oath, Fiaschetti admitted that Varotta beat all the suspects—meaning that those waiting to be questioned heard their shrieks. For himself, he conceded only to giving Raffaele "a couple of slaps."[6] According to Lavine, his role was to break in on his detectives beating a suspect, chase them out in apparent anger, and then try to gain the prisoner's confidence. Lavine wrote that among the hundreds of victims of gang attacks he saw as a reporter, he'd never observed such severe injuries. "Their faces seemed swollen to at least twice the normal size and were completely out of alignment," he wrote.[7] After twelve hours of meting out the third degree, detectives still had no idea where Joseph was.

"These men have no hearts," a weary Nicoletti said of the five defendants as they were taken to court in the morning. "There is no question in my mind that at least one of them knows where little Giuseppe is being held."[8]

Nicoletti was the woman of the hour—she'd played the key role in breaking a case the whole city was watching. The *Times* praised her "cunning, effective detective work." Her photo on the front page of the next day's *Daily News* showed her as a short, athletically built young woman with dark hair in a fashionably short cut, a broad-brim hat with a sash, a black dress with a scooped neck and lacy collar, and a resolute look in brown eyes a little sleepy from forty-eight straight hours of detective work.[9]

FIGURE 21.1. Rae Nicoletti, the NYPD's first policewoman of Italian origin, was praised for her key role in arrests of suspects in the kidnapping of Joseph Varotta. No one was happy about the outcome of the case, however. Photo credit: *New York Daily News*, June 4, 1921.

Fiaschetti had feared from early on that the kidnappers would never free Joseph because he was so smart; they'd know he'd be able to provide clues to police. And then on June 11, the bad news came that a little boy's decomposed corpse had been found in the shallows of the Hudson River near Piermont, twenty-five miles north of the city. It was indeed Joseph, as his father confirmed when he arrived at the morgue in Nyack with Detective Angelo Trezza. He was clothed in the sailor outfit, with the same little red garters, suspenders, and little brown shoes, except that the worn-through soles had been replaced. The medical examiner found that drowning was the cause of death—the fate the blackmail letters had threatened.[10]

Roberto Raffaele was the first to be convicted of first-degree murder; he was sentenced to death. He then testified against Marino and Cusamano in their separate trials; both were convicted and sentenced to die. The charges against Ruggieri had to be dropped. Melchionne was ruled mentally incompetent for trial and sent to Matteawan State Hospital for the Criminally Insane.

Two other defendants were included in the murder-kidnapping indictment, identified only as "John Doe" and "Richard Roe." Looking back on the case in a law review article, the prosecutor who successfully argued for the three convictions before the state's top court noted that these two men were the actual kidnappers and murderers, never caught.[11]

Raffaele gave a small clue to "Doe" and "Roe." At one point, he saw two men he didn't recognize with the kidnappers who recruited him. "They were handsomely dressed, and they appeared to be of Italian parentage and they were very good-looking," he testified.[12] They were the slick swells who'd used some worn-out workmen to fleece another poor man of his imagined wealth. Whoever was behind the kidnapping was educated enough to write unusually elegant if extremely violent Black Hand letters, with a flowing Italian script. "They were written in imitation of the Sicilian dialect by a person of some education who was not a Sicilian," Assistant District Attorney Robert Coleman Taylor wrote.

And then there was the suspect Fiaschetti says he mistakenly sent his way the night of the arrests. He was young, clean-cut, and out of place among the shabbily dressed workers who waited for Raffaele in front of the Varottas' building on the night of June 2. In a straightforward way, the young man said he was related to one of the other men, and had stopped by only to chat. Fiaschetti let him walk.

Eventually, his memoir says, he got a tip that led him to conclude that the handsome youth he released had killed Joseph Varotta—"my biggest mistake."[13]

* * *

The Varotta case put Italian defendants on the cutting edge of law enforcement innovation once again. The appeals prosecutor, Taylor, acknowledged that the arrested suspects were likely locked up in the Tombs when the murder occurred, making the capital punishment imposed on them, "as far as this writer is aware, unprecedented." The Court of Appeals upheld the death sentences without explanation, as it did 150 times from 1911 to 1923. Ultimately, the defendants were not executed; Governor Al Smith commuted their sentences to life in prison on the request of the district attorney and sentencing judge.[14]

The case lives on, however, as a textbook example of police brutality, the result of a startling statement Fiaschetti made in his 1930 memoir. He related that after Joseph's corpse was found, he went to the jail aching for vengeance. The passage was quoted in a report by the first national commission to investigate police practices, the Wickersham Commission, as an example of "police lawlessness": "I went to the Tombs and got myself a sawed-off baseball bat and walked in on those dogs. Yes; they came through with everything they knew." Fiaschetti and the Italian Squad were not alone in this. The same groundbreaking report charged that "the third degree is widely and brutally employed in New York City."[15]

Nicoletti received a department commendation, but the case left a bitter aftertaste for all involved. "Persons familiar with police history" told the *Herald* that the breakup of the old Italian Squad impeded the investigation. "There is an Italian squad now, under command of Detective Michael Fiaschetti, but it does not contain a single man of the detectives who made the Italian squad terrible to the blackmailers, kidnappers and counterfeiters of a decade ago." Petrosino and Vachris deserved credit for the past success, the *Herald* said. And it listed the names of fourteen detectives still in the department who worked for them but weren't detailed to the new squad, including Charles Corrao, Ralph Micelli, and John Crowley. For Fiaschetti, it was an ominous development to have a major newspaper like the *Herald* question his leadership.[16]

"The Most Famous of Detectives"

BARTOLO FONTANA stormed into police headquarters on Friday night, August 12, 1921, raving about a gangland plot to murder him. "I know too much! They sent out the word to 'burn' me," he shouted at Fiaschetti, promising to help police investigate the gang that was after him.

Fontana was thirty years old, slender and dapper and, at five feet, three inches tall, a good nine inches shorter than the detective. Fiaschetti would have known from his speech that he was Sicilian, as Fontana was, a native of Castellammare del Golfo. Nearly a decade after he arrived in New York, the old family rivalries from that beautiful fishing village were haunting him.

Fiaschetti told Fontana to come back the next day, but made sure to get his address, 36 St. Marks Place near Second Avenue. Then he assigned a detective to trail the man. Frazzled Fontana showed up on Saturday, still with plenty to say—but not what Fiaschetti needed to hear. "I talked with him again, but he wouldn't tell me anything," Fiaschetti said later. He assigned one of his best investigators, James Pellegrino, to stay with Fontana.

Pellegrino, born in Newark and raised in Manhattan's Little Italy, was the son of Italian immigrants. At age thirty-seven, he had served in the NYPD for twelve years. He caught Fiaschetti's eye in Magistrate's Court as they waited on separate cases. Pellegrino had shown up with multiple knife slashes, there to testify against a notoriously violent bandit who'd attacked him after he broke up a brawl. He'd taken thirty-one stitches, but Mulberry Street, where Pellegrino's mother lived, came to the officer's aid—to the point that it took six police officers who arrived on the scene to prevent the crowd from lynching the assailant. Pellegrino was the kind of cop Fiaschetti admired, and not long after, Pellegrino was transferred from patrol duty to work for him at police headquarters.[1]

Pellegrino took Fontana to the Broadway Central Hotel. Early Sunday morning, Fontana tossed in his sleep and cried out, "They made me kill Camillo. They will kill me next. I know too much"—or so Fiaschetti later told the *Daily News*. Pellegrino shook Fontana awake and proceeded to question him for the rest of the night, getting nothing. They returned to headquarters in the morning and that, according to Fiaschetti, was when he broke down during questioning.

He told of how gangsters from his hometown had forced him to murder his friend Camillo Caiozzo. "It all started in some family squabble in Sicily," Fiaschetti told a *News* reporter. ". . . I questioned Fontana until I had his full story of how the band had worked and what they had done."[2]

* * *

The "family squabble" Fiaschetti referred to was a war between Mafia clans—the Buccellatos, and the intermarried Bonventre-Magaddino-Bonanno families—in Castellammare del Golfo. "If the Bonannos did not find a natural explanation for an event, they blamed the Buccellatos, and vice versa," mob boss Joseph Bonanno wrote in his autobiography.[3] Eye-for-an-eye warfare broke out in Castellammare in 1916, leading to the murder of one of the Magaddinos, Pietro. Camillo Caiozzo was said to have been an accomplice in that slaying.

The dispute boiled over into Brooklyn and Detroit, where both families had relatives. Pietro Magaddino's brother Stefano, living at 105 Roebling Street in the Sicilian enclave on the North Side of Williamsburg, thus took on responsibility to avenge his brother's death when Caiozzo fled to New York, arriving on June 28, 1921. He knew just the man who could do the job: fellow Castellammarese Bartolo Fontana, who stood a chance of catching Caiozzo with his guard down since they were friends. Fontana agreed, feeling he had no choice.[4]

The "full story" Fiaschetti had referred to was shocking. Fontana's confession involved not only the Caiozzo slaying in New Jersey, but seven more murders in New York City and nine in Detroit, carried out by a gang called the "Good Killers." Within two days, the headlined tally inflated from seventeen to 125, mostly because Detroit police attributed seventy slayings in their Italian community to the Buccellato-Bonventre feud, a vastly inflated figure.[5]

Fiaschetti used his willing contacts in the press to juice an already juicy story. Embellishing the early version, he said that he, not Pellegrino, was the one overnighting with Fontana when he admitted the murder in his sleep. That became the story, repeated countless times in the press. There were added touches: that Fontana was sleepwalking, that he said he'd seen the ghost of his slain friend, that Fiaschetti saved him from jumping out the window in his hallucinatory frenzy.

The ghost story was a sensation, and helped Fiaschetti keep his investigation in the papers everyday. He also invoked the greatest mystery the Italian Squad faced, claiming Fontana had given him a lead to solve Joseph Petrosino's murder. The next day, Fiaschetti was the news: he showed off a death threat he'd received in the mail, featuring the skull and crossbones, a heart pierced with a dagger, a bomb with lit fuse and a handgun, and the price of $5,000. "I get lots of such valentines," he said. "I suppose that is the price that has been put on my head."

Fiaschetti did indeed receive many death threats, much as Petrosino, Vachris, and Corrao had. Even so, his address and phone number were listed in the Brooklyn directory. It stood out as a three-line listing rather than the usual one line: "Dect Sergnt—Police Dept City NY." Given Petrosino's fate, the danger he faced was not to be dismissed lightly. This may be why the Italian Squad and Bomb Squad cops were first in line to receive "steel corsets"—body armor—when they were introduced into the NYPD a few months later.[6]

Fiaschetti introduced Jane Dixon, a *Telegram* feature writer, to Fontana when she visited his basement office in police headquarters. She described the informer as looking boyish, "harmless enough, his deep eyes burning feverishly in their deep sockets, his curly mop of hair disarranged by his nervous fingers."

"And has the ghost of your friend departed now that you have told your secret?" she asked. Fiaschetti translated Fontana's answer: "Yes. Now I am afraid only of the living."

In her article, Dixon waxed over Fiaschetti, with his "shoulders of a ring champion, straight, shining black hair, eyes like the blue of his native Mediterranean under a noonday sky, dark curtains of lashes casting their shadows to add a touch of mystery, and the olive skin-tones that belong to South countries." His alpaca coat, his "aura of extreme kindness," his voice "soft as a summer breeze," the "Nemesis of these harpies of the underworld": practically a god from Roman mythology.[7]

* * *

Fiaschetti waited to put out the story of Fontana's cooperation until he could test his veracity. He had the informant telephone Stefano Magaddino and say he needed money to get away from police. They arranged to meet in Grand Central Station. Sure enough, Magaddino showed up, gave Fontana thirty dollars, and told him to take a train to Buffalo, where "the chief" would help him elude police. "We have plenty of money. You will be defended by the best lawyers if arrested," he added—a remark that Detective Silvio Repetto, disguised as a suitcase-toting traveler, was close enough to overhear. Detectives Repetto, Fiaschetti, Eugene Scrivani, and Jack Rue from Monmouth County, New Jersey, swept in at that moment to subdue Magaddino, who fought back before the gathering crowd.[8]

Police rounded up the rest of the gangsters Fontana said had forced him to murder Caiozzo and helped dispose of his body. In addition to Magaddino and Vito Bonventre, the suspects were three henchmen from Manhattan: Mariano Galante, Giuseppe Lombardi, and Francesco Puma. Bartolomeo DiGregorio, of 117 Roebling Street, was held on a weapons charge.

Fiaschetti, Pellegrino, and Repetto questioned the suspects for much of the night at police headquarters and, according to the *Times*, police said three of them admitted to complicity in the Caiozzo murder. But

FIGURE 22.1. Informant Bartolo Fontana (right) informed on the "Good Killers" gang, creating a frenzy. From left: the bandaged Stefano Magaddino, Detective Silvio Repetto, Francesco Puma, Giuseppe Lombardi, baker Vito Bonventre, and Mariano Galante. Photo credit: *Kansas City (KS) Kansan*, August 28, 1921.

three of the suspects were badly bruised when they showed up before Magistrate Joseph Corrigan in the Tombs Police Court. Magaddino, with a big white bandage on his head, looked especially bad. Fiaschetti said Magaddino had to be beaten back after he attacked Fontana. Detectives had lined up all of the men—including Fontana—in the fingerprinting room, probably a tactic to provoke the suspects. According to police, Magaddino lunged at Fontana, grabbed him by the throat, kicked him to the ground. Magaddino, age thirty, was said to have kicked Fiaschetti in the stomach as detectives pried him away from Fontana. Fiaschetti reportedly knocked him unconscious with a blackjack. When he revived, Magaddino supposedly shouted at Fontana, "I'll burn you for this"—according to Fontana, alluding to the gang's practice of burning the bodies of its murder victims in the oven of Vito Bonventre's bakery at 115 Roebling Street in Williamsburg, Brooklyn.[9]

* * *

Meanwhile, Monmouth County prosecutor Charles F. Sexton sifted through the investigative files and prepared for trial. The defendants had actually been held on a complaint filed by one of *his* detectives, Jack Rue. Sexton was disturbed at the way Fiaschetti had used the case to promote himself. He didn't believe that Fontana had revealed the murder mystery to Fiaschetti in his sleep. Nor did he like the way Fiaschetti grabbed all credit for the case, since the Monmouth County detectives had done some important sleuthing of their own. For example, they found that the sandstones used to weigh down the victim's body in the Shark River— where a crabber found it on August 8, 1921—had come from a pile of rocks used for clambakes at a nearby "resort." That led to the arrest of Salvatore Cieravo, the owner of the Neptune City business, which Sexton believed to be a front for prostitution and gambling. Further, they identified Caiozzo from scraps of paper found in his pockets.

From there, it would not have been difficult to identify Fontana as the killer after contacting Caiozzo's worried relatives, who filed a missing persons report with the NYPD on August 8. The detectives in New Jersey provided their information to Fiaschetti; it's unclear how detailed it was. The NYPD Annual Report's Italian Squad highlights for 1921 simply says, "On August 12, 1921, confidential information reached this Squad that one Bartolo Fontana . . . was recently implicated in a murder perpetrated in the State of New Jersey." That is the same date that Fontana first went to Fiaschetti at police headquarters. At a minimum, Fiaschetti was armed with some very useful background from the New Jersey investigators when he questioned Fontana. The chagrin in the New Jersey office paralleled the reaction that Akron, Ohio, detectives had to working with Fiaschetti.[10]

In March 1922, Fontana testified for the first time in open court as a government witness; Cieravo was being tried as an accessory-before-the-fact to murder. According to Fontana, Cieravo lent him the shotgun to murder his victim, then later helped him and two of the New Yorkers, Puma and Lombardi, to dispose of the corpse in the river. Before proceedings began, Fontana pleaded "no contest" to murder and was sentenced to life in prison.

Fontana testified that when he told Cieravo he was afraid to kill Caiozzo, he suggested that he take his target duck-hunting and murder him then. Caiozzo, age twenty-six, was a blond-haired Sicilian who stood five feet, five inches tall. On the way back from hunting, he suddenly became fearful, according to Fontana.

"Oh mother, oh mother, somebody is going to kill me," Caiozzo lamented.

"What's the matter? What did you say that for?" Fontana asked.

"Benny," he said, using Fontana's nickname, "we better go to California because someone is framing us up." Fontana said that's when he shot Caiozzo dead, fearful that Caiozzo knew he was being set up and would try to kill him first. There were other witnesses, including Fiaschetti, but the case rested on Fontana's credibility—which was quickly shattered.

The jury acquitted Cieravo after four hours of deliberation. Sexton dropped further charges against Cieravo. Fontana went to Trenton State Prison, not to be used again as a witness—a flop in his out-of-town debut. The rest of the case against the fearsome gang rounded up on Fontana's word went nowhere.[11]

* * *

The "Good Killers" case opened a window on the early development of the American Mafia, demonstrating connections to the Sicilian Mafia and, through family ties, some links among gangs in several US cities.[12] This is really what Italian Squad detectives had been fighting to stop ever since Petrosino headed the unit. The so-called "Black Hand" was never some many-armed monster run by Mafia or Camorra bosses in Sicily or Naples, but there were some criminal elements with links to the Old World—the Lupo-Morello gang, especially. These were the gangs that especially concerned Petrosino, and he lost his life trying to eliminate them early on.

Of the "Good Killers" suspects, Stefano Magaddino, in particular, went on to a long career as an organized crime boss based in Buffalo, which was ideally situated for liquor smuggling across the Canadian border. Joe Bonanno, who had moved with his parents to Williamsburg's Roebling Street as a boy in 1908 and then gone back with them to Sicily after staying thirteen years, returned in 1924 and began his rise to "family" boss. His mother was a Bonventre; her mother was a Magaddino.[13]

In hindsight, a more painstaking investigation of Fontana's disclosures was needed rather than quick arrests—he'd given no more than a road map. It's hard to avoid the conclusion that Fiaschetti chose the course that would yield the most spectacular headlines. He was acclaimed, and in yet another Sunday newspaper profile, it was asserted that "through his activities in Italy and various American cities Mike Fiaschetti has become one of the most famous of detectives. His fame is even greater, and his medals and recognitions more numerous, than his predecessor, Petrosino."[14]

If Fiaschetti had been able to build on the raw intelligence Fontana gave him, he might have been able to make major inroads against the budding American version of the Mafia. He didn't get the chance.

23

"Broken Up"

SHORTLY after Mayor Hylan began his second term on January 1, 1922, Commissioner Enright announced what newspapers described as the biggest shake-up in the Police Department's history—seen as a tacit admission that New York, like other major cities, was struggling to stop a postwar crime wave. Some moves modernized the department, but Enright also continued his practice of rewarding friends and punishing enemies. "Enright has always been a politician rather than a policeman," the *Brooklyn Standard Union* asserted.[1]

The Italian Squad was collateral damage. Lieutenant James J. Gegan, commander of the Bomb Squad, was among those rewarded. On February 4, Enright announced that the Italian Squad would be merged with the Bomb Squad; Gegan, who'd been promoted to lieutenant six weeks earlier, would command the unit. Fiaschetti was to be his assistant. Gegan was a son of Irish immigrants; once again, Italian workers had an Irish foreman.

"Greater efficiency and broader activities" were the reasons Enright gave for the decision. "Conditions which seemed to require the formation of the nationality organization of detectives some years ago have to a large extent disappeared, it was said, and the present work required different methods and supervision," the *Times* observed.[2]

But this change in "methods and supervision" would in effect halt aggressive investigation of Italian organized crime in New York just as it was growing powerful, on the way to morphing into an American Mafia that would do much to corrupt business, labor, and politics—and do long-term damage to the reputation of all Italian Americans.

Gegan was a friend of Enright and, like the commissioner, very much the politician. As president of the Lieutenants' Benevolent Association,

Enright created the mold for New York's outspoken police union chiefs. Gegan followed his path as president of the Sergeants' Benevolent Association. He did the heavy lifting to get the state legislature to approve Enright's plan to give New York City detectives raises and to make their jobs permanent—thus cementing Enright's appointments. Further, the legislation would give the police commissioner the right to promote a low-level detective to permanent commander of the Detective Bureau—a post that Enright's critics suggested was designed for Hylan's detective/brother-in-law.

Gegan lined up a powerful sponsor, Senate Majority Leader Clayton Lusk, a Republican from upstate Cortland. Other police unions, former commissioners, and newspapers (with the exception of the Hearst papers) opposed the bill, leaving the puzzling question of why a senator from the heart of apple country had become so involved in police politics in the city. Lusk could do no better than to say "for personal reasons" when a reporter queried.[3]

A more specific answer would involve the silver set that Gegan presented to Lusk's wife the morning after a dinner the union gave to honor the upstate senator, attended by a thousand people. As Gegan later testified before New York City's commissioner of accounts, the silver set, each of the 153 pieces engraved with an "L" and contained in a mahogany box lined with green velvet, had cost the detective union $1,131 (equivalent to $17,764 in 2022 dollars). (The "permanent detective bill" failed after Hylan reluctantly exercised a "home rule" veto that existed at the time. He praised the measure but said the city couldn't afford the pay increase because of a budget deficit.)[4]

While Gegan ingratiated himself with Enright, Fiaschetti did not. Fiaschetti's influence was not in police politics or in the mayor's office, but in the newspapers, which lionized him. He followed his predecessors in establishing strong connections to reporters; Petrosino, Vachris, and Corrao had done the same. Press access was one way the Italian detective commanders could offset the ethnic obstacles they faced within the department.

Shortly after he took office in 1918, Enright issued orders barring police from speaking with reporters without the department's permission. During the 1921 mayoral campaign, Enright was especially sensitive about any news coverage that told the public there had been a crime wave on his watch. He even urged the city's district attorneys to prosecute the *Herald* for breaking a law against "furnishing false information," articles that listed unsolved homicides on Enright's watch.[5]

Meanwhile, Fiaschetti made headlines by telling reporters about the massive number of homicides he was investigating. "Two Hundred Murders in New York City Laid to Camorra" topped a glowing profile of Fiaschetti that ran just as the fall campaign was starting. No one kept horrifying crime news on the front page as well as Fiaschetti, and that could not have endeared him to the boss.[6]

* * *

The Bomb Squad that the Italian Squad detectives joined was really a Red Squad specializing in surveillance of radicals and mass arrests of political dissidents. Detectives spent many hours infiltrating radical meetings—some 221 meetings in 1920. What Enright really wanted was a "secret police," as he called it, to be devoted to espionage investigations. This was needed, his 1920 annual report stated, because the expected postwar resurgence of immigration would include "a large percentage of malcontents, agitators and virulent anarchists, thirsting for sensationalism and violence to shore up their insane propaganda and wicked doctrines."[7]

Predictably, the Italian Squad detectives did little of their previous work once they joined the Bomb Squad. Gegan's squad found time to investigate jewelry and securities thefts, however—a lucrative assignment because insurance companies paid awards to the detectives if goods were recovered.[8]

Fiaschetti contributed to arrests made in the robbery of banker Albert R. Shattuck in his home at 19 Washington Square North on April 2, 1922. The robbers fled with $75,000 in jewelry, leaving Shattuck, his wife, and eight servants to a very uncertain fate, locked inside a vault. They were able to survive because the seventy-year-old banker figured out how to unlock the vault from inside. According to the *Daily News*, Fiaschetti got a lead on the case by following an "exceedingly comely young Corsican woman" who was the lady friend of one of the gunmen. The case topped the list of the Police Department's most important arrests of 1922. Meanwhile, investigation of serious crime in the Italian community was scattershot.

* * *

This became clear when shooting broke out in the early-evening rush on Grand Street a block east of police headquarters on May 8, 1922. As factories emptied thousands of workers into the streets, five men were seen rushing out of the doorways to shoot at bootlegger Umberto Valenti and an associate, Silvio Tagliagamba, who fired back. Pedestrians dropped to the ground, five of them wounded by stray bullets. Tagliagamba was shot in the back and later died. His boss, Valenti, fled unscathed. Police who happened to be going by caught one of the assailants; a detective sitting in an unmarked police car reached out the window and snagged him by the collar as he ran past. The "collar" was identified through fingerprints: Joseph Masseria, then aged thirty-five and striving to rise to the top of the underworld.

In August, gunmen in a stolen blue Hudson touring car shot at Masseria at close range. His straw hat took two bullets but he fell to the ground unharmed, appearing dead. Then the gunmen shot a path through a crowd of three hundred striking cloakmakers at Second Avenue and Fifth Street, wounding eight people, one fatally.[9]

Three days later and seven blocks away, Masseria was avenged; his bootlegging rival Umberto Valenti was shot dead. Once again, passersby fled in fear. A child visiting from New Haven, nine-year-old Agnes Egglinger, was shot in the chest in front of her grandparents' stoop; Joseph Schepis, a street cleaner and immigrant from Messina, Sicily, was shot in the neck. (Both survived.)[10]

Such wanton shooting smacked of a return to the bad old days on the Lower East Side, when politically connected gangs sprayed shots at each other across the streetscape. Fiaschetti, working with the respected commander of the homicide squad, Arthur Carey, tried to find the shooters. But he didn't get far: just when his skills were really needed, he was booted out of the Detective Bureau.

* * *

Michael Fiaschetti was keen to unravel a kidnapping melodrama that played out in the newspapers during the summer of 1922. Salvatore Iavarone, a butcher, had come to him with a tearful story of how his beautiful twenty-eight-year-old wife, Maria, and their three-year-old son, Anthony, went missing on June 23, leaving behind daughters Jean, age six, and Tessie, age four. Iavarone told Fiaschetti that the family's $40,000 in bank savings was also missing, as well as $10,000 worth of jewelry kept in a safe deposit box. Then he received a phone call, he said, that led him to pay $200 in ransom to get his son back. Shortly after, Maria's mother, Tessie Volpicella, received a letter from Maria, telling her, "Dear mother, forgive me for what I have done. They have hold of me and I cannot get away. I am crying for the children. When they let me go I'll come home."

Fiaschetti suspected that Maria Iavarone had conspired in some Black Hand plot to steal away not only the butcher's wife, but the Iavarones' ample savings. On August 5, he arrested longshoreman Vincenzo Damiani, whom Fiaschetti believed to be the middleman in taking the ransom from Iavarone in return for handing over his son on July 7. Two other men were arrested in Utica, New York, one supposedly Maria's brother and the other, Samuel Contarino, said to be the brother of the man "who is reported to be with Mrs. Iavarone," John Contarino.[11]

But the big catch was the star of the saga, Maria Iavarone. The day after the three arrests were made, she hired a lawyer, Lorenzo C. Carlino, who was already representing Damiani. Fiaschetti told him that he needed to see Mrs. Iavarone and, according to Carlino, promised she

FIGURE 23.1. Michael Fiaschetti (center) met his match in Maria Iavarone, whom he suspected of taking part in an extortion conspiracy aimed at her husband. After roughing up her lawyer at a meeting in police headquarters, he escorted her to the lockup. She spoke to reporters along the way. Photo credit: *New York Daily News*, August 8, 1922.

wouldn't be arrested if she came in voluntarily; the lawyer would have wanted to arrange bail in advance so she wouldn't be jailed. When they arrived, Carlino brought his client to Gegan's office. They were speaking when Fiaschetti charged in and hustled Maria Iavarone into his own office because it was *his* case. He locked Carlino out; the lawyer said he could hear him threatening her. When Fiaschetti opened the door because another detective had knocked, Carlino barged in and confronted Fiaschetti, who told him that his client was now under arrest on a grand larceny charge. Carlino shouted that this meant she'd be put in the Tombs pending arraignment, which he'd tried to avoid, and warned his client not to answer any questions.

At that point, Fiaschetti punched Carlino in the chest. The detective, eight inches taller than the lawyer, grabbed his collar, dragged him to the door, and heaved him out. Carlino was not accustomed to getting the bum's rush, and he was a man with friends. He was born and raised in Buffalo, where his father, an immigrant from Messina, Sicily, was a civic leader and successful real estate businessman. An article that appeared in one of the Buffalo newspapers in 1920 after Lorenzo Carlino was appointed assistant district attorney in Manhattan gives a glimpse of the family's influence. There was "a big dinner given by politicians in the Bowery district" at the Italian Garden at 341 Broome Street, the restaurant where influential Italians gathered to celebrate their successes.[12]

Carlino went straight to Inspector Coughlin, the chief of detectives. He made Fiaschetti apologize to the lawyer. Meanwhile, Marie Iavarone was in the hallway speaking with another woman of about her age, *Telegram* reporter Elisabeth Smith. She wisely gave her side of the story to Smith: that she had left her husband because he'd cheated on her and threatened her. Any money she took was hers: "I worked in my husband's butcher shop. For nine years I worked there. I cut meat. I worked like a man—just as hard, I tell you."

It was mostly Mrs. Iavarone's style that the reporter admired. She was dressed in a "decidedly modern and smartly New Yorkish black Canton crepe gown, with a cape trimmed with black fur, a platinum wedding ring and a diamond, set in platinum, and carries the accepted bead bag that thousands of women the city over have likewise appropriated. Not a trace of Naples remains in her costume."

And she cast Iavarone as the star of a story "cut straight from the thrilling pages of a Prosper Merimée romance"—the Cornell grad apparently referring to the popular French writer's novel that became the basis for the Bizet opera *Carmen*. "Its central figure, in an aura of tragic torrid light, is the wife and mother, beautiful dusky-haired Marie Iavarone, with eyes of smouldering fire." Salvatore "beside her appears comparatively insignificant," the writer added.[13]

Then it was time for Fiaschetti to take Marie Iavarone to the Tombs jail. Along the way, she made her case to the court of public opinion. "I learned there were other women," she told reporters. "At first, I would not believe. I begged him to come back, to be Marie's Salvatore again, as he was when we were poor. He threatened me. Once he threw the cleaver at me. It missed and buried itself in the ice box." As for the charge against her: "Steal what? Money? Iavarone's money? Who worked for it? Who made the home and nursed the babies? Who made Iavarone what you call in America, the success?"

At the jail, her husband showed up with their three children, who hugged and kissed their mother, as reporters witnessed. Then she was separated from the children and led away to her cell.

"Maybe tomorrow, I bail her out," Salvatore said lamely. And he did post her $2,500 bail.[14]

* * *

The hammer fell on August 25. Buried somewhere in an order effecting the transfer of 135 officers, Acting Detective Sergeant First Grade Michael Fiaschetti was reduced to patrolman and transferred to the Williamsburg precinct where he last walked a beat in uniform. His salary was cut by a third. Reporters were astonished that the detective who "has done some of the best work in the history of the department . . . is reduced to the ranks, ordered into uniform and assigned to ordinary patrol duty."[15] It's a sign of the times that the reporters didn't think to connect the demotion to the roughing up Fiaschetti administered to a defense lawyer who was trying to advise his client, which their own papers had reported two weeks earlier. Apparently, that wasn't considered a serious infraction.

"News of Fiaschetti's demotion stunned the entire Police Department last night," the Daily News declared. When there was some explanation, it focused on a falling out between Fiaschetti and Gegan. "Fiaschetti became a subordinate of Lieut. Gegan's, and as he had ruled the Italian squad since 1918 he found it hard to realize, it was said yesterday, that he was now on the same footing as other first grade detectives," the Herald commented. "Some of his men have taxed him with domineering and with receiving credit for work performed by others."[16]

Fiaschetti had no sponsor in the department to save him from falling off his high wire. He played the papers to get "cheap publicity," Inspector Coughlin complained privately to a Secret Service agent. But both Fiaschetti and Carlino thought that Enright demoted the detective because of the lawyer's complaint. Fiaschetti said so in his memoir, noting that Carlino had the influence to back up his charges. "The Italian Squad was broken up," he lamented.

Nearly four months after Fiaschetti was demoted, the *Tribune* explained what was behind a move "which puzzled many and angered some." Carlino told the paper that Fiaschetti was disciplined for assaulting him and also his client Damiani, whom he said suffered internal injuries from being kicked in the stomach. Charges were drawn up against him and were pending, he said.[17]

Fiaschetti was supposed to report for patrol duty the day after the demotion was announced, but instead he quickly arranged to take a vacation. He never actually did uniform duty because he was able to arrange assignment to the Manhattan district attorney's office, where he worked on the Varotta kidnapping and then on homicide cases. He stayed long enough for Vincenzo Papaccio's trial in Naples in 1923 and retired on June 3, 1924.[18]

Putting the Italian Squad under Gegan failed—the NYPD's annual report for 1922 shows no notable successes in dealing with Italian underworld crime at a time when it was criss-crossing Italian neighborhoods with gunfire. With Fiaschetti's departure, the other detectives were either transferred to patrol or quietly absorbed into the homicide squad. The Italian Squad's story was over.[19]

* * *

Having brought the Italian Squad back to life and then led it to its demise, Fiaschetti began mythologizing it. In mid-September, newspapers across the country started publishing his syndicated series, "Crimes That I Have Solved." He'd hit it off with *World* feature writer Prosper Buranelli, who mastered the hardboiled style and turned out stories for the storied detective. National magazine articles and a memoir, *You Gotta Be Rough*, followed. Buranelli was brilliant and eclectic, born in Texas and remembered mostly for popularizing the newspaper crossword puzzle. He wrote fiction and books with the boxing champion Gene Tunney, among others.[20] The articles and book that Buranelli and Fiaschetti created were filled with exaggeration and error, hype that has often become history.

The Italian Squad was mythologized even during Joseph Petrosino's lifetime, then more so after the unit's passing. But the true story, with its many gray areas, can be more compelling and more instructive.

Conclusion

A Bridge to an Alienated Community

THE New York City I covered as a daily newspaper reporter in the 1980s and '90s does not seem so different from the city the Italian Squad policed: tabloid war, crime wave, political corruption scandals, and poor relations between police and minority communities. Calls for the death penalty, mandatory sentences, more police. After the 2001 attack on the World Trade Center, Arab immigrants came to be seen as a "problem."

That's not to say the two eras are entirely alike. One key difference is that in the early twentieth century, racist eugenics theory was considered respectable. It buttressed the assumption that southern Italians, among other "races," were inherently inferior and therefore unfit to be American. The Dillingham Commission's 1911 report referred to "the not unfounded belief that certain kinds of criminality are inherent in the Italian race."[1]

This mindset seeped into the way journalists, judges, jurors, prosecutors, police, and elected officials reacted to crime among southern Italians, making for a criminal justice system the immigrants rightly viewed as stacked against them. Italian Squad leaders often used their access to the press to argue against this supposition that Italians were a "problem." Interviewed at the height of his celebrity in 1921, Michael Fiaschetti spoke at length on this:

The Italian people are good, hard-working, emotional, artistic and kindly. You can walk along Mulberry or Roosevelt Street, the most congested Italian districts in New York, at any hour of the day or night, in perfect safety. The Italians work so hard they have to retire early. They attend to their own affairs, are devout in their religion and make good citizens . . . lawlessness is not only found among the Sicilian provincials of the Italian people. You will find it among all peoples—all nationalities. America has its hold-up men, who will kill without provocation and who will beat their victims unmercifully. . . . France has its Apaches [the Parisian underworld], who murder with spiked mitts and daggers. England has its Whitechapel district, which produces a repellent class of murderous characters. So you see, the Italians are not alone in crime.[2]

Petrosino fought the same battle. He clearly disappointed a *Times* reporter in 1906 when he'd be interviewed only in defense of Italian immigrants, rather than talk about their crimes: "It does not take an Italian long to save money and contribute his mite to the Government. He works hard, has simple pleasures, loves the things that are beautiful, and sends his children to the public schools. He is worth enlightening."[3]

At the same time, Petrosino and his successors were extremely disappointed at the difficulty of persuading Italian immigrants to cooperate with police. Petrosino wrote a memo discussing the "sacred duty of every honest and hard-working citizen" to cooperate with police. If Italians did so, the trust they generated "would result in commercial improvement, intellectual development" and "political power." This was Petrosino's essential mission, but he was so frustrated that he suggested anyone failing to notify police about a blackmail threat be held legally responsible for the disaster of a bombing, or, in a case where money is paid and no bomb is planted, for concealing a crime.[4]

The situation persists. Harvard University's Executive Session on Policing and Public Safety found, for example, that "it remains surprisingly difficult to get residents of poor minority neighborhoods to engage constructively with police due to a history of strained relationships, continued skepticism of the sincerity of the police, and fear of reprisals from local criminals when cooperating with police."[5] For immigrants, stricter immigration laws pose another reason not to interact with police.

Without cooperation from the Italian community, American police were "powerless," wrote the journalist Luigi Barzini, Sr. "For this, Petrosino was more furious with the victims than the criminals. He called them 'sheep.' He launched fierce invectives at them. He felt abandoned, left alone in an enormous struggle."[6]

* * *

The Italian Squad has entered law enforcement history as ancestor to some problematic undercover units. When he was sued in 1971 over the NYPD Special Services Division's spying on African American, anti-war, and leftist organizations, Police Commissioner Patrick V. Murphy traced his controversial intelligence unit back to the Italian Squad and its investigation of the "Black Hand Society."[7]

It's not an apt comparison; police and the FBI were trying to undermine political dissent that the Constitution protects; the Italian Squad targeted obviously illegal activity such as extortion. Tunney's Bomb Squad was the true ancestor to the 1960s undercover ops. Amedeo Polignani cleared the way for Gene Roberts, the Black rookie cop who posed as Malcolm X's bodyguard.[8]

Petrosino's Italian Squad did parent the many rackets squads that followed, starting with the Italian or Black Hand squads in other major cities. Petrosino and the Italian Squad commanders who followed him were often in touch with like units, whether formally established or not, in Chicago; Buffalo; Pittsburgh and Pittston, Pennsylvania; New Orleans; Detroit; Boston; and Akron, Ohio. Eventually, organized-crime units were at work all over the country. They inevitably focused on Italian American suspects, as did news coverage of organized crime.[9]

My experience as a reporter leaves me with mixed feelings about this. As a cub reporter at the *Hudson Dispatch* covering Union City, New Jersey, in the late 1970s, I had to catch up quickly on the Mafia because the Genovese crime family was such a hidden power there. Certainly, I could not have covered the corrupt Teamsters Union local there without that knowledge. The same applied to the city government; the mayor, school board president, and housing authority director were convicted in a scheme to take more than a half million dollars in payoffs from a construction company that a Genovese mobster secretly controlled. The payoffs were skimmed from the public school system. The power of the Mafia was real, and needed to be taken down.

In retrospect I realize that reporters, including this one, and law-enforcement experts acted as if only Italians engaged in organized crime. This was captured in 1970 when the Manhattan district attorney's office investigated bookmaker Hugh Mulligan, a son of Irish immigrants suspected of masterminding a long-standing network of dishonest cops. When a *Times* reporter asked how such a big figure in the city's underworld could be so little known, a source in the DA's office explained, "We never really heard about him. When we went after organized crime, we only went after Italians."[10]

The President's Commission on Law Enforcement and Administration of Justice took a similar view in 1967. "Today the core of organized crime in the United States consists of 24 groups operating as criminal cartels in large cities across the Nation," it asserted. "Their membership is exclusively Italian."[11] The commission called for the creation of organized-crime intelligence units in attorneys general offices and big-city police departments, and urged metropolitan-area newspapers to create an organized crime beat. The panel also opened the way for the Racketeer Influenced and Corrupt Organizations Act, passed in 1970—a tool that would have greatly helped Italian Squad detectives to break up the Lupo-Morello combine before it evolved into the "first family" of the American Mafia.[12]

RICO is a powerful and controversial law; though passed in reaction to the crimes of Italian American gangsters, it applies to everyone, of course. As a reporter, I witnessed great successes and serious civil liberties infringements as a result of the statute. Take the famous heroin-trafficking case dubbed "Pizza Connection." The US attorney who brought the case in 1983, Rudolph Giuliani, minted that term at the urging of a creative *Daily News* reporter—the press again playing a role in framing how the public perceived crimes committed by Italians, as the newspapers did in creating the "Society of the Black Hand" eighty years earlier.[13] Twenty-two defendants were tried in a massive racketeering-conspiracy case that lasted seventeen months from 1985 to 1987. It was one of the signal victories of the Justice Department campaign against the mob, but Giuliani's publicity-seeking "mega trial" tactics in this and other cases led to some backlash from judges against expansive use of RICO.

In announcing the complaint, Giuliani labeled a minor defendant, rural Illinois pizza man Joe Trupiano, one of the "chief lieutenants." As it turned out, he was such a minor figure that only twenty minutes of the long trial concerned him. He was convicted, only to have a three-judge federal appeals court panel unanimously overturn his verdict for lack of evidence. He'd already served his time, nine and a half months. To RICO opponents, he was a victim of guilt by association, framed for something he did not do.[14]

The RICO law—applied to members of Congress, bankers, stock brokers, even people who cheat on college admissions—is among many advances in prosecutorial power created at the expense of mafiosi. For example, in 1987 the Supreme Court set aside concerns about due process to allow Giuliani to hold Genovese crime family figure Anthony Salerno without bail on grounds that he was a danger to the community following his indictment on rackets charges.[15]

This all follows from the legacy of the Italian Squad: organized-crime intelligence units; the need for tougher laws; the ensuing decimation of the once-powerful American Mafia; the accompanying civil liberties questions. The Italian Squad also has found a place in the history of police violence, mainly due to Fiaschetti's pronouncements about his "treat 'em rough" tactics. As the Wickersham Commission made clear, Fiaschetti was not alone in this. The commission cited a letter that Robert H. Elder, the former Brooklyn prosecutor, published in 1929 charging that "the third degree has now become established and recognized practice in the police department of the city of New York. Every police station in the city is equipped with the instruments to administer the torture incident to that process."[16]

The newspapers often accepted police violence when employed against Italian suspects. For example, a 1908 *Eagle* article praises the Brooklyn Italian Squad's use of the "third degree" for Italian suspects: "The horrors of the Inquisition might have been bad but when Vachris and his men get at a fellow who dodges the truth when they know that he is perverting it, there is something doing. Vachris deals with most of the liars single-handed, and he manages them with wondrous vigor and effect."[17]

Through connections with the Italian immigrant community, Vachris and other veteran detectives on the squad knew a great deal more than they could prove in court. Often enough, people in the Italian community felt able to confide in them, even if they were unwilling to testify in public. This may explain, although certainly not excuse, their use of harassment and violence against men they firmly believed to be a danger to the community.

The Italian Squad cops were outsiders within their own department. The same obstacles that Italians encountered in dealing with the Irish in church, waterfront and construction work, and unions applied in the police workplace as well. That's not to compare it with the racism that New York's first Black police officer, Samuel Battle, faced after joining the force in 1911. The Italian detectives' lot improved from the days when bosses routinely called Petrosino "the Dago," but except for the years when Theodore Bingham was commissioner, they did not get the promotions they deserved. Throughout this book, there are accounts of acclaimed officers who had difficulty in getting on the force, in being promoted, or in keeping the positions they'd won. It's difficult to say whether discrimination was at work in individual cases, but in the big picture, there is strong evidence of bias. It shows, for example, in how few experienced Italian detectives were able to advance to first-grade status.

One reason is that they lacked political sponsors. The Democrats in Tammany Hall were no friends of the Italian Squad, a wild card in a deck that was otherwise marked in Tammany's favor. The Italian detective commanders' political leanings tended toward the Teddy Roosevelt Republican-Progressive movement; that's where the sympathies of Vachris, Fiaschetti, and Petrosino went. Corrao was at home with his brother's Brooklyn Democrats.

Tammany was seen as an obstacle because of its ties with the gangs that provided "repeater" voters and political muscle when needed. Looking back on the days when he worked closely with his friend Petrosino, Detective Ralph Micelli wrote in 1915:

> I will not dwell on the early struggles of the Italian squad. It is history now and belongs to an era when conditions at police headquarters were not as pleasant as they are today. Then the ward leader and politician with pull could always gain the commissioner's ear and many wires were pulled so taut that they made the life of the policemen dangling from them almost unbearable.[18]

The Republican Bingham was a staunch supporter of the Italian Squad, but his inflammatory declarations about immigrant criminals in New York were fodder for eugenicists and nativists such as the influential sociologist Edward A. Ross. He noted that Bingham referred to New York's southern Italian criminals as including "as many ferocious and desperate men as ever gathered in a modern city in time of peace— medieval criminals who must be dealt with under modern law." To Ross, this meant Italians should be treated as s second-class people who "lack the power to take rational care of themselves."[19] Ross published this claptrap in the same year he became president of the American Sociological Society; the following year, he helped found the American Association of University Professors. Such views are anathema in academia now, but Ross's notion of "race suicide" has outlived him.

So, too, has the belief that immigrants are crime-prone; it's the most common complaint about the social problems that immigration alleg- edly causes.[20] It's true that poor screening in both Italy and the United States allowed some Italian criminals to escape the harsh justice of their homeland for the streets of New York. In their missions to Italy, Vachris and Petrosino had worked out a solution—but there wasn't a political will to see it through. Had appropriate laws and practices been estab- lished, perhaps the chokehold quotas of the 1924 immigration law would not have seemed to be the solution. American society faces similar ques- tions today: the achievements and contributions of generations of Italian American citizens, a people so maligned a century ago, should well be considered in debates about limiting immigration, and about "replace- ment," "crimmigration," border walls, and the like.

As we've seen throughout this account, the Italian Squad detectives could be only as effective as the local politics allowed. The failure to make use of the criminal records that Anthony Vachris obtained in Italy was especially egregious. Several hundred Italians who'd arrived in New York with serious criminal records, in violation of US immigration law, could have been deported. On top of that, Police Commissioner Baker ignored the connection that Vachris had arranged with Italian police, even after State Department officials reminded him of how important it could be. Likewise, the spiteful decision Commissioner Waldo made to destroy Vachris's career was a deep setback for good policing; Va- chris was an effective commanding officer whose work was admired by judges, prosecutors, and the Italian community. But he wasn't shy about speaking out. The trouble with New York detectives, Vachris once said, was that "they are not well managed. There is no management at all. Or those that could manage them are interfered with and they are not al- lowed to use their own judgment."[21]

Hyped-up news coverage played a pivotal role in the Italian Squad's story by setting an agenda that politicians and police brass had to respond to. Stories and lurid graphics about the supposed Black Hand "society" created the political need to form the squad in 1904. And there was in fact a law-enforcement need for some kind of unit that would investigate crimes in Italian immigrant neighborhoods; the larger Police Department didn't show the ability or even inclination to do so. When the squad was abolished in 1911, it was also for political reasons—it had lost the one-time support it had from some of the most influential political and business leaders in the Italian community. But the law-enforcement need for it persisted, and so the unit survived in a shadow existence until the Italian Squad was officially reinstated in 1919. There were more police officers of Italian origin on the force by then, but a special unit was still needed for in-depth investigation of organized criminal gangs. Under Fiaschetti's leadership, the Italian Squad was positioned to do that. But political priorities dictated that much of the detectives' energy be directed elsewhere—to low-level Prohibition enforcement and intrusive surveillance of political radicals. That, in turn, led the department to merge what was by then a famed unit into the Bomb Squad, where its mission (and commander) were subordinated to the more politically pressing work of harassing anarchists and communists. In the meantime, organized crime boomed.

The Italian Squad was a pioneer in the long law-enforcement effort to uproot organized and transnational crime. It demonstrated the necessity for some kind of specialized investigative team; the decision to end the Italian Squad in 1922 contributed to the collapse of New York police efforts to investigate the city's criminal underworld—just at the point when gangs of various ethnic combinations began prospering in the illicit liquor trade. By the 1930s an American Mafia had cohered. As a result, the smearing taint of organized crime tarnished the reputation of Italian Americans even after they gained acceptance in American society in the years after World War II. High-profile investigations by the US Senate's Kefauver and McClellan committees during the 1950s defined organized crime in ethnic terms: Italian.[22]

In the big picture, the Italian Squad detectives fought forces beyond their control. Their mission was summed up in the telegram consul William Henry Bishop sent to announce Petrosino's murder: "Dies martyr . . . protecting peaceful Italian[s] in America." This was the cause that Vachris, Corrao, and Fiaschetti all took up in ways that often went beyond the call of duty. But when they nabbed the arsonists, bombers, and kidnappers who plagued their immigrant community, their successes put Italian American criminals on the front page. Having an "Italian" squad heightened the crimes' identification with an ethnic group. The Italian detectives protected many an Italian immigrant, but despite their courageous example, they could not protect the reputation of their people against the eugenicist claim they they were inherently un-American. When the Immigration Act of 1924 passed, it cut Italian migration down to under six thousand people a year, dividing families in the process. "It was best for America that our incoming immigrants should hereafter be of the same races as those of us who are already here," the measure's Senate sponsor, David Reed, explained.[23]

There were victories along the way, but their greatest quest—to solve Petrosino's murder—eluded the detectives. Petrosino remained with the squad in spirit—and as a reminder of the hazards the detectives faced. No, the Italian Squad detectives weren't able to change the way the larger society viewed Italian immigrants. They weren't able to stop the development of what became the American Mafia. Where the Italian Squad detectives succeeded, though, was in the work they did with individual crime victims. Frustrated as the detectives were by the often meager cooperation they received, they still served as a bridge for an alienated immigrant community. They helped people who were in the grip of traumatic events: Maddalena Finizio, the bride who was raped and whose husband was murdered shortly after they arrived in America, and who put her life back together; Joseph Longo, Michael Scimeca, and other kidnapped children; Ciro Pecoraro, the father targeted for a bomb because he refused to let his daughter marry a gangster; Francesco Spinella, the immigrant businessman from East Eleventh Street, and the many like him—grocers, milk dealers, bankers, landlords, a great operatic tenor—who faced dire threats because their hard work had produced some material success. Petrosino, Vachris, Corrao, Fiaschetti, and the detectives who worked with them were willing to take great risks for them and many others like them. That is what made their work valuable and memorable.

Epilogue

THE men believed responsible for the unsolved plot to murder Joseph Petrosino met bitter ends. Giuseppe Morello spent the last decade of his life helping Joseph Masseria become the most powerful figure in New York's Italian underworld. Masseria's greed prompted the much-romanticized Castellammarese War in 1930; Morello was one of the casualties. The 1960s FBI informant Joseph Valachi said a hitman he knew only by nickname told him how Morello died in his East Harlem office on August 15, 1930: "Buster told me that this Morello was tough. He said he kept running around the office, and Buster had to give him a couple of more shots before he went down."[1] Masseria's luck ran out on the afternoon of April 15, 1931, when he was shot in the back and head while playing pinochle in the Nuova Villa Tammara restaurant in Coney Island.[2] Two hoodlums close to Masseria, Luciano and Vito Genovese, had betrayed him. They went on to become Mafia bosses.

Ignazio Lupo likewise returned to crime after his counterfeiting sentence was commuted in 1921; he was returned to prison in 1936. He was released ten years later, broken and broke, and died January 13, 1947.[3] Vito Cascio Ferro, Petrosino's "dreaded criminal," became arguably Sicily's most powerful Mafia figure until he was arrested in 1926; he died in prison in 1943.

Some say that Cascio Ferro admitted he himself murdered Petrosino with a single shot. As author Luigi Barzini, Jr., put it, Cascio Ferro, who "brought the organization to its highest perfection without undo recourse to violence," shot the lawman "not for money, but for the honor, prestige and preservation of the società. The man had challenged the Mafia as a whole and had to be killed personally by Don Vito and nobody else." There is reason to doubt that this claim was anything more than a boastful attempt by an over-the-hill don to romanticize his life of crime; Cascio Ferro's role was more likely to coordinate the New York–Sicilian connection behind the murder.[4]

William J. Flynn, nemesis of the Lupo-Morello gang, became head of the Secret Service. While in that post, he began writing syndicated Sunday feature stories that celebrated his successes. Flynn knew hype. In one article, he wrote about "the worldwide power of the Black Hand," extending the reach of small-time hoodlums around the globe.[5] Similarly, when the Secret Service began investigating espionage, he asserted in a newspaper interview that Germany had 250,000 spies inside the United States. His bloviating alienated German and Irish Americans, and in November 1917, he resigned his post. After the bombing of Attorney General A. Mitchell Palmer's home, he was called in to head the federal Bureau of Investigation, the early FBI, in 1919. Flynn led the "Palmer raids," another public relations mess, and resigned in 1921. He went into writing crime fiction, and made his mark as editor of *Flynn's Weekly*. He died at age sixty in 1928.[6]

Michael Fiaschetti opened Fiaschetti International Detective Agency, 401 Broadway. He was also quite busy inflating his reputation, with writer Prosper Buranelli's help. Fiaschetti, who loved the action, was trying to find out how Judge Joseph Force Crater disappeared—he told the *Daily News* that Crater was still "alive and well"—when Mayor Fiorello La Guardia hired him in 1934 as third deputy commissioner of markets. His job was to get the racketeers out of the produce markets. He returned to his detective agency in 1938.[7]

After his wife Jennie died in 1905, Fiaschetti did not remarry until April 2, 1943, when he was wed in Brooklyn to Jean Melillo. He died July 29, 1960, at the Veterans Administration Hospital in Brooklyn.

Many of the Italian Squad detectives remained to serve out successful, productive careers in the Police Department. Charles S. Corrao was promoted to lieutenant. When a testimonial dinner was held for him in 1922, hundreds of people, including the future mayor La Guardia, gathered in his honor. Joseph Longo, the kidnapped boy he'd rescued eleven years earlier, wrote a letter thanking him. Corrao's brother Frank died in 1927, never realizing his ambition for a judgeship or elected office. Charles Corrao served the last of his thirty-nine years in the department as a lieutenant in the Bay Ridge, Brooklyn, precinct at Fifth Avenue and Eighty-Sixth Street, working not far from the home he shared with his wife, Nellie. He died while still on the force, on October 8, 1934, a victim of blood poisoning following appendix surgery. Headlines summed up: he was "Corrao, Police Hero."[8]

Of the original Italian Squad detectives, Ralph Micelli, an expert marksman, was noted for his innovations in pistol instruction. He became a handwriting expert as well, and retired as a deputy inspector in 1939 after forty years in the NYPD. He died in 1944 at the age of sixty-six.[9] Peter Dondero also served for forty years, retiring as a lieutenant working from the Bay Ridge police station. He died at the age of seventy-two in 1949.[10] Rocco Cavone compiled such a record of "Black Hand" arrests that when Enright demoted him to lower-paid patrol duty in 1923 in one of his purges of the Detective Bureau, newspapers likened it to an earthquake at police headquarters. The one-time Petrosino protege was still on the job when he died of a heart attack at the age of fifty in 1932.[11] Michael Mealli started a detective agency that provided security on the docks; he died in 1939 at the age of sixty-three. His brother Andrew, who became a police lieutenant, died a year earlier.[12] Joseph DiGilio retired in 1924 after thirty years of service; he died at home in Astoria in 1935 at the age of seventy.[13] Governor Al Smith pardoned Paul Simonetti for his perjury conviction in 1926; he died eight years later at the age of sixty-six.[14]

John Archiopoli, another original Italian Squad member, was renowned for his linguistic ability; it was said he could speak fourteen languages. The "cop diplomat" was remembered for using that talent to work out a truce in a Chinatown tong war. He died as a captain in 1929, his twenty-fifth year in the department. In 1924, Archiopoli was at the hospital bedside of his brother-in-law, Bernardino Grottano, a former Italian Squad detective who died after being shot in the chest during a gunfight with robbers on Brooklyn's Fulton Street shopping district. He was forty-two.[15]

Even after he retired from the department, Anthony Vachris continued to have a rocky relationship with the police hierarchy. He started a waterfront security agency; his guards, who carried guns, were known by their yellow cloaks and shields emblazoned with Vachris's name. The company ran into trouble when Vachris lost a contract to guard the Italian Line piers at West Fifty-Seventh Street after the Police Department refused his repeated requests to cooperate with his guards. Testifying before the Meyer Committee state legislative probe of the NYPD in 1921, Vachris said his problem was that he "didn't have the pull."

The reason was that a police inspector, Dominick Henry, was in the process of steering the steamship company to another security firm that a retired inspector owned. The Italian Line's general manager testified that gratuities totalling $1,000 were paid to Inspector Henry.

Vachris suffered many personal losses. His wife, Rafaella, whom he'd written about with so much feeling during his mission to Italy, died in 1915. They had three children, Charles, Jennie, and Lena. The following year, he married twenty-six-year-old Laura Carasole; he was fifty-six.[16] They had one child, Robert Elder Vachris, named for the former Brooklyn prosecutor Vachris had worked with; they lived along with Vachris's mother, Maria, in the Brooklyn neighborhood now called Dyker Heights at 1459 Seventy-Third Street (an area where many of the Italian Squad detectives settled). This was where Laura Vachris died of pneumonia in 1920 at the age of twenty-nine. Later the same year, Vachris married Angela DeMartini; they moved to River Edge, New Jersey, in suburban Bergen County in 1922.

Vachris created the borough's police department and served as its first chief. He was occasionally involved in controversy, as when he made a traffic stop to search a well-known and politically influential minister. Then there was the flap over his chickens—"'War' Resumed over Chickens," the local paper declared after neighbors' complaints that his chicken coops were reducing property values. "These chickens are a little hobby of mine and I don't see why I can't have a hobby," Vachris responded.[17] Indeed, after so many years of death threats, high-pressure cases, and big-city police politics, it was hard to argue that he didn't deserve a chance to live the suburban American Dream, his way. He died on January 6, 1944, at Hackensack Hospital at the age of seventy-seven. Obituaries noted he was survived by his four children, eight grandchildren, and eight great-grandchildren, as well as his wife, Lydia—he had married again, apparently to Angela's sister. Tony Vachris was not one to give up easily.

* * *

The struggle of the Italian Squad detectives to explain their ethnic community to the police and the police to their ethnic community never really ended. Police officers Black, Latino, Asian, Arab, and from many other ethnic or religious backgrounds continue on. If anything, the pressure is greater than ever to improve the relationship between police and minority communities.

Jason Rivera understood that, and wanted to make a difference. He was one of two police officers fatally shot on January 21, 2022, when they responded to a domestic call. Rivera, the twenty-two-year-old son of immigrants from the Dominican Republic, grew up in a predominantly Dominican neighborhood. He touched on that in a letter to the commander of the Police Academy entitled "Why I Became a Police Officer":

Growing up in Inwood, Manhattan, the community's relationship between the police and the community was not great. I remember one day when I witnessed my brother being stopped and frisked. I asked myself, why are we being pulled over if we are in a taxi? I was too young to know that during that time, the NYPD was pulling over and frisking people at a high rate. My perspective on police and the way they police really bothered me. As time went on, I saw the NYPD pushing hard on changing the relationship between the police and the community. This was when I realized that I wanted to be a part of the men in blue; [to] better the relationship between the community and police.[18]

ACKNOWLEDGMENTS

THIS book grew from a previous work I did with New York University Press, a history of the bumpy relations between New York's Irish and Italians. So it's a further exploration of the world my Italian-born grandparents and their six surviving children lived in at various locations on Mott and Prince Streets in lower Manhattan. It was eye-opening to learn more about the violence that surrounded them. In their honor, the book is written in memory of one of the six children, the late Leonard T. Muscato, who intrigued me with bits and pieces of information about his work as an investigator on Manhattan district attorney Frank Hogan's Rackets Squad.

This book is dedicated to four people who entered this world—and brightened mine—during the years I was at work on it: Pete Moses, Charlie Bowser, Minna Moses, and Owen Bowser. God bless 'em.

As always, I'm very grateful to the literary agent Steve Hanselman and to Julia Serebrinsky, who made this book possible, as they did the two previous books we did together. Working with New York University Press now for the second time has again been a great experience. The NYU team is very impressive. Special thanks go to Clara Platter, the senior editor for History and Law, who is so open to new ideas, supportive to writers, and enthusiastic. I've been very pleased to work with her, Veronica Knutson, and Dan Geist.

Since some of the research was done amid COVID-related shutdowns, online archives and above-and-beyond help from archivists for records otherwise unavailable were essential. Many thanks to the New York Public Library's Research Division, the New York City Municipal Archive, the New-York Historical Society, the Brooklyn College Library, the Lloyd Sealy Library at John Jay College, the Archives at Yale, the

National Archives and Records Administration, the Herbert Hoover Presidential Library, the Archivio di Stato di Palermo, and the Archivio di Stato di Napoli.

There are more historical documents accessible online than ever before. Special thanks go to the City Record Project, an amazing resource created by the NYU Tandon School of Engineering under direction of Professor Jonathan Soffer. It digitized the *City Record* newspaper's daily, fine-print chronicle of the city government's minutiae. Other important sources of information were Newspapers.com, Ancestry.com, the Library of Congress's *Chronicling America*, New York State Historic Newspapers, FultonHistory.com, HathiTrust Digital Library, Unz.org, the Internet Archive, Google Books, and the Center for Research Libraries.

Richard Esposito kindly shared difficult-to-find Police Department documents that he gathered for his book on the NYPD's Bomb Squad. Painstaking research by authors David Critchley, Mike Dash, Thomas Hunt, and Salvatore Lupo provided a foundation for my own work, which explores some of the same organized-crime history, but from the perspective of the Italian immigrant detectives.

Thank you to outside reviewers for NYU Press; they contributed a great deal through their suggestions. Many thanks to Tom Robbins, Scott Johnson, Marina Cacioppo, Heather Barr, Valerie Carelli, Jeanne-Marie Byington, Jane Cramer, Mark Price, Amy Reytar, Craig Wright, Michael Frost, James Moses, and Anthony Mancini.

I've been very fortunate to have access to records that were passed down through the family of Lieutenant Anthony Vachris, whose story plays such a large role in the saga of the Italian Squad. I'm indebted to Alfred Vachris, Robert Vachris, and Ann Witherow. Thank you!

Similarly, I am grateful to Joseph Petrosino's granddaughter Susan Burke for preserving his personal papers and to documentary filmmaker Anthony Giacchino for curating them and sharing the files with me.

Dr. Francesco Landolfi, an Italian scholar who is expert on transnational crime, helped me time and again as I sought out records in Italy and tried to understand the politics and justice system in the early twentieth century. I also learned much from watching him develop his doctoral thesis and book on New York's Italians and Prohibition. Grazie mille!

I am so grateful to my family for such steady support and love, and occasional expertise. My son, Matthew Moses, is a writer with a great sense for the arc of a story. It was good to talk it through with him. His wife, Lisa Loen, a costume designer, provided guidance on some of the period clothing. My son-in-law, Geoffrey Bowser, is an attorney who coached me on some of the legal fine points. And my daughter, Caitlin Bowser, always made me smile. My mother, Anne Moses, was the youngest of her siblings and is now the family raconteur. Her stories helped make the past come alive for me. Most of all, thanks to my wife, Maureen. It sounds cliché, but it's absolutely true: I never could have done this without her.

NOTES

Abbreviations

Curran—*Stenographers Minutes. Special Committee of the Board of Aldermen of the City of New York, Appointed to Investigate the City's Police Department. Pursuant to resolution dated Aug. 5, 1912.*
NARA—National Archives and Records Administration
NYMA—New York City Municipal Archive
RG—Record Group

Newspapers

ABJ—Akron (Ohio) Beacon Journal
BSU—Brooklyn Standard Union
BT—Brooklyn Times
BTU—Brooklyn Times Union
Citizen—Brooklyn Citizen
CR—City Record
Eagle—Brooklyn Daily Eagle
Herald—New York Herald
NYT—New York Times
Post—New York Evening Post
Sun—New York Evening Sun
Telegram—New York Evening Telegram
Tribune—New York Tribune

Chapter 1. "Dies Martyr"

1   William Bishop to Robert Bacon, Assistant Secretary of State, March 20, 1909, Numerical and Minor Files of the Department of State, 1906–1910, NARA, RG 59, M862, Roll 845, Frame 701; *La Giustizia* (Milan), March 15, 1909, 1; *Corriere della Sera* (Milan), March 14, 1909, 3; *La Stampa* (Turin), March 14, 1909, 3; "Omicidio di Giuseppe Petrosino," March 16, March 24, April 2, 1909, Archivio di Stato di Palermo, Questura, Archivio Generale, box 1584, folder 352; Mike Dash, *The First Family: Terror, Extortion, Revenge, Murder and the Birth of the American Mafia* (New York: Random House, 2009), 189; William Henry Bishop Papers (MS 83), Series III, Diaries, Box 19, Folder 89, Manuscripts and Archives, Yale University Library. See entries for March 13–14, 1909.
2   *Herald*, March 13, 1909, 1; *Telegram*, March 13, 1909, 1.

3 Bingham to Secretary of State, March 13, 1909. NARA, RG 59, M862, Roll 845, Frame 593; Lloyd Griscom to Secretary of State, March 13, 1909; W. L. Baker to Secretary of State, March 13, 1909, Frame 595.

4 *Tribune*, March 14, 1909, 3.

5 Anthony Vachris to Charles F. Vachris, May [?] 1942, Vachris archive; US naturalization record for Anthony Vachris, New York, NY, October 5, 1887.

6 *Telegram*, March 13, 1909, 1; *Tribune*, March 14, 1909; *NYT*, March 14, 1909; *Eagle*, March 8, 1908, 24.

7 *BSU*, January 28, 1904; *Herald*, August 16, 1904, 1.

8 Paul Moses, *An Unlikely Union: The Love-Hate Story of New York's Irish and Italians* (New York: New York University Press, 2015), 140.

9 Michael Fiaschetti, *You Gotta Be Rough: The Adventures of Detective Fiaschetti of the Italian Squad* (New York: Doubleday, 1930), 19, 81.

10 *BSU*, March 14, 1909, 1; Bingham to Secretary of State, March 13, 1909, NARA, RG 59, M862, Roll 845, Frame 603.

Chapter 2. "On the Dead Quiet"

1 *NYT*, August 25, 1904, 6; Moses, *Unlikely Union*, 131.

2 *Il Progresso*, December 27, 1906, 1.

3 Moses, *Unlikely Union*, 121.

4 Gino C. Speranza, "How It Feels to Be a Problem," *Survey*, May 7, 1904, 457. The Du Bois essay appeared in the *Atlantic*, www.theatlantic.com, accessed January 13, 2022. For an overview of Du Bois's writings on Italian immigrants, see David R. Roedinger, "Du Bois, Race and Italian Americans," in *Are Italians White? How Race Is Made in America*, edited by Jennifer Guglielmo and Salvatore Salerno (New York: Routledge, 2003), 259–63.

5 *Report of the Department of Commerce and Labor, Government Printing Office* (Washington, DC, 1907), 138.

6 *Corriere della Sera*, March 15, 1909, 3.

7 Griscom to State Department, March 13, 1909, NARA, RG 59, M862, Roll 845, Frame 595.

8 *Herald*, September 13, 1903, 3; *Tribune*, September 14, 1903, 12; *World*, September 18, 1903, 5; 1920 US Census for Nicolo Cappielo, Brooklyn, NY; *NYT*, January 6, 1908.

9 Robert M. Lombardo, "The Hegemonic Narrative and the Social Construction of Deviance: The Case of the Black Hand," *Trends in Organized Crime* (2010), 270–73.

10 Arthur H. Warner, "Amputating the Black Hand," *Survey*, April 3, 1909, 166; *World*, August 8, 1904, 5; *Tribune*, August 14, 1904, 4.

11 James Lardner and Thomas Reppetto, *NYPD: A City and Its Police* (New York: Henry Holt and Company, 2000), 144; Critchley, *Origin*, 40–41.

12 *CR*, September 21, 1904, 6242; *CR*, January 30, 1904, Supplement; 1910 US Census for Rocco Cavone, Brooklyn, NY; *Herald*, August 9, 1914, 4; Stephan Talty, *The Black Hand: The Epic War between a Brilliant Detective and the Deadliest Secret Society in American History* (Boston: Houghton Mifflin, 2017), 63. Bonnoil was later promoted to lieutenant.

13 *NYT*, August 28, 1904, 44.

14 George B. McClellan, Jr., *The Gentleman and the Tiger: The Autobiography of George B. McClellan, Jr.* (Philadelphia: J.B. Lippincott, 1956), 211.

15 *NYT*, December 14, 1906, 10; *NYT*, March 17, 1891, 4.

16 *NYT*, December 20, 1906, 12; *NYT*, December 21, 1906, 8; *Annual Report of the Police Commissioner of the City of New York for the Year Ending December 31, 1907* (New York: M. B. Brown, 1908), 24; *CR*, January 31, 1908, 1309.

17 *NYT*, February 21, 1907, 18.

18 McClellan, *Gentleman*, 296; *Sun*, February 27, 1907, 5; *Tribune*, February 27, 1907, 4.

19 McClellan, *Gentleman*, 264–65.

20 *Eagle*, December 23, 1906, 12.

21 Theodore A. Bingham, "Foreign Criminals in New York," *North American Review*, September 1908, 385; *Sun*, March 31, 1908, 2; *Eagle*, March 3, 1908, 1; *BSU*, March 1, 1909, 1.

22 *NYT*, January 6, 1906.

23 *NYT*, February 22, 1909, 8.

24 *Tribune*, February 2, 1909, 5; *Sun*, February 20, 1909; *Herald*, February 20, 1909, 6; *Telegram*, February 19, 1909, 1; *Il Progresso*, February 21, 1909, 2.

25 *NYT*, March 21, 1909, SM1.

26 Arthur H. Woods to Robert Bacon, January 15, 1909, NARA, RG 59, M862, Roll 845, Frame 489.

Chapter 3. "The Same Fate as Petrosino"

1 *Tribune*, March 15, 1909, 1; *Post*, March 13, 1909, 1; *World*, March 13, 1909, 2; *Eagle*, March 15, 1909, 1.

2 *Sing Sing Prison Admission Register, 1865–1939* (hereafter Sing Sing Admission Register) for Joseph DePriemo, March 17, 1903, New York State Archives; William J. Flynn, *The Barrel Mystery* (New York: James A. McCann Company, 1919), 18–22; *Sun*, October 24, 1905, 5; *NYT*, October 24, 1905, 5; *Sun*, July 29, 1909, 4; *BSU*, February 24, 1908, 1; Pernetti v. People, 99 App. Div 391 (New York Appellate Division, 1904).

3 *NYT*, December 3, 1908, 11; *NYT*, March 17, 1909, 1.

4 *World*, March 16, 1909, 2; *World*, December 28, 1908, 1; *NYT*, March 17, 1909, 1.

5 *Eagle*, March 15, 1909, 1.

6 Bingham to Secretary of State, March 16, 1909, NARA, RG 59, M862, Roll 845, Frame 637; *Il Progresso*, March 18, 1909, 1.

Chapter 4. "We Are on the Ground and He Is Not"

1 1910 US Census for Charles A. Peabody, New York, NY; *NYT*, May 13, 1942, 19;
   Sun, January 16, 1908, 2; *Sun*, November 13, 1908, 7.
2 Arthur A. Carey, *Memoirs of a Murder Man* (Garden City, NY: Doubleday, 1930),
   126.
3 *World*, March 22, 1909, 1.
4 Anthony F. Vachris, *Journal from Italy Trip*, March 16, 17, 20, 22, 23, 24, 25, 26, 27,
   1909. The events Vachris describes in the journal track closely to the information
   in State Department files.
5 Lloyd C. Griscom, *Diplomatically Speaking* (New York: Literary Guild of America,
   1940), 15, 278, 341, 328; Vachris, *Journal*, March 27, 1909.
6 *NYT*, June 27, 1942, 13.
7 Arrigo Petacco, *Joe Petrosino*, trans. Charles Lam Markmann (New York:
   Macmillan, 1974), 130.
8 Philander Knox to Lloyd C. Griscom, March 15, 1909, NARA, RG 59, M862, Roll
   845, Frame 611.
9 Wilson to Bingham, April 2, 1901, NARA, RG 59, M862, Roll 845, Frame 693.
10 Vachris, *Journal*, April 11, 1909.
11 Bingham to Knox, May 1, 1909, NARA, RG 59, M862, Roll 845, Frame 837.
12 Vachris, *Journal*, May 2, 1909.
13 *Boston Globe*, January 1, 1909, 5; *Boston Globe*, March 20, 1909, 10; Telegrams,
   Griscom to Secretary of State, March 18, 1909, NARA, RG 59, M862, Roll 845,
   Frame 661; March 21, 1909, Frame 561.
14 Bishop Papers (MS 83), Series III, Diaries, Box 19, Folder 90, entry for May 13,
   1909; Arthur Woods, "The Problem of the Black Hand," *McClure's*, May 1909, 44.
15 Leonardi to Griscom, May 22, 1909; NARA, RG 59, M862, Roll 845, Frame 961;
   Bingham to Secretary of State, May 10, 1909, Frame 875.
16 *Eagle*, February 21, 1909; *Eagle*, May 15, 1909, 2; *Eagle*, May 16, 1909, 7; Vachris,
   Journal, May 2, 1909.
17 Griscom to Knox, June 3, 1909, NARA, RG 59, M862, Roll 845, Frame 956.
18 Curran, 3814; *Eagle*, August 20, 1909, 12.
19 *Newark Star*, August 18, 1909, 2; *NYT*, August 20, 1909, 4; *Telegram*, August 19,
   1909, 3; *Tribune*, August 20, 1909, 12; *Sun*, August 20, 1909, 3.
20 Curran, 3814.
21 Garrett to Knox, August 13, 1909, NARA, RG 59, M862, Roll 845, Frame 1087.
22 *Eagle*, August 20, 1909, 12; Curran, 3816.

Chapter 5. "He Got Me Some Clerical Work"

1 Curran, 3815.
2 McClellan, *Gentleman*, 59.
3 *NYT*, November 4, 1903, 8; *NYT*, December 25, 1903, 6; *Tribune*, December 24,
   1903, 1.

4   McClellan, *Gentleman*, 185, 232, 285; *Buffalo Commercial*, January 9, 1904, 6; *Buffalo Courier*, December 22, 1894, 2; *World*, May 3, 1895, 1; *NYT*, April 5, 1905, 18.

5   George B. McClellan, Jr., *Autobiography*, unpublished manuscript, (193-), 503, Mss. collection, New-York Historical Society.

6   William J. Gaynor, "Lawlessness of the Police in New York," *North American Review*, January 1903, 25; Mike Wallace, *Greater Gotham: A History of New York City from 1898 to 1919* (New York: Oxford University Press, 2017), 620.

7   Bertillon System, New York State Division of Criminal Justice Services, www.criminaljustice.ny.gov, accessed July 21, 2021.

8   Bingham v. Gaynor, complaint, contained in Record on Appeal from Interlocutory Judgment Appellate Division of New York State Supreme Court, First Department, filed November 10, 1910.

9   *Citizen*, June 7, 1909, 1; Bingham, "Foreign Criminals," 385; McClellan, *Gentleman*, 296; Jenna Weissman Joselit, *Our Gang: Jewish Crime and the New York Jewish Community, 1900–1940* (Bloomington: Indiana University Press, 1983), 72–74.

10   *Eagle*, July 12, 1909, 1; *NYT*, July 13, 1909, 5; Daniel G. Slattery, "General Bingham as Head of the Police," *Boston Evening Transcript*, July 14, 1909, 16; Curran, 3944; *Annual Report of the Police Commissioner City of New York for the Year Ending December 31, 1908* (New York: M. B. Brown, 1909), 23.

11   *Eagle*, July 2, 3, 1909, 1; *Tribune*, July 3, 1909, 3; *American*, July 3, 7, 1909, 1; *Tribune*, July 13, 1909, 12. For records of transferred officers, see listings for Harry Bertini at *CR*, March 5, 1909, 2953; *CR*, May 6, 1909, 48; *CR*, July 30, 1910, 357; *CR*, December 6, 1911, 10133; John M. Dondero at *CR*, March 5, 1909, 2595; and Walter S. Lerocker at *CR*, March 26, 1909, 3506; *CR*, May 25, 1909, 2238; *CR*, July 2, 1909, 7762.

12   *BSU*, July 17, 1909, 4.

13   Salvatore Lupo, *The Two Mafias: A Transatlantic History, 1888–2008* (New York: Palgrave Macmillan, 2015), 21; "Omicidio di Giuseppe Petrosino," May 16, 1909, Archivio di Stato di Palermo, Questura, Archivio Generale, box 1584, folder 352.

14   *Tribune*, April 7, 1909, 3; *Eagle*, December 10, 1908, 2; Petacco, *Joe Petrosino*, 182; *La Sentinella* (Thomas, WV), August 19, 1911, 2.

15   Emanuel H. Lavine, *Secrets of the Metropolitan Police* (Garden City, NY: Garden City Publishing, 1937), 143.

Chapter 6. "Petrosino Is Dead, but the Black Hand Lives"

1   *Goshen (NY) Independent Republican*, May 28, 1909, 1; *Buffalo Enquirer*, January 21, 1909, 1; *Buffalo Courier*, 1; Passenger Lists of Vessels Arriving at New York, New York, 1820–1897; *Duca di Abruzzi*, January 19, 1909.

2   *Citizen*, June 23, 1909, 1.

3   *Johnstown (NY) Daily Republican*, November 13, 1909, 1; *Sun*, November 17, 1909, 5; 1930 US Census for Madeline Mancinelli, Clifton, NJ; People v. Barobuto, Court of Appeals of the State of New York, November 9, 1909, accessed September 6, 2021, at www.casemine.com. Union Hill is now part of Union City, NJ.

4 *NYT*, May 1, 1909, 6; *Tribune*, May 12, 1909, 5; *Citizen*, May 16, 1909, 6; New York State Archives, Albany, NY, Sing Sing Prison, 1852–1938, Box 18, Volume 46.

Chapter 7. "They Have Those Responsible for the Murder of Detective Petrosino"

1 Lupo, *Two Mafias*, 21–22.
2 Bingham to Bacon, February 1, 1909, NARA, RG 59, M862, Roll 968, Frame 940; Bacon to Bonaparte, February 4, 1909, Frame 944; Bingham to Secretary of State, December 17, 1908, M862, Roll 845, Frame 403.
3 Petrosino archive; Critchley, *Origin*, 42–44; *Hartford Courant*, July 28, 1909, 1; *Eagle*, July 28, 1909, 1; *Bridgeport (CT) Times and Evening Farmer*, December 11, 1909, 1.
4 *Sun*, June 5, 1909; *Tribune*, June 5, 1909; *Buffalo News*, Associated Press, June 5, 1909, 1.
5 Flynn, *Barrel Mystery*, 32; *Daily Reports of Agents, 1875–1937* (hereafter *Daily Reports*) William Flynn, February 9, 1910, *Records of the Secret Service*, NARA, RG 87, September 9, 1909, T915, Roll 116, 1st series, Frame 455; September 11, 1909, Frame 470; October 9, 25, 1909, Frames 769, 970, 988; Matt Birkbeck, *The Quiet Don* (New York: Berkeley Books, 2013), 42–52; *Pittston (PA) Gazette*, May 24, 1911, 1.
6 Dash, *First Family*, 209–10; Flynn, *Barrel Mystery*, 216; *NYT*, November 16, 1909, 1; *Sun*, November 16, 1909, 6.
7 *Sun*, November 13, 1909, 6; *NYT*, November 13, 1909, 1; Critchley, *Origin*, 33.
8 *Binghamton (NY) Press*, November 18, 1909, 1; *Il Progresso*, November 19, 1909; *Sun*, November 18, 1909, 12.
9 Declaration of Intention for Antonio Viola Comito, April 10, 1911, Baltimore, MD; Arriving Passenger and Crew List for Antonio Viola Comito, June 29, 1907, New York, NY; *Daily Reports*, Flynn, January 4, 1910, T915, Roll 116, 1st series, Frame 1968.
10 *Daily Reports*, Flynn, January 16, 1910, Roll 116, 2nd series, Frame 154; *Eagle*, February 8, 1910, 2.
11 Lawrence Richey Papers, *Black Hand Confessions, 1910*, Herbert Hoover Presidential Library, box 1, 58–59, 69–70, 80–81.
12 *Binghamton (NY) Press and Sun-Bulletin*, February 25, 1910, 1; *Binghamton (NY) Press and Sun-Bulletin*, June 3, 1912, 1.
13 *Sun*, February 17, 1910, 5.
14 *Daily Reports*, Flynn, February 8, 1910, T915, Roll 116, 2nd series, Frame 493; February 10, 1910, Frames 514, 523.
15 *Tribune*, February 20, 1910, 1; *Citizen*, February 20, 1910, 1.
16 *NYT*, March 17, 1909, 1; *Daily Reports*, John J. Henry, April 15, 1910, Reel 116, 2nd series, Frame 1148.
17 Bencivenni, Marcella. *Italian Immigrant Radical Culture: The Idealism of the Sovversivi in the United States, 1890–1940* (New York: New York University Press,

2011), 31; Emelise Aliandri, *The Italian-American Theatre of New York City* (Chesterton, SC: Arcadia, 1999), 49–54; *NYT*, March 11, 1910, 4.

18 Petrosino archive, Agreement between Mrs. Adelina Petrosino and Henry A. Bonori, November 16, 1909; Receipt, Henry A. Bonori to Mrs. Adelina Petrosino, March 16, 1910; *Eagle*, March 5, 1910, 16; *Eagle*, March 14, 1910, 19; *Sun*, March 14, 1910, 4; *NYT*, March 14, 1910, 5.

Chapter 8. "The Impotence of the Metropolitan Police"

1 People v. Antonio Misiani, Supreme Court, Appellate Division, Second Department, Volume 1437, fols. 52–56; *Eagle*, March 6, 1910, 5.

2 *Misiani*, fols. 152–62.

3 *BSU*, November 23, 1896, 1; *Eagle*, February 28, 1897, 1; *BSU*, November 24, 1896, 2; *Eagle*, June 7, 1896, 5; *Eagle*, March 24, 1909, 1; *NYT*, March 25 1909, 7.

4 *Eagle*, July 24, 1902, 1; *Eagle*, January 12, 1904, 20.

5 Royal Embassy of Italy to Secretary of State, January 19, 1909, NARA, RG 59, M862, Roll 968, Frame 928.

6 *Buffalo Courier*, March 17, 1910; *Eagle*, March 16, 1910, 1.

7 *Eagle*, March 6, 7, 9, 16, 1910; *Citizen*, March 9, 1910, 12; *BSU*, March 25, 1910, 1; *San Francisco Call*, March 13, 1913, 1; *Bridgeport (CT) Evening Farmer*, March 24, 1913, 2.

8 People v. Cincotta, 163 App. Div. 863 (1914); *Eagle*, February 16, 1915, 4.

9 *Il Progresso*, February 22, 1910, 2.

10 Flynn, *Barrel Mystery*, 28; *Daily Reports*, Flynn, February 9, 1910, NARA, RG 87, Roll 116, 2nd series, Frame 523.

11 *Misiani*, fol. 171.

12 *Ireland, Select Births and Baptisms, 1620–1911*; US Census for 1910, Arthur Gloster, New York, NY; US naturalization record index card for Arthur Gloster, October 11, 1894; *CR*, July 29, 1903, Supplement, 100; *CR*, January 26, 1906, 932; *CR*, February 21, 1902, 928. Gloster's reprimand: *CR*, April 23, 1897, 1531. Gloster's loss of pay: half day, *CR*, June 22, 1897, 2732; two days, *CR*, April 23, 1897, 153; half day, *CR*, May 11, 1897, 1788; two days, *CR*, March 5, 1898, 1011; half day, *CR*, June 20, 1899, 3744; three days, *CR*, October 16, 1899, 6068.

13 See Moses, *Unlikely Union*, 113–54.

14 Flynn to Gaynor, April 7, 1910, Gaynor Collection, NYMA, Box 45, Folder 399; *Tribune*, April 19, 1910, 3.

Chapter 9. "The Policeman's Club"

1 *NYT*, January 28, 1910, 3; *Il Progresso*, January 29, 1910, 2; Marilynn S. Johnson, *Street Justice: A History of Police Violence in New York City* (Boston: Beacon Press, 2003), 99–107.

2 Baker to Gaynor, February 9, 1910, William J. Gaynor Collection, NYMA, Series I, Box 45, Folder 394; Schmittberger to Baker, August 30, 1910, Gaynor Collection,

NYMA, Series I, Box 47, Folder 410; 1900 US Census for Henrietta Hyman, New York, NY; 1905 New York State Census for Henrietta Hyman, New York, NY; *CR*, December 10, 1910, 11320; *NYT*, August 7, 1911, 9; *NYT*, October 4, 1911, 6.

3 Moses, *Unlikely Union*, 119; Johnson, *Street Justice*, 122–24, 105; *Sun*, March 14, 1909, 2; *NYT*, August 28, 1904, 23.

4 *Eagle*, August 8, 1910, 2.; William R. Hochman, "The Shooting of Mayor Gaynor," *New York History* 93, no. 1 (Winter 2012): 53–69.

5 *Philadelphia Inquirer*, December 5, 1930, 18.

Chapter 10. "My Boy Will Be Cut to Pieces"

1 *Eagle*, June 22, 1910, 4; *NYT*, June 22, 1910, 1; US passport application for Mariano and Michael Scimeca, June 16, 1923; 1905 New York State Census for Mariano Scimeca, Brooklyn, NY; 1910 US Census for Mariano Scimeca, New York, NY; New York, NY, Marriage Index for Leonilda Petrella, November 24, 1904.

2 People v. Vito Micelli, Court of Appeals of the State of New York, Volume 135 (1915), fol. 113.

3 *Eagle*, June 25, 1910, 2; *Il Progresso*, June 28, 1910, 2; *NYT*, September 4, 1910, SM5.

4 *Eagle*, November 21, 1909, 43.

5 *Citizen*, June 22, 1910, 1; *Tribune*, June 24, 1910, 14; *Eagle*, June 30, 1910, 1; *Tribune*, August 1, 1910, 4; *Eagle*, August 2, 1910, 17.

6 Alberto Pecorini, *Gli Americani nella Vita Moderna Osservati de un Italiano* (Milano: Editrice Treves, 1909), 117, 325; *L'Italia*, December 25, 1909, 1; *NYT*, September 4, 1910, SM5.

7 *Post*, September 10, 1910, 2; *NYT*, September 10, 1910, 2; *NYT*, November 27, 1910, 10; *Il Progresso*, September 11, 1910.

8 International News Service, *Buffalo (NY) Courier*, December 12, 1910, 2; US passport application for Michael Scimeca and Mariano Scimeca, June 16, 1923. It confirms that they lived in Palermo until May 1911.

9 People v. Pettanza, Court of Appeals of New York State, Vol. 38 (1913), fol. 35.

10 *Eagle*, November 24, 1910, 4; Index to Death Certificates, New York, NY, for Maria Longo, November 19, 1910. The official cause of death was paralysis from chronic endocarditis.

11 *Tribune*, November 23, 1910; *Eagle*, November 28, 1910, 1; *Eagle*, December 3, 1910, 1.

12 People v. Rappa, New York State Supreme Court, Appellate Division, Vol. 1586 (1913), fols. 45–51.

13 *Tribune*, December 10, 1910, 1; *BTU*, December 27, 1910, 1; *Eagle*, December 9, 1910, 2; *Pettanza*, fols. 169–77.

14 *Rappa*, fol. 131; *Eagle*, June 23, 1913, 1; *NYT*, August 2, 1914, 15.

15 *Eagle*, November 1, 1911, 2.

16 *World*, December 1, 1910, 12; *Post*, October 25, 1910; *NYT*, October 30, 1910, 38; 1910 US Census for William J. Flynn, Bronx, NY.

Chapter 11. "Where Is Tony Vachris?"

1 *Sun*, January 16, 1911, 2; *Eagle*, January 16, 1911, 16; *NYT*, January 8, 1911, 10; *Sun*, January 8, 1911, 12; *NYT*, February 14, 1911, 6.

2 *Tribune*, November 18, 1910, 3.

3 *Daily Reports*, Richard H. Taylor, February 16, 1911, NARA, RG 87, Roll 277, Frame 1142; March 10, 1911, Frame 1501.

4 *Eagle*, February 11, 1911, 1; *BSU*, February 12, 1911, 5; *NYT*, February 12, 1911, 16.

5 *Pittston (PA) Gazette*, February 13, 1911, 1; *Daily Reports*, Taylor, February 9, 1911, NARA, RG 87, Roll 277, Frame 1040. Lucchino survived—that time. He became a Pittston police detective and was murdered in 1920. Two men were executed in 1922 for the slaying. For a summary, see the Officer Down Memorial Page, www.odmp.org/officer/22961-detective-samuel-lucchino.

6 *Eagle*, July 20, 1911, 6.

7 *NYT*, February 15, 1911, 8.

8 *Post*, February 21, 1911, 1; *World*, February 21, 1911, 10.

9 *Sun*, February 7, 1908, 2; *BSU*, February 7, 1908, 3; *Buffalo (NY) Commercial*, February 7, 1908, 9; 1910 US Census for John J. Freschi, New York, NY; *BSU*, December 20, 1910, 9.

10 *Italoamericana: The Literature of the Great Migration, 1880–1943*, ed. Francesco Durante and Robert Viscusi (New York: Fordham University Press, 2014), 715; *Il Progresso*, December 16, 1910, 1.

11 *Immigrants and Crime: Reports of the Immigration Commission* (Washington, DC: Government Printing Office, 1911), 1–8. Instead of comparing the proportion of violent crimes committed by Italians and other nationalities, the commission examined *what percent of crimes within each nationality* involved violence, such as homicide or assault. Italians didn't have the large number of drunk-and-disorderly offenses that other groups had (since alcoholism was not a major problem for them). This raised the percentage of crimes involving violence higher. Further, the commission did not include armed robbery in the category of violent crimes; this offense was much more prevalent among native-born Americans.

12 *Il Progresso*, December 16, 1910.

13 *Il Progresso*, December 16, 1910.

14 *BT*, April 27, 1911, 1; *Sun*, April 28, 1911, 1; *BSU*, April 27, 1911, 1; *BSU*, May 23, 1911, 1.

15 Curran, 3804–22; *Citizen*, June 21, 1911, 14; *Citizen*, September 22, 1911, 1; *Eagle*, July 12, 1911, 2; *World*, June 30, 1911, 9; *BTU*, June 30, 1910, 10.

16 *Eagle*, June 25, 1911, 14.

17 Johnson, *Street Justice*, 290–91.

18 *Post*, February 17, 1912, 1.

Chapter 12. "The Temperament of Your Race"

1 *NYT*, June 28, 1908, 14.

2 *Sun*, September 6, 1911, 1; *Washington Star*, September 6, 1911, 1; *Washington Post*, September 7, 1911, 6.

3 *NYT*, October 5, 1911, 5; *World*, October 11, 1910, 1; 1910 US Census for James E. Brande, New York, NY; Sing Sing Admission Register for Giuseppe Costabile, October 19, 1911.

4 1910 US Census for Salvatore Siragusa, New York, NY; *World*, September 15, 1911, 1; New York State Archives, Great Meadow Correctional Facility Registers, 1906–1942, for Giovanni Rizzo, December 6, 1912; *Annual Report of the Chief Clerk of the District Attorney's Office County of New York for the Year Ending December 11, 1911* (New York: M. B. Brown, 1912), 55.

5 *NYT*, September 28, 1911, 5; *NYT*, September 29, 1911, 8.

6 New York State Rifle & Pistol Association v. Kevin P. Bruen, U.S. Supreme Court, 20–843.

7 The 70 percent figure, often cited in the gun debate, comes from a 1990 study published by the Second Amendment Foundation, which opposes gun control laws. See Brendan F. J. Furnish, "The New Class and the California Handgun Initiative: Elitist Developed Law as Gun Control," in *The Gun Culture and Its Enemies*, ed. William R. Tonso (Bellevue, WA: Merrill Press, 1990), 133. For a rebuttal: Patrick J. Charles, "A Historian's Assessment of the Anti-Immigrant Narrative in NYSRPA v. Bruen," Duke Center for Firearms Law, August 4, 2021, https://perma.cc/H7NG-W4UJ, accessed November 11, 2021.

8 *Report of the Secretary of State on Statistics of Crime in the State of New York* (Albany, NY: J.B. Lyon, 1913), 177, 192, 217, 222.

9 See Carolyn Moehling and Anne Morrison Piehl, "Immigration, Crime, and Incarceration in Early Twentieth-Century America," *Demography* (November 2009), 759: "Even taking the younger age distribution into account, Italian immigrants appear to have been disproportionately involved in more serious crimes."

Chapter 13. "Arrested by One of His Own Countrymen"

1 *Sun*, May 19, 1912, 8; *Tribune*, May 19, 1912, 1; *NYT*, September 24, 1911, SM8; *Washington Post*, September 7, 1911, 6.

2 *Citizen*, June 4, 1896, 1.

3 *Eagle*, June 7, 1896, 5. Corrao transferred from Cullen's Eleventh Precinct to the Brooklyn Detective Bureau in 1898: *CR*, April 29, 1898, 1938.

4 *Eagle*, June 10, 1896, 12; *Citizen*, June 4, 1896; 1870 US Census for Daniel Farrell, Perth Amboy, NJ.

5 *NYDN*, January 26, 1964, 584.

6 *Eagle*, January 19, 1902, 5; *Eagle*, February 13, 1902, 7; *CR*, March 25, 1902, 1783; *Citizen*, February 25, 1902, 1.

7 *Eagle*, October 11, 1911, 18.

8 *Eagle*, October 12, 1911, 2; *BTU*, October 12, 1911, 13; *Eagle*, September 12, 1911, 2; *Eagle*, September 13, 1911, 6.

Chapter 14. "This Is Another Administration"

1 *CR*, July 24, 1912, 6371; *CR*, July 31, 1913; *CR*, June 19, 1913, Supplement, 5916; *Herald*, August 5, 1912, 4.

2 *Tribune*, July 18, 1912, 2; *NYT*, July 24, 1912, 1.

3 *World*, January 24, 1906, 5; *Washington Post*, January 26, 1906, 6.

4 Andy Logan, *Against the Evidence: The Becker-Rosenthal Affair, a Great American Scandal* (London: Weidenfeld & Nicholson, 1970), 22.

5 *World*, July 25, 1912, 1; *NYT*, July 25, 1912, 1.

6 *Sun*, December 23, 1917, 47; *CR*, November 30, 1908, 12760; 1910 US Census for Francis J. Upton, New York, NY.

7 *NYT*, July 26, 1912, 1; *NYT*, July 31, 1912, 1.

8 *Herald*, August 5, 1912, 4.

9 Jenna Weissman Joselit, *Our Gang: Jewish Crime and the New York Jewish Community, 1900–1940* (Bloomington: Indiana University Press, 1983), 10, 75–84.

10 *Eagle*, May 13, 1912, 3.

11 *CR*, June 19, 1913, 5914.

12 *Sun*, February 14, 1913, 4; *Citizen*, February 28, 1913, 1; Curran, 3622–23, 3804–12, 3942.

13 *Eagle*, August 26, 1913, 5; *Eagle*, December 24, 1913; *Citizen*, October 30, 1913, 12.

14 The Curran Committee report is at *CR*, June 19, 1913, 5912–42.

15 *Tribune*, September 4, 1913, 6; *Sun*, September 5, 1913, 1; *Eagle*, December 31, 1913, 1.

16 *Tribune*, July 31, 1915, 1.

17 Logan, *Against the Evidence*, 17.

18 *Eagle*, January 6, 1914, 1; *Post*, January 6, 1914, 3.

Chapter 15. "That Is the Stuff"

1 People v. Angelino Sylvestro, New York State Supreme Court Appellate Division, First Department, Case on Appeal, fols. 1310–11, 1303.

2 *Sylvestro*, fol. 57.

3 *Sun*, October 11, 1913, 2.

4 *Eagle*, February 2, 1914, 7.

5 *Sylvestro*, fols. 933–36.

6 *Sylvestro*, fol. 454.

7 *Paterson (NJ) Morning Call*, September 25, 1913, 1; *Passaic (NJ) News*, October 6, 1913, 1.

8 *Annual Report of the Chief Clerk of the District Attorney's Office County of New York for the Year Ending December 31, 1914* (New York: M. B. Brown, 1915), 6; Sing Sing Admission Register for Pietro Giambruno, March 6, 1914.

9 *Sylvestro*, fols. 1408–13.

10 *Tribune*, March 18, 1912, 1; *CR*, May 23, 1914, 4531.

11 *NYT*, September 24, 1911, SM8.

12 *Herald*, May 10, 1914, 8; *Citizen*, September 6, 1913.

13 *NYT*, August 2, 1914, 8.

14 *NYT*, December 30, 1906, 21.

15 *Tribune*, July 30, 1914, 14.

16 *World*, December 1, 1914, 16; *Tribune*, December 12, 1914, 16.

17 *Tribune*, May 5, 1913, 1; *Tribune*, April 11, 1913, 2.

18 World War I draft registration, Liborio Gambardella, September 12, 1918.

19 People v. Oresto Shilitano, Court of General Sessions, New York County, testimony of Liborio Gambardella, 319. Accessed at www.lib.jjay.cuny.edu.

20 *Shilitano*, 23, 6, 229.

21 *Eagle*, June 30, 1916, 12.

22 *NYT*, January 17, 1913, 7; Curran, 3807–8.

23 Thomas J. Tunney, *Throttled!: The Detection of the German and Anarchist Bomb Plotters in the United States* (Boston: Small, Maynard & Company, 1919), 3–4.

Chapter 16. "Framed for Something He Did"

1 *Tribune*, March 5, 1915, 5; Eleanor Booth Simmons, "Young Wife Not Afraid Pulignano Will Meet Same Fate as Petrosino," *Tribune*, March 4, 1915, 14; 1910 US Census for Lucy Madden, New York, NY.

2 *Telegram*, March 3, 1915, 8.

3 *Cronaca Sovversiva*, March 13, 1915; *Cronaca Sovversiva*, April 10, 1915; *Cronaca Sovversiva*, April 24, 1915.

4 F. M. White, "Joe Petrosino: Scourge of the Black Hand," *The Scrap Book*, Vol. 4, Part I, October 1907, 716.

5 People v. Frank Abarno and Carmine Carbone, Supreme Court, Appellate Division, First Department, Vol. 3653, fol. 589.

6 *NYT*, July 5, 1914.

7 Tunney, *Throttled*, 43.

8 Nunzio Pernicone, *Carlo Tresca: Portrait of a Rebel* (Oakland, CA: AK Press, 2010), 77.

9 *Tribune*, October 14, 1914, 1.

10 *CR*, January 26, 1912, 761; *CR*, April 23, 1913, 3722, 3725; *CR*, May 1, 1913, 4033; *CR*, May 28, 1913, 5041; *CR*, November 15, 1913, 10560; *CR*, December 29, 1913, 12169; *CR*, January 31, 1914, Supplement; *Abarno*, fols. 406–9.

11 Tunney, *Throttled*, 45; *Abarno*, fols. 413–15.

12 *Abarno*, fols. 187, 590.

13 "In re Carlo Tresca: Resume of Activities," M. J. Davis, May 7, 1920, 9, Tresca FBI File, Part 1 of 10.

14 People v. Mills (178 NY 274, 284), April 26, 1904. The Supreme Court case is Sorrells v. United States, 287 U.S. 435, 53 S.Ct. 210, 77 L.Ed. 413 (1932).

15 *Abarno*, fols. 2084–89.

16 Author's recollection from covering trials with Kempton.

17 *World*, April 13, 1915, 11.

18 *CR*, July 30, 1927, Supplement, 423; *New York Evening Journal*, July 2, 1928, 2; *NYDN*, June 26, 1932, 306.

19 Tunney, *Throttled*, 68; *World*, June 3, 1919, 1; *NYT*, June 3, 1919, 1.

20 David J. Gottfried, "Avoiding the Entrapment Defense in a Post-9/11 World," *FBI Law Enforcement Bulletin*, January 12, 2012, https://leb.fbi.gov.

21 Jesse J. Norris and Hanna Grol-Prokopczyk, "Estimating the Prevalence of Entrapment in Post-9/11 Terrorism Cases," *Journal of Criminal Law and Criminology* 105, no. 3 (2015): 616.

Chapter 17. "They'll Get Theirs"

1 Fiaschetti, *Rough*, 111–13; US passport application for Giosue Gallucci, June 7, 1906; *Tribune*, May 18, 1915, 1; *NYT*, May 25, 1915, 10.

2 Dash, *First Family*, 239–40, citing Nat J. Ferber, *A New American: The Life Story of Justice Salvatore A. Cotillo* (New York: Farrar & Rinehart, 1938), 20.

3 Fiaschetti, *Rough*, 103; *Herald*, January 7, 1917, Magazine Section, 2; Critchley, *Origin*, 109–19.

4 People v. Pellegrino Marano, Court of Appeals of the State of New York, Vol. 107 (1921), fol. 738.

5 *Herald*, July 28, 1913, 12; *World*, July 26, 1913, 4; Critchley, *Origin*, 116.

6 *BSU*, March 14, 1915; *CR*, March 31, 1915, 2652; *CR*, July 31, 1917.

7 People v. Alessandro Vollero, Court of Appeals of the State of New York, Vol. 41 (1919), fol. 799; *BSU*, March 7, 1918, 2.

8 *Vollero*, fols. 347, 2233.

9 *Vollero*, fols. 510–13, 756.

10 *Sun*, November 28, 1917, 1; *Tribune*, November 28, 1917, 16; New Jersey Births and Christenings Index for Amalia A. Valvo, Jersey City, NJ, January 15, 1898.

11 *BSU*, March 17, 1917, 1.

12 *Vollero*, fols. 2000–2, 2242–45; *BSU*, April 20, 1917; *Citizen*, April 21, 1917; *BSU*, June 1, 26, 1917; *BTU*, May 26, 1917.

13 *NYDN*, August 5, 1928, 5; *Citizen*, November 11, 1917, 2; *BSU*, February 17, 1918, 16.

14 *Nevada State Journal*, December 6, 1945, 2; *Reno (NV) Gazette-Journal*, October 11, 1917, 8, November 2, 1917, 6.

15 *Morano*, fols. 760, 614–15; *Vollero*, fols. 1760, 4357.

16 *Vollero*, fols. 882–92.

17 *BSU*, September 8, 1916, 3; *Eagle*, July 24, 1917, 5.

18 Andrew Paul Mele, *The Italian Squad: How the NYPD Took Down the Black Hand Extortion Racket* (Jefferson, NC: McFarland, 2020), 26–27.

19 *Tribune*, February 16, 1918, 15; *Vollero*, fols. 497, 698, 1814; *Eagle*, July 24, 1917, 5.

20 Sing Sing Admission Register for Agidia Damico, June 7, 1915; *Tribune*, December 24, 1914, 4; *Eagle*, January 5, 1915, 8.

21 *CR*, May 28, 1912, 4521; *BSU*, April 25, 1912, 4; *CR*, January 30, 1914, 1063; *Eagle*, May 3, 1912, 7; *Eagle*, January 20, 1921, 1.

Chapter 18. "The Man with a Hole in His Hand"

1 Michael Fiaschetti, "The Man with the Hole in His Hand," *Collier's*, February 14, 1925, 16–17, 43; *ABJ*, December 24, 1917; *ABJ*, December 24, 1917; *ABJ*, March 12, 1918; Mark J. Price, *Mafia Cop Killers in Akron: The Gang War before Prohibition* (Charleston, SC: History Press, 2017), 38, 44, 49, 52, 60; *ABJ*, February 14, 1916, 1.

2 *Sun*, July 30, 1911, 1; *BTU*, July 29, 1911, 2.

3 *CR*, November 20, 1913, 10698; *BSU*, October 20, 1914, 1; *BTU*, October 20, 1914, 1; *Tribune*, July 26, 1915, 12.

4 *Herald*, January 4, 1916, 1; *Sun*, January 4, 1916, 3; *NYT*, January 4, 1916, 4.

5 Price, *Cop Killers*, 106.

6 Price, *Cop Killers*, 109–10.

7 *ABJ*, May 13, 15, 1918, 1; *ABJ*, June 14, 1918, 1; *Akron (OH) Evening Times*, June 20, 1918, 1; Price, *Cop Killers*, 112.

8 *ABJ*, May 14, 1918, 1.

9 *ABJ*, June 8, 1912, 12; *Akron (OH) Evening Times*, June 13, 15, 1918.

10 US passport application for Benjamin Di Nicola, November 1, 1923; 1920 census for Benjamin Nicola, Shaker Heights, Ohio; *ABJ*, August 10, 1918, 1; *ABJ*, August 12, 1918, 1.

11 Michael Fiaschetti as told to Prosper Buranelli, "Blood Money for Bluecoats," *Liberty*, June 8, 1929, 43.

12 *Akron (OH) Evening Times*, August 15, 24, 1918; *ABJ*, August 16, 20, 1918.

13 *Akron (OH) Evening Times*, October 5, 1918, 1; Price, *Cop Killers*, 140–43.

14 *ABJ*, November 22, 23, 1965.

15 *World*, September 13, 1918, 9.

16 *ABJ*, September 24, 1918, 13; *Tribune*, September 4, 1921, 2; Prosper Buranelli, "How Detective Fiaschetti 'Got Some Information,'" *Washington Star*, June 25, 1922, Part 4, 3; Alexander Herman, "Italian Sherlock Holmes Amuses Self by Flirting with Death Daily," *Bartlesville (OK) Examiner*, 2. The latter story appeared in dozens of papers.

17 Roetzel to Enright, June 17, 1918, in Fiaschetti, *Rough*, 301.

Chapter 19. "Appreciation and Thanks"

1 *Newsday*, August 1, 1960, 87.

2 *BTU*, June 14, 1919, 6; *BTU*, January 21, 1920, 1; *Herald*, May 15, 1919, 4.

3 Fiaschetti, *Rough*, 158–60; *Eagle*, June 14, 1919, 3.

4   *Sun*, May 15, 1919, 4; *Eagle*, April 12, 1919, 4; *Montreal Gazette*, May 16, 1919, 22; *Police Department of the City of New York Annual Report for 1919*, 83–84; Michael Fiaschetti, "The Ditch Digger's Hat," *Collier's*, March 28, 1925, 38.

5   *Eagle*, June 14, 1919, 1; *Eagle*, June 15, 1919, 7; *Citizen*, June 17, 1919, 1; *NYPD Annual Report for 1919*, 112.

6   *BTU*, July 21, 1919, 5; *Herald*, July 22, 1919; *Telegram*, July 21, 1919, 7.

7   *Citizen*, February 27, 1913, 6.

8   Terry Golway, *Machine Made: Tammany Hall and the Creation of Modern American Politics* (New York: Liveright, 2014), 226; *NYT*, July 7, 1918, 1.

9   *Outlook*, February 6, 1918, 201.

10 *Tribune*, November 27, 1921, 8; *Police Department of the City of New York Annual Report for 1918*, 18.

11 *NYT*, April 21, 1918, 15.

12 *Sun*, January 24, 1918, 1; *CR*, January 1, 1918; *CR*, July 31, 1918.

13 *Eagle*, January 23, 1918, 2; *Tribune*, January 23, 1918, 1; *Herald*, January 24, 1918, 1.

14 *Police Department of New York Annual Report for 1920*, 101.

15 Fiaschetti, "The Ditch Digger's Hat," 38; Fiaschetti, *Rough*, 168–69; *Queens (NY) Daily Star*, May 6, 1921, 1.

Chapter 20. A "Vast and Complex" Mission to Naples

1   *Book World of the Sun and Herald*, February 1, 1920, 9.

2   Dash, *First Family*, 271, 280; Critchley, *Origin*, 155; Sing Sing Admission Register for Giuseppe Masseria, May 26, 1913; 1920 US Census for Joseph Masseria, New York, NY; New York City Landmarks Preservation Commission, "New York Curb Exchange," https://s-media.nyc.gov, accessed February 3, 2022; *NYT*, October 13, 1920, 1.

3   *Herald*, November 7, 1919, 8. See also *Eagle*, November 16, 1919, 1; *World*, January 6, 1920, 2.

4   *NYDN*, January 3, 1920, 2.

5   *BTU*, December 3, 1920, 1; *Joplin (MO) Globe*, January 9, 1921, 6.

6   *Herald*, September 22, 1921, 8; *Tribune*, December 10, 1920, 1; *BTU*, November 23, 1921, 3.

7   *Herald*, September 22, 1921, 8. Twenty-three of the forty-five victims in a list of Brooklyn's unsolved murders for 1920 have Italian surnames.

8   *Eagle*, October 18, 1920, 2.

9   1920 US Census, analyzed by New York City Department of Planning, www1.nyc. gov, accessed February 5, 2022.

10 Arthur C. Train, *Courts, Criminals and the Camorra* (New York: Scribner's, 1912), 224.

11 *NYDN*, March 8, 1920; *NYDN*, March 9, 1920.

12 *Baltimore Sun*, March 17, 1920, 11; People v. Papaccio, 140 Misc. 696 (NY General Sessions, 1931); *Eagle*, October 28, 1920, 18, Fiaschetti, *Rough*, 307; "Vincent

Papaccio, 2 copy photos, 1 w/infor frm Det. Bur. Buffalo," pde_0261, NYMA; Archivio di Stato di Napoli, Tribunale di Napoli, Tribunale penale, 1923, Box 8, Folder 310, Processo penale a carico di Vincenzo Papaccio per duplice omicidio in danno di Lena Spinelli e Josephine Gentile (Hereafter, Archivio di Stato di Napoli).

13 Fiaschetti, *Rough*, 256–57; US passport application, Irving A. O'Hara, New York, NY, November 23, 1923; *Eagle*, October 28, 1920, 18.

14 Fiaschetti, *Rough*, 259.

15 *Olean (NY) Times Herald*, December 16, 1920, 1; *NYT*, December 16, 1920, 2; *NYT*, December 16, 1920, 2; *BSU*, December 19, 1920, 11; *Tribune*, March 27, 1921, 12; *Boston Globe*, March 2, 1921.

16 Fiaschetti, *Rough*, 267–89.

17 Michael Fiaschetti, "Crimes I Have Solved—No. 6," *Buffalo (NY) Times*, September 23, 1922, 6. The State Department birth record for Byington's daughter corroborates his presence in Naples around this time. *Report of Birth of Children Born to American Parents* for Janice Joy Byington, Naples, Italy, March 28, 1921. Byington's descendants have no knowledge of such an incident.

18 Archivio di Stato di Napoli; *Papaccio*, 140 Misc. 696.

19 Repetto to Fiaschetti, January 17, 1921, Archivio di Stato di Napoli; *Eagle*, January 2, 1921, 10.

20 *Philadelphia Inquirer*, February 19, 1921, 2; *Eagle*, June 13, 1922, 2; *NYT*, June 13, 1922, 1.

21 *Papaccio*, 140 Misc. 696.

Chapter 21. "Cunning, Effective Detective Work"

1 People v. Cusamano, Court of Appeals of New York State, Vol. 41 (1923), fols. 242, 677–80; *World*, June 3, 1921, 1; Mary Sullivan, *My Double Life: The Story of a New York Policewoman* (New York: Farrar & Rinehart, 1938), 105–6; Sing Sing Admission Register for Antonio Marino, June 28, 1922.

2 *Herald*, June 14, 1921, 1.

3 *Cusamano*, fols. 279, 934, 1041.

4 *Cusamano*, fol. 786.

5 Emanuel H. Lavine, *The Third Degree: A Detailed and Appalling Exposé of Police Brutality* (Garden City, NY: Garden City Publishing Company, 1930), 118–19; People v. Roberto Raffaele, New York Court of Appeals, 233 NY 590, fols. 725–30; Petition for Naturalization for Salvatore Varotta, Providence, RI, August 17, 1922.

6 *Cusamano*, fol. 910.

7 Lavine, *Third Degree*, 121.

8 *NYT*, June 4, 1921, 8.

9 *NYDN*, June 4, 1921, 1.

10 *Cusamano*, fols. 74–66, 301–3.

11 Robert Coleman Taylor, "The Kidnapping and Murder of the Varotta Boy," *Virginia Law Review* (April 1923), 433.

12 *Cusamano*, fol. 964.

13 Fiaschetti, *Rough*, 240–41, 235. There is no corroboration for this, and the memoir is wrong in stating that the perpetrator stabbed Joseph, whose body showed no marks. But there seems little reason for Fiaschetti to make up such a blunder.

14 Taylor, "Varotta Boy," 439, 442.

15 National Commission on Law Observance and Enforcement, Volume IV (Washington, DC: US Government Printing Office, 1931), 90–92, citing Fiaschetti, *Rough*, 242.

16 *Herald*, June 18, 1921, 5. There was one detective who also worked for Petrosino, Silvio Repetto.

Chapter 22. "The Most Famous of Detectives"

1 World War I draft registration for Bartolomeo Fontana, New York, June 5, 1917; World War I draft registration for James Pellegrino, New York, NY; 1910 US Census for James Pellegrino, New York, NY; *CR*, July 6, 1918, 3480; *CR*, July 31, 1922; *World*, May 26, 1920, 16; *World*, July 23, 1920, 6; *BTU*, November 14, 1929, 11.

2 *NYDN*, August 18, 1921, 2.

3 Joseph Bonanno with Sergio Lalli, *A Man of Honor: The Autobiography of Joseph Bonanno* (New York: Simon & Schuster, 1983), 30.

4 *NYPD Annual Report for 1921*, 248.

5 *World*, August 17, 1921, 1; *Herald*, August 20, 1921, 1.

6 *Tribune*, August 21, 1921; *Tribune*, August 22, 1921; *NYT*, October 15, 1921, 8.

7 Jane Dixon, "Thrilling Adventures of the Nemesis of the Blackhanders," *Telegram*, August 21, 1921, 16.

8 *Tribune*, August 17, 1921, 3; *Asbury Park (NJ) Press*, August 17, 1921, 1.

9 *Telegram*, August 17, 1921, 1; *BSU*, August 17, 1921, 1.

10 *Asbury Park Press*, August 10, 1921, 1; *Long Branch (NJ) Daily Record*, August 18, 1921, 1; *NYPD Annual Report for 1921*, 248; *NYDN*, August 18, 1921, 2.

11 *Asbury Park Press*, March 25, 1922, 1.

12 For detailed analysis, see Critchley, *Origin*, 216–30, and Thomas Hunt and Michael A. Tona, "The Good Killers: 1921's Glimpse of the Mafia," American Mafia, https://mafiahistory.us, accessed February 13, 2022.

13 Lupo, *Two Mafias*, 52–55.

14 Roy A. Giles, "Two Hundred Murders in New York City Laid to Camorra," *Tribune*, September 4, 1921, 11.

Chapter 23. "Broken Up"

1 *Tribune*, January 18, 1922, 10; *Herald*, January 15, 1922, 1; *BSU*, January 17, 1922, 10.

2 *NYT*, February 5, 1922, 9; *CR*, December 24, 1921; *CR*, January 17, 1922, 335.

3 *BSU*, April 14, 1921, 10; *BSU*, May 3, 1921, 10.

4 *Tribune*, July 26, 1921, 1.

5 Enright to Hylan, September 27, 1921, NYMA, Hylan Collection, Series I, Box 143, Folder 1532.

6 Giles, *Tribune*, September 4, 1921.

7 *NYPD Annual Report for 1920*, 99, 167–68.

8 Irving O'Hara cashed in on this, bringing in much more than his salary. *World*, July 3, 1922, 3; *CR*, June 2, 1922, 3698; *CR*, June 22, 1922, 4431.

9 *World*, May 9, 1922, 2; *Tribune*, May 9, 1922, 1; *Herald*, August 9, 1922, 1; *NYT*, August 9, 10, 1922; *World*, August 10, 1922, 22; Patrick Downey, *Gangster City: The History of the New York Underworld 1900–1935* (Fort Lee, NJ: Barricade, 2004), 2092, Kindle.

10 *Herald*, August 12, 1922, 14; 1930 US Census for Agnes Egglinger, New Haven, Conn.; World War II draft registration card for Joseph Schepis, Queens, NY. See Critchley, *Origin*, 154–56, on Masseria's rise.

11 *Tribune*, July 21, 1922, 24; *World*, August 5, 1922, 2.

12 *Tribune*, December 16, 1922, 9; *Buffalo Courier*, January 4, 1920, 34.

13 Elisabeth Smith, "Beautiful Neapolitan Scoffs at Charge That She Was Held for Ransom by Mafia," *Telegram*, August 9, 1922, 4.

14 *Utica (NY) Observer-Dispatch*, August 5, 1922, 9.

15 *World*, August 25, 1922, 1.

16 *NYDN*, August 26, 1922, 3; *Herald*, August 26, 1922.

17 *Daily Reports*, Joseph La Palma, October 18, 1922, NARA, RG 87, Roll 605, Frames 972, 978, 986; Fiaschetti, *Rough*, 292; *Tribune*, December 16, 1922, 9.

18 *CR*, June 24, 1924.

19 *NYT*, November 12, 1922, 5; *Eagle*, November 10, 1922, 3.

20 *Record* (Hackensack, NJ), June 20, 1960, 4.

Chapter 24. Conclusion

1 *Reports of the Immigration Commission*, 209.

2 Giles, *Tribune*, September 4, 1921, Part II, 2. See also Fiaschetti, *Rough*, 82, 86; Marina Cacioppo, *"If These Sidewalks Could Talk." Reinventing Italian-American Ethnicity: The Representation and Construction of Ethnic Identity in Italian-American Literature* (Torino: Otto Editore, 2005), 38, 42.

3 *NYT*, December 30, 1906, 21.

4 Petrosino archive, undated. It appears to be a draft of a memo to Bingham, written in Italian.

5 Anthony A. Braga and Rod K. Brunson, "The Police and Public Discourse on 'Black-on-Black' Violence," *New Perspectives in Policing* (May 2015), US Dept. of Justice, Office of Justice Programs, www.ojp.gov.

6 Pier Cepetto, *L'Assassinio Del Detective* (New York: Francesco Tocci/Emporium Press, 1909), 139.

7 Handschu v. Special Services Division, 605 F. Supp. 1384 (1985).

8   See Les Payne and Tamara Payne, *The Dead Are Arising: The Life of Malcolm X* (New York: Liveright, 2020), 486–87.

9   Robert M. Lombardo, "Fighting Organized Crime: A History of Law Enforcement Efforts in Chicago," *Journal of Contemporary Criminal Justice* 29, no. 2 (2013): 1–21, 2; *Chicago Tribune*, March 15, 1910, 3.

10 Luciano Iorizzo and Salvatore Mondello, "Origins of Italian-American Criminality: From New Orleans through Prohibition," *Italian Americana* 1, no. 2 (Spring 1975): 216–36, 217; *NYT*, July 24, 1970, 1; 1920 US Census for Hugh Mulligan, New York, NY.

11 "The Challenge of Crime in a Free Society," President's Commission on Law Enforcement and Administration of Justice (Washington, DC: US Government Printing Office, 1967), 192.

12 As Mike Dash titled his excellent book on this gang.

13 Lombardo, "Case of the Black Hand," 270–72. "minted that term": the author was present for the conversation.

14 *Newsday*, November 19, 1989, 8.

15 U.S. v. Salerno, 481 U.S. 739, 107 S. Ct. 2095 (1987).

16 National Commission on Law Observance and Enforcement, Vol. 4, "Report on Lawlessness in Law Enforcement" (Washington, DC: US Government Printing Office, 1931), 53, 90–91.

17 *Eagle*, March 8, 1908, 24.

18 Ralph Micelli, "Joe Petrosino, the Martyr," *Pittsburgh Press*, September 19, 1915, 65.

19 Edward Alsworth Ross, *The Old World in the New: The Significance of Past and Present Immigration to the American People* (New York: Century, 1914), 111, 113. See Peter D'Agostino, "Craniums, Criminals, and the 'Cursed Race': Italian Anthropology in American Thought, 1896–1924," *Comparative Studies in Society and History* (April 2002), 319–43.

20 Charles Jaret, "Troubled by Newcomers: Anti-Immigrant Attitudes and Action during Two Eras of Mass Immigration to the United States," *Journal of American Ethnic History* 18, no. 3 (Spring 1999): 30.

21 Curran, 3829.

22 Dash, *First Family*, 273; Richard D. Alba, *Blurring the Color Line: The New Chance for a More Integrated America* (Cambridge, MA: Harvard University Press, 2009), 65–67.

23 *NYT*, April 27, 1924, 3.

Epilogue

1   Peter Maas, *The Valachi Papers* (New York: Putnam's, 1968), 89.

2   *NYDN*, April 16, 1931, 2.

3   Dash, *First Family*, 308.

4   Luigi Barzini, *The Italians* (New York: Bantam, 1964), 275.

5   *Lexington (KY) Herald*, June 17, 1915, 13.

6 Dash, *First Family*, 295–98.

7 *NYDN*, October 24, 1933, 3. Crater went missing in 1930.

8 *BSU*, March 15, 1922, 4; *BTU*, October 9, 1934, 1.

9 *NYT*, April 20, 1944, 19.

10 *Eagle*, August 1, 1949, 7.

11 Associated Press, *Buffalo (NY) Morning Express*, February 4, 1923, 39; *Eagle*, February 4, 1923, 5.

12 *NYT*, July 25, 1939, 26; *Eagle*, July 25, 1939, 5.

13 *BTU*, February 1, 1935, 10.

14 New York State Archives; Executive Orders for Commutations, Pardons, Restorations, Clemency and Respites, 1869–1931, April 13, 1926.

15 *Eagle*, March 31, 1929, 16; *Citizen*, May 24, 1924, 1; *BTU*, May 26, 1924, 1.

16 New York, NY, Extracted Marriage Index for Laura Carrasale, October 12, 1916; New York, NY, Index to Birth Certificates, December 15, 1890.

17 *Record* (Hackensack, NJ), July 13, 1933, 9.

18 Probationary Police Officer, Company #20–62 to Commanding Officer, Police Academy, accessed via Tina Moore and Patrick Reilly, "Slain NYPD Rookie Wanted to Improve Relations between Cops and Communities," *New York Post*, January 22, 2022, https://nypost.com.

SELECTED BIBLIOGRAPHY

Major sources and informative context, excluding news coverage, which is cited in the Notes.

Bingham, Theodore A. "Foreign Criminals in New York." *North American Review*, September 1908, 383–94.

Birkbeck, Matt. *The Quiet Don*. New York: Berkeley Books, 2013.

Cacioppo, Marina. "Early Representations of Organized Crime and Issues of Identity in the Italian American Press (1890 to 1910)." *Italian American Review* 6, no. 1 (Winter 2016): 54–75.

———. *"If These Sidewalks Could Talk." Reinventing Italian-American Ethnicity: The Representation and Construction of Ethnic Identity in Italian-American Literature*. Torino: Otto Editore, 2005.

Carey, Arthur A. *Memoirs of a Murder Man*. Garden City, NY: Doubleday, 1930.

Corradini, Anna Maria. *Joe Petrosino, a 20th Century Hero: A Documented Account of His Assassination in Palermo*. Palermo: Provincia Regionale di Palermo, 2009.

Critchley, David. *The Origin of Organized Crime in America: The New York City Mafia, 1891–1931*. New York: Routledge, 2009.

Czitrom, Daniel. *New York Exposed: The Gilded Age Police Scandal That Launched the Progressive Era*. Oxford: Oxford University Press, 2016.

D'Agostino, Peter. "Craniums, Criminals, and the 'Cursed Race': Italian Anthropology in American Thought, 1896–1924." *Comparative Studies in Society and History* 44, no. 2 (April 2002): 319–43.

Dash, Mike. *The First Family: Terror, Extortion, Revenge, Murder and the Birth of the American Mafia*. New York: Random House, 2005.

———. *Satan's Circus: Murder, Vice, Police Corruption and New York's Trial of the Century*. London: Granta Books, 2007.

Downey, Patrick. *Gangster City: The History of the New York Underworld 1900–1935*. Fort Lee, NJ: Barricade Books, 2004.

Durante, Francesco, ed. *Italoamericana: The Literature of the Great Migration, 1880–1943*, American edition edited by Robert Viscusi. New York: Fordham University Press, 2014.

Esposito, Richard, and Ted Gerstein. *Bomb Squad: A Year Inside the Nation's Most Exclusive Police Unit*. New York: Hyperion, 2007.

Fiaschetti, Michael. *You Gotta Be Rough: The Adventures of Detective Fiaschetti of the Italian Squad. As Told to Prosper Buranelli*. New York: Doubleday, Doran & Company, 1930.

Flynn, William J. *The Barrel Mystery*. New York: James A. McCann Company, 1919.

Gaynor, William J. "Lawlessness of the Police in New York." *North American Review*, January 1903, 10–26.

Golway, Terry. *Machine Made: Tammany Hall and the Creation of Modern American Politics*. New York: Liveright, 2014.

Hunt, Thomas. "Badges in Little Italy: Joseph Petrosino and New York's Italian Squad." American Mafia, https://mafiahistory.us/a015/f_italsquad.html.

———. "Caged Wolves: The History of New York's Morello Mob." American Mafia, https://mafiahistory.us/cagedwolves.

Hunt, Thomas, and Michael A. Tona. "The Good Killers: 1921's Glimpse of the Mafia." American Mafia, https://mafiahistory.us/a014/f_goodkillers.html.

Immigrants and Crime: Reports of the Immigration Commission. Washington, DC: Government Printing Office, 1911.

Iorizzo, Luciano, and Salvatore Mondello. "Origins of Italian-American Criminality: From New Orleans through Prohibition." *Italian Americana* 2, no. 1 (Spring 1975): 216–36.

Johnson, Marilyn S. *Street Justice: A History of Police Violence in New York City*. Boston: Beacon Press, 2003.

Landolfi, Francesco. *Politics, Police and Crime in New York during Prohibition: Gotham and the Age of Recklessness, 1920–1933*. New York: Routledge, 2022. (Reviewed in manuscript form, courtesy of the author.)

Lardner, James, and Thomas Reppetto. *NYPD: A City and Its Police*. New York: Henry Holt, 2000.

Lavine, Emanuel H. *The Third Degree: A Detailed and Appalling Exposé of Police Brutality*. Garden City, NY: Garden City Publishing Company, 1930.

Logan, Andy. *Against the Evidence: The Becker-Rosenthal Affair, a Great American Scandal*. London: Weidenfeld & Nicholson, 1970.

Lombardo, Robert M. "Fighting Organized Crime: A History of Law Enforcement Efforts in Chicago." *Journal of Contemporary Criminal Justice* 29, no. 2 (May 2013): 296–316.

———. "The Hegemonic Narrative and the Social Construction of Deviance: The Case of the Black Hand." *Trends in Organized Crime* 13, no. 4 (2010): 263–82.

Lupo, Salvatore. *The Two Mafias: A Transatlantic History, 1888–2008*. New York: Palgrave Macmillan, 2015.

McCarthy, Kevin E. "Cops in Court: Assessing the Criminal Prosecutions of Police in Six Major Scandals in the New York City Police Department from 1894 to 1994." PhD diss. City University of New York, 2016.

McClellan, George B., Jr. *The Gentleman and the Tiger: The Autobiography of George B. McClellan, Jr.* Philadelphia: J.B. Lippincott, 1956.

Mele, Andrew Paul. *The Italian Squad: How the NYPD Took Down the Black Hand Extortion Racket*. Jefferson, NC: McFarland, 2020.

Moehling, Carolyn, and Anne Morrison Piehl. "Immigration, Crime, and Incarceration in Early Twentieth-Century America." *Demography* 46, no. 4 (November 2009): 739–63.

Moses, Paul. *An Unlikely Union: The Love-Hate Story of New York's Irish and Italians.* New York: New York University Press, 2015.

Nicaso, Antonio. "Organized Crime and Italian Americans." In *The Routledge History of Italian Americans*, edited by William J. Connell and Stanislao G. Pugliese. New York and London: Routledge, 479–92.

Oliver, Wesley MacNeil. "The Neglected History of Criminal Procedure, 1850–1940." Widener Law School Legal Studies Research Paper Series no. 09–26 (2009). Accessed at https://papers.ssrn.com/sol3/papers.cfm?abstract_id=1463746.

Oller, John. *Rogues' Gallery: The Birth of Modern Policing and Organized Crime in Gilded Age New York.* New York: Dutton, 2021.

Petacco, Arrigo. *Joe Petrosino*, trans. Charles Lam Markmann. New York: Macmillan, 1974.

Pozzetta, George E. "Another Look at the Petrosino Affair." *Italian Americana* 1, no. 1 (Autumn 1974): 80–92.

Price, Mark J. *Mafia Cop Killers in Akron: The Gang War before Prohibition.* Charleston, SC: History Press, 2017.

Reppetto, Thomas. *American Mafia: A History of Its Rise to Power.* New York: Henry Holt, 2004.

Ribak, Gil. "'The Jew Usually Left Those Crimes to Esau': The Jewish Responses to Accusations about Jewish Criminality in New York, 1908–1913." *AJS Review* 38, no. 1 (April 2014): 1–28.

Roedinger, David R. "Du Bois, Race and Italian Americans." In *Are Italians White? How Race Is Made in America*, edited by Jennifer Guglielmo and Salvatore Salerno. New York: Routledge, 2003, 259–63.

Speranza, Gino C. "How It Feels to Represent a Problem." *The Survey*, May 7, 1904. Reprinted in Durante, *Italoamericano*, 52–58.

Sullivan, Mary. *My Double Life: The Story of a New York Policewoman.* New York: Farrar & Rinehart, 1938.

Talty, Stephan. *The Black Hand: The Epic War between a Brilliant Detective and the Deadliest Secret Society in American History.* Boston: Houghton Mifflin, 2017.

Taylor, Robert Coleman. "The Kidnapping and Murder of the Varotta Boy." *Virginia Law Review* 9, no. 6 (April 1923): 432–45.

Train, Arthur C. *Courts, Criminals and the Camorra.* New York: Scribner's, 1912.

Tunney, Thomas J. *Throttled!: The Detection of the German and Anarchist Bomb Plotters in the United States. As Told to Paul Merrick Hollister.* Boston: Small, Maynard & Company, 1919.

Vellon, Peter. *A Great Conspiracy against Our Race: Italian Immigrant Newspapers and the Construction of Whiteness in the Early 20th Century.* New York: New York University Press, 2014.

Wallace, Mike. *Greater Gotham: A History of New York City from 1898 to 1919.* New York: Oxford University Press, 2017.

Woods, Arthur. "The Problem of the Black Hand." *McClure's*, May 1909, 40–47.

Websites

"The American Mafia." Documented organized crime history from researcher-writer Thomas Hunt. mafiahistory.us.

ancestry.com. Access to a broad range of public records, including census, naturalization, passport, travel, draft, probate, and New York State prison admission and pardon records.

Center for Research Libraries. Access to *Il Progresso Italo-Americano*. http://catalog.crl. edu/record=b2844061~S5.

The City Record, official newspaper of city government, source for NYPD personnel information. http://cityrecord.engineering.nyu.edu.

Fulton History, for access to newspapers, especially in New York State. fultonhistory. com.

Google Books offers access to court cases heard in the New York State Court of Appeals and Appellate Division. books.google.com.

Hathi Trust Digital Library. Access to annual reports of the NYPD and many other documents. hathitrust.org.

Library of Congress Chronicling America, https://chroniclingamerica.loc.gov.

NARA, nara.gov. Relevant collections of State Department and Secret Service records available online.

newspapers.com. Access to many previously unavailable New York newspapers, among others.

New York State Historic Newspapers, https://nyshistoricnewspapers.org.

Unless otherwise noted, ancestry.com is the source for birth, baptismal, census, death, and marriage records; New York State prison records; and draft registration, passport, and travel records.

Transcripts of court cases heard by the New York State Court of Appeals and the New York State Supreme Court Appellate Division were accessed at books.google.com.

Records of Joseph Petrosino that remained in his family are identified as coming from the Petrosino archive, courtesy of Petrosino's granddaughter Susan Burke and filmmaker Anthony Giacchino. Papers retained in the Vachris family are identified as coming from the Vachris archive, courtesy of Alfred Vachris, Ann Witherow, and Robert Vachris.

INDEX

Abarno, Frank, xii, 151, 153, 157–61

African Americans, 135, 228, 231

Ahern, William, 179

Akron Beacon Journal, 180

Akron, Ohio police murders, xii, 174–80, 213

Albanese, Alphonse "Frank Perry", 64

Aldermen, NYC Board of, 48, 61, 110; opposition to Bingham, 24–27; Curran Committee hearings, 135–37

Alfano, Enrico, 67

American Mafia, 142, 191, 230, 234–35; and "Good Killers" case, 214–16, 263n12

anarchists, xii, 23, 27, 218, 234; and St. Patrick's Cathedral bomb plot, 151–61

Archiopoli, John, ix, 19, 239

Asbury, Herbert, 145

Bacon, Robert, 29, 67–68

Baker, William F., x, 47–48, 52, 58–59, 61, 90–91, 96, 233

Barbuoto, John, 64–65

Barlow, Peter, 72

Barra, Cesare, 104

"Barrel Murder," xi, 6, 67–69, 86, 89; and connection to Petrosino slaying, 31–33

Barsotti, Carlo, xiii, 111–12

Barzini, Luigi, Jr., 237

Barzini, Luigi, Sr., 228

Battle, Samuel, 231

Becker, Charles, xii, 130, 134–38

Bellavia, Giuseppe, 106

bias in criminal justice system, 15, 21, 27, 76, 138

Biddle, Mrs. A. J., Jr., 202

Bingham, Theodore, x, 27, 35–36, 57, 67–68, 87, 131, 231–32; and Petrosino slaying, 5, 7, 12, 28–30, 33; appointed police commissioner, 22–23; "secret service" and, 24–26, 55–56, 59–60; and Vachris mission, 41–50, 52, 61

Biondo, Lorenzo, xii, 177–79

Biondo, Pasquale, xii, 177–78; execution of, 180

Bishop, Sheba, 43, 45

Bishop, William Henry, xiii, 37, 45–46, 49, 51; on Petrosino slaying, 5, 7, 16, 43–44, 66, 235

Black Hand (*Mano Nera*), 15, 27–28, 45, 51, 67, 88–89, 120, 141, 147–48, 175, 197; false portrayals of, 9, 13–14, 18, 50, 65–66, 101, 214, 228, 234, 238; origins of, 17–18; and Italian Squad, 20, 24, 71, 116; and kidnappings, 96, 98, 100–104, 201–2, 206

Bomb Squad, 125, 148, 155, 162, 210, 228; Italian Squad merged into, 216–18, 234

Bonanno, Joseph, 209, 215

Bonaparte, Charles, 68

Bonnoil, Maurice, ix, 19, 249n12

Bonori, Henry A., 79

Bonventre, Vito, xiii, 211–12

Borgia, Filomena, 174

Borgia, Rosario, xii, 174, 177, 179–80

Boston Evening Transcript, 58

Bozzuffi, John, 103

Bozzuffi, Tony, 103

Brande, James E., 120–21, 142

Bresci, Gaetano, 154–55

Bresci Circle, 154–57, 161

ABOUT THE AUTHOR

P AUL MOSES is Professor Emeritus of Journalism at Brooklyn College and author of *An Unlikely Union: The Love-Hate Story of New York's Irish and Italians* and *The Saint and the Sultan: The Crusades, Islam and Francis of Assisi's Mission of Peace*, which won the 2010 Catholic Press Association award for Best History Book. He worked in daily journalism for twenty-three years, serving as City Hall bureau chief and city editor at *Newsday*, where he was the lead writer on a team that won a Pulitzer Prize.